STUDY GUIDE

STUDY GUIDE

CLAYTON MacKNIGHT

TUTTLE Publishing
Tokyo | Rutland, Vermont | Singapore

Contents

Part One: The Basics

Part Two: Essential Grammar Points

Part Three: Vocabulary and Kanji

Part Four: **Reading Comprehension**

Part Five: **Listening Comprehension**

Appendices

Free Bonus audios and online resources* can be downloaded.

How to Download the Bonus Material of this Book.

1. You must have an internet connection.
2. Type the URL below into to your web browser.

https://www.tuttlepublishing.com/jlpt-study-guide

For support email us at
info@tuttlepublishing.com.

*Some of the online resources are password locked. The password can be found on page 9.

Part One
The Basics

How to Use This Book

JLPT Study Guide is designed to be the complete guide to passing the 日本語能力試験N5 or JLPT N5. The guide prepares you for every part of the exam. Not only does it cover all the necessary grammar, but there are also dedicated sections for vocabulary, reading and listening, so that you can practice your comprehension and test-taking skills.

This book can be used by beginners or by those who have previously studied the language for self-study or in a classroom setting. If you have studied Japanese for some time, the JLPT-style questions will help you narrow down your focus before the big test. If you are just starting out, there is romaji available to help you read all of the Japanese text.

Manga Story

Throughout **JLPT Study Guide**, you will be following along with Matt and Yu, in their misadventures. Matt has just started studying in Japan, while Yu is living and working in Japan. They will be introducing the major N5 grammar points at the start of several lessons in the book.

Grammar Section

The grammar section covers all of the essential grammar for the N5. Each lesson starts with a quick conversation that introduces the major grammar points. From there we will be going over common mistakes for each grammar point. You will also have the chance to practice the grammar with some simple exercises. At the end of every lesson, there are JLPT-style questions to help you get comfortable with answering real questions from the test.

Vocabulary, Reading and Listening Sections

Each of these sections will walk you through valuable strategies on how to improve your score on the test, as well as improve your listening and reading comprehension skills. There are also numerous JLPT-style questions just like the kind you will see on the N5, so that you will be prepared.

Contents of the online materials

- 3 full practice tests* with answer keys and listening scripts
- audio recordings and listening scripts for all of the listening exercises
- audio flashcards that cover all the key sentences from the book
- audio recordings for all of the introductory conversations in the grammar sections
- full kanji editions of all the grammar conversations
- answer keys for all of the questions in the book
- translations and romaji for all the reading passages
- grammar, kanji, kana, and vocabulary flashcards

How to get started

If you have just started studying Japanese, you should start with the hiragana flashcards and mnemonics. In order to pass the test, you will need to be pretty comfortable with hiragana. There is no English or romaji on the test; the entire test is in hiragana, some kanji, and a little katakana. Don't feel like you have to master the hiragana before starting though. There is romaji throughout the book to help you read the key phrases and expressions.

After familiarizing yourself with the hiragana, dive into the grammar section starting with lesson 1. The lessons are cumulative, each lesson builds on past lessons, so you will need to understand the grammar points in the previous lessons, before moving on to the next. At the end of each chapter, there are 10 JLPT-style questions that cover the lesson's main grammar points.

Once you have finished the grammar section, you can move on to the vocabulary, reading and listening sections. All of these sections presume you have knowledge of N5 vocabulary and grammar. Only the vocabulary section requires that you read kanji though. The reading section will have furigana—hiragana above the kanji—to help you with difficult kanji. The listening section only uses hiragana.

After you have completed the main guide, you can move on to the practice tests available online. Each test is full-length and has detailed answer explanations that can help you discover your weak points before you take the actual test.

If you have been studying Japanese for a period of time, and are looking to refine your understanding of the test, it is best to start with one of the practice tests available online, and find out where your weaknesses are. Knowing your weaknesses, you can then focus on the specific sections of the JLPT that you need to improve to pass the test.

Whether you are just starting out, or have some experience with Japanese, use the audio flashcards to help you reinforce the grammar as well as get some

*Use this password to access the practice tests: **PasstheJLPT**.

regular-focused listening practice. These can be used while commuting on the train, on the car, walking or doing housework.

The JLPT does not cover the writing of kanji. For instance, you do not need to know the exact stroke order or all the readings for a particular kanji. However, it might be easier to recognize kanji if you practice writing them out with the practice sheets included with the online materials.

SYMBOLS AND ABBREVIATIONS USED IN THIS BOOK

PARTS OF SPEECH

Part	Symbol	Examples
名詞 **meishi** *noun*	*N*	おべんとう, 本, つくえ **obentō, hon, tsukue** *bento, book, desk*
い形容詞 **ikeiyōshi** い *-adjective*	い *A*	あかい, おいしい, すずしい **akai, oishii, suzushii** *red, delicious, cool*
な形容詞 **nakeiyōshi** な *-adjective*	な *A*	べんり, しずか, きれい **benri, shizuka, kirei** *convenient, quiet, pretty*
動詞 **dōshi** *verb*	*V*	する, 行く, 食べる **suru, iku, taberu** *to do, to go, to eat*

Japanese is a little unusual in that it actually uses two different kinds of adjectives—い-adjectives and な-adjectives. The reason for the difference is that な-adjectives are actually loanwords from Chinese. They are typically written in more complicated kanji without any okurigana—hiragana that typically follows kanji in other Japanese words.

VERB FORMS

Form	Symbol	Examples
ます形 **masukei** ます *-form*	*V* ます	行きます, 食べます, 来ます **ikimasu, tabemasu, kimasu** *go, eat, come*
辞書形 **jishokei** *dictionary form*	*Vdict*	行く, 食べる, 来る **iku, taberu, kuru** *to go, to eat, to come*
て形 **tekei** て *-form*	*V* て	行って, 食べて, 来て **itte, tabete, kite** *go, eat, come*

Form	Symbol	Examples
た形 **takei** た -form	*Vpast*	行った，食べた，来た **itta, tabeta, kita** *went, ate, came*
ない形 **naikei** ない -form	*V ない*	行かない，食べない，来ない **ikanai, tabenai, konai** *not go, not eat, not come*
連用形 **renyōkei** *verb stem*	*Vstem*	行き，食べ，来 **iki, tabe, ki** *go, eat, come*

PLAIN FORM

Symbol	Affirmative		Negative	
	Non-past	Past	Non-past	Past
Vplain	行く **iku** *go*	行った **itta** *went*	行かない **ikanai** *not go*	行かなかった **ikanakatta** *didn't go*
	食べる **taberu** *eat*	食べた **tabeta** *ate*	食べない **tabenai** *not eat*	食べなかった **tabenakatta** *didn't eat*
い *plain*	高い **takai** *tall/expensive*	高かった **taka katta** *was tall/expensive*	高くない **takaku nai** *not tall/expensive*	高くなかった **takaku nakatta** *wasn't tall/expensive*
な *plain*	べんりだ **benri da** *convenient*	べんりだった **benri datta** *was convenient*	べんりじゃない **benri ja nai** べんりではない **benri dewa nai** *not convenient*	べんりじゃなかった **benri ja nakatta** べんりではなかった **benri dewa nakatta** *wasn't convenient*
Nplain	学生だ **gakusei da** *a student*	学生だった **gakusei datta** *was a student*	学生じゃない **gakusei ja nai** 学生ではない **gakusei dewa nai** *not a student*	学生じゃなかった **gakusei ja nakatta** 学生ではなかった **gakusei dewa nakatta** *wasn't a student*

The plain form, or casual form, is often used in conversation between friends, in most printed material like books and magazines or in clauses. Before using it in conversation, you might want to listen to what others use. And, generally speaking, this form is never used at work or in business situations, even between friends.

One of the biggest faux pas people make when starting at a Japanese company is to use casual Japanese too much. To make matters worse, your co-workers might not want to embarrass you by pointing that out. No matter how friendly you are with them outside of work, it's important to try to use polite Japanese at work.

POLITE FORM

Symbol	Affirmative		Negative	
	Non-past	Past	Non-past	Past
Vpolite	行きます **ikimasu** *go*	行きました **ikimashita** *went*	行きません **ikimasen** *not go*	行きませんでした **ikimasen deshita** *didn't go*
	食べます **tabemasu** *eat*	食べました **tabemashita** *ate*	食べません **tabemasen** *not eat*	食べませんでした **tabemasen deshita** *didn't eat*
い polite	高いです **takai desu** *expensive /tall*	高かったです **takakatta desu** *was expensive/ tall*	高くないです **takaku nai desu** 高くありません **takaku arimasen** *not expensive/tall*	高くなかったです **takaku nakatta desu** 高くありませんでした **takaku arimasen deshita** *wasn't expensive/tall*
な polite	べんりです **benri desu** *convenient*	べんりでした **benri deshita** *was convenient*	べんりじゃないです **benri ja nai desu** べんりではないです **benri dewa nai desu** べんりじゃありません **benri ja arimasen** べんりではありません **benri dewa arimasen** *not convenient*	べんりじゃなかったです **benri ja nakatta desu** べんりではなかったです **benri dewa nakatta desu** べんりじゃありませんでした **benri ja arimasen deshita** べんりではありませんでした **benri dewa arimasen deshita.** *wasn't convenient*
Npolite	学生です **gakusei desu** *a student*	学生でした **gakusei deshita** *was a student*	学生じゃないです **gakusei janai desu** 学生ではないです **gakusei dewanai desu** 学生じゃありません **gakusei ja arimasen** 学生ではありません **gakusei dewa arimasen** *not a student*	学生じゃなかったです **gakusei ja nakatta desu** 学生ではなかったです **gakusei dewa nakatta desu** 学生じゃありませんでした **gakusei ja arimasen deshita** 学生ではありませんでした **gakusei dewa arimasen deshita** *wasn't a student*

Most of the test will be in polite or formal Japanese. It is used in almost every business situation and when meeting people for the first time. You should also always use it with people who are older than you or are your superior, like your teacher or an instructor.

Introduction to the JLPT

The 日本語能力試験, or JLPT test, consists of 5 levels. The N5 level is the easiest level and is meant to test your ability to understand some basic Japanese. At this level, most test-takers are able to understand typical everyday conversations as well as read basic sentences written in hiragana, katakana and kanji.

The JLPT tests passive skills only—reading and listening. You will not be required to produce any sentences for the test. Instead, there are various kinds of multiple-choice questions that are designed to test your understanding of different aspects of the material that is covered. The grammar, vocabulary and kanji may seem easy, but the test will be testing your knowledge of not only the meanings, but the small differences between two very similar grammar points, vocabulary words or kanji.

For reading, the test will check your ability to use hiragana, katakana and around 100 kanji. The kanji covered at this level are the ones that are normally used in basic daily communication. Your ability to comprehend longer passages and basic context clues will also be tested.

For listening, the test will cover basic situations involving common classroom and home situations. The dialogues will be at a slower pace, fairly short and test your ability to comprehend key points, as well as common responses to everyday phrases and expressions.

So, why should you take the N5?

The JLPT helps you set clear goals with your studies. The N5 level covers a certain set of grammar, vocabulary and kanji, giving you focus in your studies. This can make it a lot easier to measure your progress and see how your studies have paid off. It can be incredibly motivating to cross off what you have learned.

Taking the test at this early level can also help you identify weak points that you can work on as you study Japanese and make progress toward a higher level. If you find yourself doing really well with kanji, but scoring low on listening, you can shift your studies to spend more time on listening. It can also show how much more effective one study strategy is than another, helping you cut out practices that are a waste of time.

What can you do after you pass?

Generally speaking, if you would like to go to work for a company that uses Japanese as its main language, you will need to pass a higher level of the test, like N2 or N1. So, it is easy to dismiss the N5 as an unnecessary step in your Japanese studies. However, don't discount it quite yet. Passing the N5 shows you have a dedicated interest in Japanese and are willing to put time and effort into studying it.

Employers will see it as proof of your interest in the language and your ability to use some simple Japanese. With the knowledge you gain from studying for the test, you will be able to make simple conversation with Japanese co-workers and survive in Japan when you come to visit.

How is the JLPT N5 organized?

The test is administered in 3 separate blocks of time on the same day. Depending on the country where you are taking the test, there are typically breaks between each block of time, with a longer lunch break between the second and third time blocks:

言語知識 (文字・語彙) **Gengochishiki (Moji • Goi)** *Language Knowledge (Vocabulary)*	言語知識 （文法）・読解 **Gengochishiki (Bunpō) • Dokkai** *Language Knowledge (Grammar) • Reading*	聴解 **Chōkai** *Listening*
25 minutes	*50 minutes*	*30 minutes*

LANGUAGE KNOWLEDGE (VOCABULARY)

The first two parts of this section will cover the readings of the N5 kanji. The first part, **Kanji Reading**, will have a sentence with an underlined word written in kanji, and you will have to choose the appropriate reading in hiragana. The only word in kanji will be the one they are testing you on.

来週 りょこう に いきます。
Raishū ryokō ni ikimasu.
Next week, (I) am going on a trip.

1 こしゅう koshū	2 こしゅ koshu	3 らいしゅう raishū	4 らいしゅ raishu

*The correct answer is 3.

NOTE: On the actual JLPT test there are no romaji/English equivalents.

The second part, **Orthography**, will give you a sentence with an underlined word written in hiragana, and you will have to choose the correct kanji or katakana. Kanji will only be used in the answers.

パンを たべました。
Pan o tabemashita.
(I) ate bread.

1 飲べました	2 食べました	3 飼べました	4 飯べました
**	**tabemashita**	**	**

*The correct answer is 2.   **There is no valid reading for these kanji.

The last two parts, written only in hiragana and katakana, cover vocabulary. In the third part, **Contextually-defined Expressions**, you must choose the word that fits in the sentence.

ここで でんしゃに（   ）。
Koko de densha ni (   ).
(I) (   ) on the train here.

1 のりました	2 つきます	3 あがりました	4 はいりました
norimashita	**tsukimasu**	**agarimashita**	**hairimashita**

*The correct answer is 1.

In the fourth part, **Paraphrases**, you must choose a sentence that has a similar meaning to the one given. The questions are designed more to test your ability to use and understand the vocabulary than just simply going over the meaning of the word.

まいあさ こうえんで はしります。
Maiasa kōen de hashirimasu.
Every morning (I) run in the park.

1 よるは ときどき こうえんで はしります。
Yoru wa tokidoki kōen de hashirimasu.
At night, (I) sometimes run in the park.
2 ごぜんちゅう ときどき こうえんで はしります。
Gozenchū tokidoki kōen de hashirimasu.
In the morning, (I) sometimes run in the park.
3 よるは いつも こうえんで はしります。
Yoru wa itsumo kōen de hashirimasu.
At night, (I) always run in the park.

4 ごぜんちゅう いつも こうえんで はしります。
Gozenchū itsumo kōen de hashirimasu.
In the morning, (I) always run in the park.

*The correct answer is 4.

LANGUAGE KNOWLEDGE (GRAMMAR) • READING

This time block actually covers two parts of the test—Grammar and Reading. There are 3 parts in the grammar section—Sentential Grammar 1, Sentential Grammar 2, and Text Grammar. This section of the exam uses N5 kanji, but all of the kanji have furigana on top to help you read them. The furigana will be in hiragana.

For the first part, **Sentential Grammar 1** (selecting grammar form), you must choose the answer that fits in the blank. Here, they will be testing your understanding of how to use particles, adverbs, and conjunctions. There will also be questions covering adjective and verb conjugations.

PARTICLES

わたしは げんかん （　　） そうじを します。
Watashi wa genkan (　　) sōji o shimasu.
I clean the entranceway.

1　が	2　を	3　に	4　の
ga	o	ni	no

*The correct answer is 4.

FORM

からい食べものを あまり （　　　　　　）。
Karai tabemono o amari (　　　　　　).
(I) (　　　　) spicy food that much.

1　食べます	2　食べました	3　食べません	4　食べています
tabemasu	tabemashita	tabemasen	tabete imasu
eat	ate	don't eat	am eating

*The correct answer is 3.

CONJUNCTIONS

よい天気です （　　　） さんぽ しましょう。
Yoi tenki desu (　　　) sanpo shimashō.
It's nice weather, (　　　) let's stroll.

1 前に	2 から	3 後で	4 のから
mae ni	kara	ato de	nokara

*The correct answer is 2.

In the second part, **Sentential Grammar 2** (sentence composition), you will be asked to put the words in the correct order. You are given 4 words that you must fill in the blanks. You then mark on the answer sheet the number of the word part that should be placed in the blank marked with a star. These questions are designed mostly to test your understanding of sentence structures. For example, they commonly test you on particle placement in a sentence:

A 「すみません。ゆうびんきょく ＿＿＿ ＿＿＿ ＿★＿ ＿＿＿ か。」
 Sumimasen. Yūbinkyoku ＿＿＿ ＿＿＿ ＿★＿ ＿＿＿ ka.

B 「あちらです。」
 Achira desu.

1 どこ	2 は	3 あります	4 に
doko	**wa**	**arimasu**	**ni**

EXAMPLE ANSWER

A 「すみません。ゆうびんきょく　2は　1どこ　4に　3あります　か。」
 Sumimasen. Yūbinkyoku wa doko ni arimasu ka.
 Sorry, where is the post office?

B 「あちらです。」
 Achira desu.
 Over there.

1 どこ	2 は	3 あります	4 に
doko	**wa**	**arimasu**	**ni**

*The correct answer is 4.

And in the third part, **Text Grammar**, you will be asked to choose the appropriate grammar point based on the context of a passage about 225~250 characters in length. You'll have to use both your comprehension skills and your understanding of the grammar points to answer the questions correctly.

…わたしは　えいがを　見たいです。えいがが　すきな　人は、いっしょに　（　　）。
…watashi wa eiga o mitai desu. Eiga ga suki na hito wa, issho ni (　　).
…I want to see a movie. People who like movies, (　　) together?

1 行きましたか	3 行って いましたか
Ikimashita ka	**Itte imashita ka**
went?	*were (you) going?*
2 行きませんか	4 行って いませんか
Ikimasen ka	**Itte imasen ka**
won't (you) go?	*aren't (you) going?*

*The correct answer is 2.

For the reading part of the *Language Knowledge (Grammar)* • *Reading* section of the test, there are 3 parts—short passages, mid-length passages, and information retrieval.

In the first part, **Short Passages**, you are presented with passages about a paragraph in length (100–125 characters) and asked basic comprehension questions about them. They may ask questions about the passage like the ones listed below:

「わたし」は、今日 何を [します/しました]か。
「Watashi」 wa, kyō nani o [shimasu/shimashita] ka.
What [is / was] "I" doing today?

いつ … あいますか。
Itsu … aimasu ka.
When … meeting?

いくら はらいますか。
Ikura haraimasu ka.
How much is (he) paying?

どの…が いいですか。
Dono … ga ii desu ka.
Which … is good?

Your answer choices may also be illustrations. For instance, a passage might describe what a store looks like. And then below it there might be 4 different illustrations of stores, followed by a question like the following:

お店は どれですか。
Omise wa dore desu ka.
Which is the store?

In the second part, **Mid-length passages**, you are presented with longer passages (225–250 characters) and asked questions that test your ability to infer meaning from the reading. Typically there are no questions that involve choosing the right illustration. Instead, they might ask questions like the following:

どうやって… [します/しました] か。
Dōyatte … [shimasu/shimashita] ka.
How [are (they) going to/did (they)] …. ?

[どうして/なぜ]… [します/しました] か。
[Dōshite/Naze] … [shimasu/shimashita] ka.
Why [are (they) going to/did (they)] …. ?

In the third part, **Information Retrieval**, you'll be asked questions about a source of information—like a pamphlet, schedule, or notice, that test your ability to scan for details. Usually, informational retrieval questions can be quite lengthy, explaining the situation and context for you to choose the correct answer.

LISTENING

The listening section is comprised of 4 parts—Task-Based Comprehension, Point Comprehension, Utterance Expressions, and Quick Response. The first two parts will test your comprehension, while the last two test your understanding of key phrases and expressions you should know at this level.

In Task-Based Comprehension, each question first explains a situation and gives you a task. After that, you'll hear a 6–10 lines of dialogue and the task again at the end. These questions are meant to test your ability to listen for details. Answer choices can be given as pictures or in hiragana. No kanji is used in the answers for this section. A typical dialogue involves two speakers narrowing down their choice for something:

いえで、男の人と 女の人が 話しています。女の人は 何を 飲みますか。
Ie de, otoko no hito to onna no hito ga hanashite imasu. Onna no hito wa nani o nomimasu ka.
At home, a man and a woman are talking. What is the woman going to drink?

男: コーヒーを 飲みませんか。
Otoko: Kōhii o nomimasen ka.
Man: Won't (you) drink some coffee?

女: コーヒーは あまり すきじゃないです。
Onna: Kōhii wa amari suki ja nai desu.
Woman: (I) don't really like coffee.

男: ああ、そうですか。おちゃは どうですか。
Otoko: Ā, sō desu ka. Ocha wa dō desu ka.
Man: Oh, okay. How about tea?

女: おねがいします。
Onna: **Onegai shimasu.**
Woman: Please.

男: つめたいのですか。
Otoko: **Tsumetai no desu ka.**
Man: A cold one?

女: はい、おねがいします。
Onna: **Hai, onegai shimasu.**
Woman: Yes, please.

女の人は 何を 飲みますか。
Onna no hito wa nani o nomimasu ka.
What is the woman going to drink?

Answer choices printed in the test booklet

1

3

2
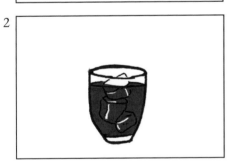

4
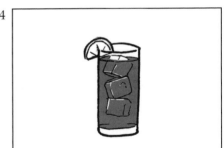

*The correct answer is 4.

Many Task-based Comprehension questions have this pattern. The different possible answers are eliminated, one by one, as one follows through the conversation until we finally arrive at the one correct answer.

Here the man offers coffee at first but the woman says that she doesn't really like coffee. So, the man then offers tea. And then, he asks her if she would like it cold (つめたい, **tsumetai**). That makes answer 4, the picture of the cold glass of tea, the best answer.

For the second part, **Point Comprehension**, you will listen to dialogues of about the same length as the Task-Based Comprehension questions, but this time you will be listening for a specific piece of information. Answers will either be in the form of pictures printed in the test booklet or as answers given in hiragana.

男の人と 女の人が 話しています。女の人は きのう、どこへ 行きましたか。
Otoko no hito to onna no hito ga hanashite imasu. Onna no hito wa kinō, doko e ikimashita ka.
A man and a woman are talking. Where did the woman go yesterday?

男： 西村さん、きのう どこへ 行きましたか。
Otoko: Nishimura-san, kinō doko e ikimashita ka.
Man: Ms. Nishimura, where did you go yesterday?

女： きのうは 新しいレストランに 行きました。
Onna: Kinō wa atarashii resutoran ni ikimashita.
Woman: Yesterday, (I) went to a new restaurant.

男： がっこうの となりのですか。
Otoko: Gakkō no tonari no desu ka.
Man: The one next to the school?

女： そうです。
Onna: Sō desu.
Woman: That's right.

男： ぼくは えいがかんに 行って えいがを 見ました。
Otoko: Boku wa eigakan ni itte eiga o mimashita.
Man: I went to the movie theater and watched a movie.

女： ほんとうですか。わたしは 今日の よる、えいがかんの 下の きっさてんで ともだちに 会います。
Onna: Hontō desu ka. Watashi wa kyō no yoru eigakan no shita no kissaten de tomodachi ni aimasu.
Woman: Really? Tonight, I am going to the cafe below the theater to meet a friend.

女の人は きのう、どこへ 行きましたか。
Onna no hito wa kinō, doko e ikimashita ka.
Where did the woman go yesterday?

Answer choices printed in the test booklet

1 レストラン	2 がっこう	3 えいがかん	4 きっさてん
resutoran	**gakkō**	**eigakan**	**kissaten**
restaurant	*school*	*movie theater*	*cafe*

*The correct answer is 1.

In Point Comprehension questions, all of the answer choices will most likely be referenced at least once in the dialogue. However, there is only one best answer. This can sometimes be quite easy because you might be able to choose the best answer without actually listening to the entire conversation.

In the conversation above, the question asks specifically about where the woman was yesterday, not the man. The woman mentions that she was at the restaurant yesterday, so that is the correct answer. She later mentions that she is going to the cafe tonight, but that is not the information we are looking for.

The last half of the listening is more focused on phrases and expressions. In the third part, **Utterance Expressions**, there will be an illustration printed in the test booklet showing the context where the expression is used. The recording will also give you some brief information about the context, and what the speaker would like to communicate. You must choose the most appropriate expression from the answer choices. No text will be given for the illustrations.

 男：ともだちは　けしゴムが　ありません。ともだちに　何と　言いますか。
Tomodachi wa keshigomu ga arimasen. Tomodachi ni nan to iimasu ka.
(Your) friend doesn't have an eraser. What do (you) say to (your) friend?

女：　1　けしゴム、かしましょうか。
　　　Keshigomu, kashimashō ka.
　　　Shall (I) lend you an eraser?

　　　2　けしゴム、つかいましょう。
　　　Keshigomu, tsukaimashō.
　　　Let's use an eraser!

　　　3　けしゴム、かしてください。
　　　Keshigomu, kashite kudasai.
　　　Lend (me) an eraser.

*The correct answer is 1.

Illustration printed in the test booklet

The girl wants to give the eraser to her friend, so answer 1 is the best. Answer 2 sounds like she is suggesting they use the eraser together to do something. And answer 3 sounds like the girl is making a request for an eraser.

In the fourth part, **Quick Response**, the listening presents you with a line of dialogue and then 3 potential responses. Again, there is nothing written in the test booklet, so you must listen carefully to all the potential answers, then mark an answer on your test answer sheet.

女：今日、何時に　かいぎですか。
Kyō, nanji ni kaigi desu ka.
Today, what time is the meeting?

男：1　5人です。
Gonin desu.
5 people.

2　1時間半です。
Ichi jikan-han desu.
One and a half hours.

3　14時です。
Jūyon ji desu.
14:00 (2:00 p.m.)

*The correct answer is 3.

The woman is asking about the time for the meeting, so answer 3 is the best answer. Answer 1 is about the number of people. Answer 2 is about the amount of time, so that is also incorrect.

TIME MANAGEMENT DURING THE TEST

The test is administered in 3 blocks of time. The first block is for the Language Knowledge (Vocabulary) section (25 minutes). The second block will be Language Knowledge (Grammar) and Reading section (50 minutes). And the final block is the Listening section (30 minutes). There is typically a longer lunch break between the reading and listening sections, but the timing of the breaks differs depending on the country where the test is conducted, so be sure to check the schedule for your area. Also keep in mind that you cannot leave the room until the test booklets and mark sheets are collected, which usually takes a few minutes.

Below is a quick breakdown of how much time to spend in each part of the test. The number in the parenthesis is the number of questions in each part of the test.

1st Section – Language Knowledge (Vocabulary) – 25 minutes total, 3 minutes to check answers

Kanji Reading (12)	Orthography (8)	Expressions (10)	Paraphrases (5)
6 minutes	4 minutes	7.5 minutes	4.5 minutes

2nd Section – Language Knowledge (Grammar) and Reading – 50 minutes total, 5.5 minutes to check answers

Grammar

Grammar Form (16)	Sentence Composition (5)	Text Grammar (5)
8 minutes	7.5 minutes	9 minutes

Reading

Short Passages (3)	Mid-length Passage (2)	Information Retrieval (1)
9 minutes	6 minutes	5 minutes

3rd Section – Listening – 30 minutes total

You don't have to worry too much about time management during the listening section since you will not be able to listen again to any of the questions. You will have about 10 seconds after each question is read out, to mark your answers before the next question begins. This is especially important for the last question of the test, since you will be instructed to put your pencil down shortly after the reading of the last question, so be sure to mark all your questions quickly during this section.

JLPT "Can-Do" Lists

A JLPT Can-do Self-Evaluation List has been made available to JLPT examinees, giving you an idea of what those who pass the N5 think they can do in Japanese. You can use them to set goals for your studies. The lessons in the grammar section of this JLPT Study Guide have been designed in line with the JLPT Can-do Self-Evaluation List.

Lesson	Can-do	Grammar Points
1	Simple Greetings and Introductions	Common N5 Expressions
2	Have a simple conversation at the store Ask simple questions Count objects	Polite Non-past Form; ある vs. いる ; Counters; Numbers; Adjective use; は vs が ; Question Words

Lesson	Can-do	Grammar Points
3	Have a simple conversation about hobbies Talk about the past Talk about what you want and want to do	Polite Past tense (verbs and adjectives); ほしい vs. 〜たい; こそあど
4	Give simple commands and directions Make polite requests Talk about locations of actions or objects	The て form; the で particle; the に particle; Something and Nothing; the へ particle; ください and くださいませんか
5	Give options or examples Make suggestions	The を particle; the と, や, and か particles; the も particle; ましょうか and ませんか; に + 行く
6	Talk about what you are doing now Talk about complete and incomplete tasks Give locations for items in a room	The negative casual form; The よ, わ and ね particles; ている and てある; もう and まだ; Location Words
7	Talk about a trip you took Talk about a sequence of events	から, まで and より; なる and する; 前に and 後で; ながら and とき; Adverbs; Conjunctions
8	Describe places and things in more detail Talk about approximate amounts	Linking Adjectives; どのくらい and ど れくらい; ぐらい vs. ごろ; The しか particle; だけ for 'Only'; 〜たり〜たり する; Clauses
9	Use transitive and intransitive verbs Understand sentence structure	Transitive vs. Intransitive Verbs; Suffixes

What is Covered in the N5

The JLPT covers a simple foundation of vocabulary, grammar, and kanji that are needed for daily conversation. The JLPT, in general, tends to be very grammar-bias, covering a lot more grammar points than vocabulary or kanji, which limits the dialogues and reading passages in the test to everyday situations like meeting up with friends or basic classroom situations. The vocabulary and kanji that is included at this level are some of the most commonly used and can help you understand the gist of most dialogues.

VOCABULARY

N5 covers vocabulary that you would use for daily activities like eating (食べる, **taberu**) and drinking (飲む, **nomu**), as well as things you do around the house like cleaning (そうじする, **sōji suru**) and doing the laundry (せんたくする, **sentaku suru**). Keeping a journal in Japanese of your activities for a few weeks is a useful way to practice a lot of these words.

Also, N5 covers a lot of the words for your immediate family, like your big brother (あに, **ani**) or little brother (おとうと, **otōto**). One thing to keep in mind here is that there are two sets of vocabulary to refer to a family—one that is usually used to refer to your own family (humble), and another that is usually used to refer to someone else's family (honorable):

父, **chichi** — (my) father (humble)
お父さん, **otōsan** — (somebody else's) father (honorable)

To practice these, you can make two family trees. For one of these trees, you can list out your family. The other tree, you can make for a friend of yours or the fictional family of your favorite TV show or movie.

N5 also introduces counters. There are over 100 counters in Japanese that are used to count everything from scenes in a play to swords. However, you will most likely only use and need to learn about 10 of the most common counters that can be used to count most objects you encounter every day. A good way to practice these is to try to use counters whenever you find yourself counting something during the day. Page 52 has a complete list of counters that will most likely come up on the test.

Finally, N5 covers vocabulary necessary for basic directions and describing the location of things. We will practice most of these in lesson 6 (p. 111). You can practice these by writing descriptions of your room describing where everything is located. Or write directions on how to get to somewhere.

GRAMMAR

The grammar for the N5 covers a lot of what you will be using on a daily basis even as you get more advanced in your studies. Keep in mind that the grammar we'll be going over in the grammar section of this book may not be tested on in the actual grammar section of the test, but you will be required to know it in order to answer questions in the listening and reading sections of the test.

Almost all sentences in Japanese use particles. Particles are small words, usually only one or two hiragana, that attach to the end of words to show their relationship to the sentence. The N5 covers all of the most common particles including は, が, も, に, へ, で and を among others. Half of the grammar section on the test will have questions on particles.

N5 also covers talking about the past, non-past progressive (be ~*ing*), conjunctions, and clauses. They also introduce casual and polite forms. All of the passages and listening will be in polite Japanese though.

KANJI

Nature Elements
山 川 天 日 空 月 木 水 火 魚 生 気 雨 金 電 花
A lot of these kanji look a lot like what they represent in nature. 山 (**yama**) looks like a mountain and 川 (**kawa**) looks like a river. You might have to be a little

imaginative with some of them, like 空 (**sora**, air). To me this kanji looks like a little guy jumping off a spring.

Directions and Locations

上 下 中 北 外 右 左 西 東 先 前 南 後 間 校 国 店 社 道 駅

A lot of the basic kanji needed for directions are covered in the test. For example, all 4 directions, 北 (**kita**, north), 南 (**minami**, south), 東 (**higashi**, east), and 西 (**nishi**, west) are covered, as well as 右 (**migi**, right) and 左 (**hidari**, left). There are also some common locations such as 店 (**mise**, store) and 駅 (**eki**, station).

Humans

人 女 男 父 母 子 友 名 目 耳 足 語 本 車

These are all involved with humans in some way. There are some basic family kanji like 父 (**chichi**, father) and 母 (**haha**, mother). Also, basic body parts 目 (**me**, eye) and 足 (**ashi**, foot/leg). Included in this category are two things related closely to human life, 本 (**hon**, book) and 車 (**kuruma**, car).

Numbers, Time and Currency

一 二 三 四 五 六 七 八 九 十 百 千 万 円 午 今 半 年 毎 時 週

Numbers in Japanese are very commonly written in the Arabic numerals that you are familiar with—0, 1, 2, 3, 4, etc. But, at some more traditional restaurants and souvenir shops you might see prices written in kanji. You may also see them used for very formal documents or monuments. At the N5 level, you will also need to know the more common kanji for time, like 年 (**nen**, year), 時 (**ji**, hour) and 週 (**shū**, week).

Adjectives

大 小 長 高 多 少 新 古 白

Only a handful of adjective kanji are introduced at this level. You have the common ones like 大きい (**ōkii**, big) and 小さい (**chiisai**, small). There are also 新しい (**atarashii**, new) and 古い (**furui**, old). They include one color—白い (**shiroi**, white).

Actions

入 出 行 来 休 食 飲 学 書 言 読 話 買 立 見 聞 何

Finally, you are left with the basic actions that you would do in everyday life. For example, you have going (行く, **iku**) and coming (来る, **kuru**). There are also eating (食べる, **taberu**), drinking (飲む, **nomu**), speaking (話す, **hanasu**) and listening (聞く, **kiku**).

The Kana Syllabary

	Hiragana	Katakana
a	あ – Draw the leaves on top, the stem down, then make a circle. **Ahh!** It's an apple with an A on it!	ア is a capital A or an **ax**.
i	い – Hawa**ii** has lots of palm trees shaped like the kana い.	イ is a set of chopsticks to **eat** with.
u	う – "**Ugh!**" the boxer said when he got hit in the gut, making a う as he bent over.	ウ is the top of a **tu**be of tooth-paste.
e	え is an **exotic** bird with a feather on its head.	エ looks like the doors of an **elevator**.
o	お is an **oasis** with a palm tree, or a golf green with a flag.	オ is an **on/off** switch.
ka	か is someone doing a **ka**rate kick to break a board.	カ is a knife blade, you can **cut** (**ka**) with.
ki	き is an old skeleton **key**.	キ is a stylized **key**.
ku	く is a beak of a **cu**ckoo bird.	ク is a **co**coon.
ke	け is a **keg**, the horizontal line is the metal binding.	ケ is a slanted **K**.
ko	こ – the two lines make a **coin**.	コ is one side of a tennis **court**.
sa	さ is someone looking right and **sob**-bing.	サ is a **sa**wddle of a horse.
shi	し is a woman's hair. **She** has lovely hair, don't you think?	シ is a lovely smile that **she** has.
su	す is a cork**su**crew.	ス is a hanger for a **suit**.
se	せ is a mother holding her child up and saying "Can you **say** mommy?"	セ is an upside down **seven** 7.

	Hiragana	Katakana
so	そ is a '2 on top of a 'C.' 2 C the future would be **so** amazing.	ソ is two stitches that someone sewed.
ta	た looks like a 't' and the top and bottom of an 'a'. That spells **ta**.	タ is a **to**mahawk.
chi	ち is someone sneezing to the left. Ha-**CH**...ooo.	チ is a **chee**rleader with a big hat.
tsu	つ is a big **tsu**nami wave.	ツ is **tsu** (2) balls and a bat.
te	て is a **te**nt blowing away in the wind.	テ is a **te**lephone pole.
to	と is someone's **to**e with a splinter in it.	ト is someone showing their hurt **to**e to somebody.
na	な is a person putting a hat on a snake. **Not** a good idea.	ナ is a bent **na**wil.
ni	に is the side view of a **knee**.	ニ – This kana has two strokes and two in Japanese is '**ni**.'
nu	ぬ looks like chopsticks picking up some **noo**dles.	ヌ is a '7.' News at 7!
ne	ね is a fisherman holding his **net**.	ネ is a knife cutting a piece off a **net**.
no	の looks like a **no**-smoking sign.	ノ is a strike through something that is **no** longer needed.
ha	は is a broken uppercase 'H' with 'a' small a in the lower right corner.	ハ is a stick, broken in **ha**lf.
hi	ひ is a big wide smile on **hea**ring a funny story.	ヒ is a man sitting down with a hand saying "**hi**."
fu	ふ is a ship with 3 sails and a flag on top. The wind makes a '**fu**' sound as it blows at the ship.	フ is a big bowl of **fo**od.
he	へ is the top of a **hay**stack.	へ is an arrow up to **hey**-ven.
ho	ほ – If you turn it counter-clockwise it spells '**HO**.' This character has just one more stroke than は.	ホ is a **ho**ly cross with two people kneeling in front.
ma	ま is a **ma**st of a sail boat.	マ is a **ma**n's big nose.

	Hiragana	Katakana
mi	み looks like 21. Look at **me**! I got 21 blackjack!	ミ is 3 notes, do-re-**mi**.
mu	む is like す but with a tail and a mark that were **mo**ved to the right.	ム is someone pumping their **mu**scle.
me	め is an eye with **ma**ke up on it.	メ is a **me**tal sword.
mo	も is a fish hook with two worms on it. **Mo**re worms means **mo**re fish.	モ is like the hiragana も, but has a higher notch for **mo**re fish.
ya	や is a **ya**k with two horns.	ヤ is a head of a **ya**k like hiragana や.
yu	ゆ is a very **u**nique (**yu**) fish.	ユ is a stretched #1. **You** are #1.
yo	よ is a hand playing with a **yo**-yo.	ヨ is a fist doing a fist bump. "**Yo**! How are you?"
ra	ら is an old lady sitting on a **ra**cking chair.	ラ is a **ra**-cket blasting into space.
ri	り looks like an 'r' and an 'i' written quickly. That spells **ri**.	リ is a **ri**-ed sticking out in a bend in the river.
ru	る is a strange road with a **loop** (**ru**) at the end.	ル is the leg and tail of a kanga-**roo**.
re	れ looks like the fisherman with his net ね, but now he has a **re**-inboot (**re**) stuck in it. The boot points to the right.	レ is a **re**-inboot.
ro	ろ is a **ro**ad.	ロ is a nut you need to **ro**tate.
wa	わ is the fisherman again, but **wha**t is he doing with that wave?	ワ – **Wah**! The toothpaste lost its cap.
o	を – を looks like someone is about to step on a frozen lake. **Wo**! Watch your step!	ヲ – **Woo**! It is a shark head.
n	ん is the lowercase '**n**' in English.	ン – The magician's assistant summons the wave up.

Part Two

Essential Grammar Points

LESSON 1
Simple Greetings & Introductions

DIALOGUE

Matt bumps into a stranger on the street. Her things scatter on the ground.

Matt: すみません。 だいじょうぶですか。
Sumimasen. Daijōbu desu ka.
Sorry. Are you okay?

Yu: だいじょうぶです。
Daijōbu desu.
I'm okay.

Matt: は…はじめまして。 あの、 マットです。
Ha... hajimemashite. Ano, Matto desu.
Ni... Nice to meet you. Aah, I'm Matt.

Yu: ああ、 はじめまして。 ゆうです。
Ā, hajimemashite. Yū desu.
Aah, nice to meet you. I'm Yu.

Matt: あなたは わたしですか。
Anata wa watashi desu ka.
You are me?

Yu:	いいえ、ちがいます。わたしの 名前は ゆうです。
	Iie, chigaimasu. Watashi no namae wa Yū desu.
	No, that's not right. My name is Yu.

Matt:	ああ、わかりました。
	Ā, wakarimashita.
	Ahh, I understand.

(一 週 間 後)
(Isshūkan-go)

(One week later)

Matt:	おさきに　どうぞ。
	Osaki ni dōzo.
	After you.

Matt and Yu:	いただきます。
	Itadakimasu.
	Thank you for the meal.

Yu:	ごちそうさまでした。
	Gochisō-sama deshita.
	That was great food.

Matt:	たのしかったです。
	Tanoshikatta desu.
	I had fun.

Roommate:	おはようございます。
	Ohayō gozaimasu.
	Good morning.

Matt:	ああ、ゆめだ。
	Ā, yume da.
	Aah, it was a dream.

'Can-do' Study Points

➡ Make simple introductions
➡ Understand simple phrases

1. GREETINGS AND OTHER EXPRESSIONS

Morning	**Midday**	**Evening and night**

おはようございます。*	こんにちは。	こんばんは。
Ohayō gozaimasu.	**Konnichiwa.**	**Konbanwa.**
Good morning.	*Good day.*	*Good evening*

➡ *おはようございます is the usual greeting when you first get to work, even if you are starting work later, for example, in the middle of the day.

At work

おつかれさまです。
Otsukare-sama desu.
Thank you for your hard work.

Coming home

Husband: ただいま。
         Tadaima.
         I'm home.
Wife: おかえりなさい。
         Okaerinasai.
         Welcome back.

When entering someone else's home

Visitor: おじゃまします。
Ojama shimasu.
Excuse me.

Owner: いらっしゃい。
Irasshai.
Welcome.

When entering a store

Sales clerk: いらっしゃいませ。
Irasshaimase.
Welcome. (more polite)

Saying goodbye

さようなら。
Sayōnara.
Goodbye.

Saying goodbye to a friend

じゃあ、また。
Jā, mata.
See you later.

Saying Good night

おやすみなさい。
Oyasuminasai.
Good night.

Leaving home for work

いってきます。
Itte kimasu.
I'm off to work./I'm going now.

Seeing someone off

お元気で。
Ogenki de.
Take care.

Visiting someone in the hospital

おだいじに。
Odaiji ni.
Get well soon

When leaving the office before others

Woman A: お先に しつれいします。
Osaki ni shitsurei shimasu.
Sorry for leaving before you.

Woman B: おつかれさまでした。
Otsukare-sama deshita.
Thanks for working hard.

Simple introductions

Businessman A:
はじめまして。どうぞ よろしく
おねがいします。
**Hajimemashite. Dōzo yoroshiku
onegai shimasu.**
*Nice to meet you. I look forward to
working with you.*

Businessman B:
こちらこそ、どうぞ よろしく
おねがいします。
**Kochirakoso, dōzo yoroshiku
onegai shimasu.**
*Nice to meet you. I look forward to
working with you.*

Introducing yourself

わたしは にしむらです。
Watashi wa Nishimura desu.
I am Nishimura.

Introducing others

こちらは スミスさんです。
Kochira wa Sumisu-san desu.
This is Ms. Smith.

Saying "please" and "thank you"

Woman outside of elevator:
どうも ありがとうございます。
Dōmo arigatō gozaimasu.
Thank you very much.

Man inside of elevator:
どう いたしまして。
Dō itashimashite.
You're welcome.

 LANGUAGE TIPS

どうも **dōmo** is often used to emphasize things. For example, you can say the following:

どうも ありがとうございます。
Dōmo arigatō gozaimasu.
Thank you very much.

But you can use it by itself in a casual situation, and the rest of this expression is implied:

どうも (ありがとうございます。)
Dōmo (arigatō gozaimasu.)
Very much (thank you.)

You can use it with other words as well:

どうも すみません。
Dōmo sumimasen.
I'm very sorry.

どうも こまりました。
Dōmo komarimashita.
I'm very troubled.

Wishing someone a happy birthday

Woman: おたんじょうび　おめでとう
ございます。
Otanjōbi omedetō gozaimasu.
Happy birthday.

Friend: ありがとうございます。
Arigatō gozaimasu
Thank you.

Before eating

いただきます。
Itadakimasu.
Thank you for giving us this meal.

After eating

ごちそうさまでした。
Gochisō-sama deshita.
That was delicious.
(lit. That was a feast.)

CULTURAL NOTES

From a very early age, Japanese school kids are taught to say ごちそうさまで
した gochisō-sama deshita after every meal. You will inevitably hear it at almost every Japanese meal you attend. But, it doesn't literally mean that the
food was delicious.

ご go at the beginning of the phrase and さま sama at the end make it
more honorable. But, what about ちそう chisō? ちそう now means 'feast,' but
long ago it meant 'to run around' usually on horses.

ちそう was written with two kanji—馳 chi (to gallop, to sail or drive a
wagon) and 走 sō (to run). So literally it means 'to gallop run.' Before an important guest came over to eat a meal, people would have to run around
town on or off horses to pick up all the things they needed for the feast. And
that's how 'running around' came to mean a feast. In the Edo period
(1603~1868) ご and さま were added to make it more honorable.

Offering to do something

Man: わたしが そうじ します。
Watashi ga sōji shimasu.
I'll clean it.
Woman: おねがいします。
Onegai shimasu.
Please (do that for me).

Offering food

Man: はい、 どうぞ。
Hai, dōzo.
Here you go.
Woman: ありがとうございます。
Arigatō gozaimasu.
Thank you.

Giving way to others

Man: おさきに どうぞ。
Osaki ni dōzo.
After you.
Woman: おさきに しつれい します。
Osaki ni shitsurei shimasu.
Sorry for going first.

Asking for the next person

おつぎのかた どうぞ。
Otsugi no kata dōzo.
Next person, please go ahead.

CULTURAL NOTES

In Japan, it is very common for people to bring back a gift or お土産 **omiyage**
from their trips. Colorful and neatly wrapped packages of food can be bought
at train stations and major tourist destinations in Japan.

These gifts should be bought for family, friends, and co-workers. Your **omiyage** needs to be something from the local area that you visited. For instance,
if you go to Kyoto, you might want to pick up 八つ橋 **yatsuhashi**, a trian-
gle-shaped Japanese sweet made from rice flour, sugar and cinnamon.

2. MANY DIFFERENT USES FOR THE WORD
すみません sumimasen

To apologize

Woman: すみません。
Sumimasen.
Sorry (for bumping into you).

To say "thank you"

Woman: すみません。
Sumimasen.
Thank you (for holding the door for me).

To call (a waitress)

Man: すみません。
Sumimasen.
Excuse me (to a waitress).

To apologize (casually)

ごめんなさい。
Gomennasai.
Sorry (in a casual situation).

📎 CULTURAL NOTES

The prayer gesture, putting your hands together in front of your face, may seem to be an odd way of apologizing in the West. However, this is a very common way to apologize casually in Japanese.

The same gesture is used when saying いただきます **itadakimasu** before a meal, or ごちそうさまでした **gochisō-sama deshita** after finishing a meal to show thanks.

JLPT Test Questions

Listen to the conversation and choose the most appropriate response.

1) ①   ②   ③

4) ①   ②   ③

2) ①   ②   ③

5) ①   ②   ③

3) ①   ②   ③

6) ①   ②   ③

Listen to the questions and choose the correct response to each question.

7) ①   ②   ③

8) ①   ②   ③

9) ①   ②   ③

10) ①   ②   ③

11) ①   ②   ③

12) ①   ②   ③

Simple Conversations at the Store

DIALOGUE

Matt stops in at the local pet store to find a new pet.

Matt: このいぬは　かわいいですね。
Kono inu wa kawaii desu ne.
This dog is cute, huh?

Clerk: そうですね。 そのいぬは　わかいです。 げんきですよ。
Sō desu ne. Sono inu wa wakai desu. Genki desu yo.
Yes, it is. That dog is young. Full of energy.

Matt: このいぬと、 そのいぬを　ください。
Kono inu to, sono inu o kudasai.
This dog and that dog, please.

Clerk: にひきですか。
Nihiki desu ka.
Two dogs?

Matt: はい。
Hai.
Yes.

(Matt leaves the pet store and goes for a walk with his dogs.)

Matt:	こんにちは。
	Konnichiwa.
	Hi.
Yu:	こんにちは。
	Konnichiwa.
	Hi.
Matt:	こんしゅうまつは　何を　しますか。
	Konshū-matsu wa nani o shimasu ka.
	What are you doing this weekend?
Yu:	ああ、ひまです。ああ、あぶない！
	Ā, hima desu. Ā, abunai!
	Uhh, I'm free. Oh, watch out!
Matt:	いたい！
	Itai!
	Ouch!
Yu:	だいじょうぶですか。
	Daijōbu desu ka.
	Are you okay?
Matt:	びょういんは　どこですか。
	Byōin wa doko desu ka.
	Where is the hospital?

'Can-do' Key Points

➡ Have a simple conversation at the store.
➡ Ask simple questions.
➡ Count objects.

POLITE NON-PAST FORM

To talk about the present and future (the non-past) politely, you can use the ま
す **masu** and です **desu** forms.

LANGUAGE TIPS

Why is this form called the non-past form? Well, Japanese only has two
tenses—past and non-past. The non-past form can be used to talk about the
present as well as the future. You will need to read and understand the context carefully in order to understand if the sentence is about the future or the
present. Pay attention to time expressions like きょう (**kyō**, today) or あした
(**ashita**, tomorrow) that can provide clues to the context.

1. VERBS

Group 1	Group 2	Group 3
書く → 書きます **kaku** **kakimasu** *to write*	食べる → 食べます **taberu** **tabemasu** *to eat*	来る → 来ます **kuru** **kimasu** *to come*
話す → 話します **hanasu** **hanashimasu** *to speak*	（学生が）いる → います **(gakusei ga) iru** **imasu** *(there) is a student, to be/exist*	する → します **suru** **shimasu** *to do*
立つ → 立ちます **tatsu** **tachimasu** *to stand*	（電車を）おりる→ おります **(densha o) oriru** **orimasu** *to get off (the train)*	
しぬ → しにます **shinu** **shinimasu** *to die*	（うわぎを）きる → きます **(uwagi o) kiru** **kimasu** *to put on (a jacket)*	
とぶ → とびます **tobu** **tobimasu** *to fly*		
飲む → 飲みます **nomu** **nomimasu** *to drink*		
かえる → かえります **kaeru** **kaerimasu** *to go back home*		
言う → 言います **iu** **iimasu** *to say*		

```
あ い う え お        ざ じ ず ぜ ぞ        は ひ ふ へ ほ        ら り る れ ろ
か き く け こ        た ち つ て と        ば び ぶ べ ぼ        わ        を
が ぎ ぐ げ ご        だ ぢ づ で ど        ま み む め も        ん
さ し す せ そ        な に ぬ ね の        や    ゆ    よ
```

If the second to last kana is from the え-row of kana (i.e. it is one of the high-lighted kana above), it is *probably* a Group 2 verb. There are exceptions to this, however. At the N5 level, the three exceptions are probably いる (for existence), おりる, and きる*. These three verbs look like they are Group 1, but they are actually Group 2.

To form the negative, you just have to remove す and add せん:

行きます → 行きません	食べます → 食べません
Ikimasu **ikimasen**	**tabemasu** **tabemasen**
(I) go *(I) don't go*	*(I) eat* *(I) don't eat*

* (for putting on clothes)

2. ADJECTIVES

	Affirmative non-past	Negative non-past
い - *adjectives*	おもしろいです **omoshiroi desu** *(it's) interesting*	おもしろくないです **omoshiroku nai desu** *(it's) not interesting*
		おもしろくありません **omoshiroku arimasen** *(it's) not interesting*
な - *adjectives nouns*	べんりです **benri desu** *(it's) convenient*	べんり［じゃ / では］ないです **benri [ja/dewa] nai desu** *(it's) not convenient*
		べんり［じゃ / では］ありません **benri [ja/dewa] arimasen** *(it's) not convenient*
いい *(irregular)*	いいです **ii desu** *(it's) good*	よくないです **yoku nai desu** *(it's) not good*
		よくありません **yoku arimasen** *(it's) not good*

➡ You can substitute でしょう for です, if you want to make a guess based on information.

EXAMPLES

- 東京に 行きます。(Group 1 verb)
  Tōkyō ni ikimasu.
  (I'm going) to Tokyo.

- ドアを しめます。(Group 2 verb)
  Doa o shimemasu.
  (I'm going) to close the door.

- 日本語を れんしゅう します。(Group 3 verb)
  Nihongo o renshū shimasu.
  (I'm going) to practice Japanese.

- 田中さんは ほそいです。(い-adjective)
  Tanaka-san wa hosoi desu.
  Mr. Tanaka is slender.

- あしたは ひまじゃありません。(な-adjective negative)
  Ashita wa hima ja arimasen.
  (I)'m not free tomorrow.

- わたしは <u>いしゃです</u>。(noun)
  Watashi wa isha desu.
  I'm a doctor.

- あの人は <u>いしゃでしょう</u>。(noun)
  Ano hito wa isha deshō.
  That person is probably a doctor.

WATCH OUT!

Note the following pairs of sentences: the sentences marked with X are incorrect.

X　このデザートは　<u>あまいじゃないです</u>。
　　Kono dezāto wa amai ja nai desu.

　→　このデザートは　<u>あまくないです</u>。
　　Kono dezāto wa amaku nai desu.
　　This dessert is not sweet.

X　このじんじゃは　<u>しずかくないです</u>。
　　Kono jinja wa shizukaku nai desu.

　→　このじんじゃは　<u>しずかじゃないです</u>。
　　Kono jinja wa shizuka ja nai desu.
　　This shrine isn't quiet.

GIVE IT A SHOT!

Rearrange the words to form the most appropriate sentence, like the example below.

れい）ビール / 毎週 / 飲みます / を

　→ <u>毎週、ビールを飲みます。</u>

1) です / は / おいしい / カレー

　→ _____

2) は / です / マイク / わたし

　→ _____

3) 本 / 読みません / を / 毎日は

　→ _____

4) きます / 今日 / を / シャツ

　→ _____

5) つまらなくない / は / これ / です

→ _____

6) たいせつ / お金(かね) / は / です

→ _____

WHAT IS THE DIFFERENCE BETWEEN あります *arimasu* AND います *imasu*?

These two verbs can both mean "to be" or "to exist," but they are not interchangeable. あります **arimasu** is used for inanimate objects (i.e. they don't move by themselves) like buildings, flowers, or parked cars, while います **imasu** is used for animate objects like humans, animals and potentially other things that move (like insects), and taxis if they are on the road moving, not parked.

EXAMPLES

■ 田中さんが います。
  Tanaka-san ga imasu.
  (There) is Mr. Tanaka.

■ 家が あります。
  Ie ga arimasu.
  (There) is a house.

WATCH OUT!

Note the following pairs of sentences: the sentences marked with X are incorrect.

X 花が います。
  Hana ga imasu.

  → 花が あります。
    Hana ga arimasu.
    (There) [is a flower / are flowers].

X いぬが あります。
  Inu ga arimasu.

  → いぬが います。
    Inu ga imasu.
    (There) is a dog.

GIVE IT A SHOT!

Finish the sentences with います or あります like the example below.

れい）いもうと　→　<u>いもうとが　います。</u>

1. ぺん　→　＿＿＿＿＿＿＿
2. 二人^{ふたり}　→　＿＿＿＿＿＿＿
3. かいぎ　→　＿＿＿＿＿＿＿
4. いしゃ　→　＿＿＿＿＿＿＿

3. NUMBERS

0	れい・ゼロ	rei/zero			
1	いち	ichi	11	じゅういち	jūichi
2	に	ni	12	じゅうに	jūni
3	さん	san	13	じゅうさん	jūsan
4	よん・し	yon/shi	14	じゅうよん・じゅうし	jūyon/jūshi
5	ご	go	15	じゅうご	jūgo
6	ろく	roku	16	じゅうろく	jūroku
7	なな・しち	nana/shichi	17	じゅうなな・じゅうしち	jūnana/jūshichi
8	はち	hachi	18	じゅうはち	jūhachi
9	きゅう・く	kyū/ku	19	じゅうきゅう・じゅうく	jūkyū/jūku
10	じゅう	jū	20	にじゅう	nijū

10	じゅう	jū	100	ひゃく	hyaku
20	にじゅう	nijū	200	にひゃく	nihyaku
30	さんじゅう	sanjū	300	さんびゃく	sanbyaku
40	よんじゅう	yonjū	400	よんひゃく	yonhyaku
50	ごじゅう	gojū	500	ごひゃく	gohyaku
60	ろくじゅう	rokujū	600	ろっぴゃく	roppyaku
70	ななじゅう	nanajū	700	ななひゃく	nanahyaku
80	はちじゅう	hachijū	800	はっぴゃく	happyaku
90	きゅうじゅう	kyūjū	900	きゅうひゃく	kyūhyaku

1,000	せん	sen	10,000	いちまん	ichiman
2,000	にせん	nisen	20,000	にまん	niman
3,000	さんぜん	sanzen	30,000	さんまん	sanman
4,000	よんせん	yonsen	40,000	よんまん	yonman
5,000	ごせん	gosen	50,000	ごまん	goman
6,000	ろくせん	rokusen	60,000	ろくまん	rokuman
7,000	ななせん	nanasen	70,000	ななまん	nanaman
8,000	はっせん	hassen	80,000	はちまん	hachiman
9,000	きゅうせん	kyūsen	90,000	きゅうまん	kyūman

ADDITIONAL LANGUAGE TIPS

When talking about numbers used to identify something like an address or a phone number, the dash (-) is pronounced の **no**:

わたしの でんわばんごうは ０７０−１２３４−５６７８です。
Watashi no denwa bangō wa zero-nana-zero-no ichi-ni-san-yon-no go-roku nana-hachi desu.
My phone number is 070-1234-5678.

This is something that will commonly come up in the listening section of the test, where they might talk about someone's phone number or address.

4. COUNTERS

Japanese has specific counters for a wide variety of objects. But, if you don't know a particular counter, you can use the native Japanese number system when counting 1–10. They can also be used for abstract things like もんだい **mondai**—problems or questions.

➡ **The Native Japanese Number System used for counting 1–10 (used as generic counters)**

1 - 一つ - ひとつ - **hitotsu**
2 - 二つ - ふたつ - **futatsu**
3 - 三つ - みっつ - **mittsu**
4 - 四つ - よっつ - **yottsu**
5 - 五つ - いつつ - **itsutsu**

6 - 六つ - むっつ - **muttsu**
7 - 七つ - ななつ - **nanatsu**
8 - 八つ - やっつ - **yattsu**
9 - 九つ - ここのつ - **kokonotsu**
10 - 十 - とお - **tō**

➡ Specific Counters

#	〜台 **dai** *Machines*	〜本 **hon** **hon** *Long Cylindrical objects*	〜人 **nin** *People*	まい **mai** *Flat things*	はい **hai** *Cupfuls*	ひき **hiki** *Small Animals*	さつ **satsu** *Books*
1	いちだい ichidai	いっぽん **ippon**	ひとり **hitori**	いちまい ichimai	いっぱい **ippai**	いっぴき **ippiki**	いっさつ issatsu
2	にだい nidai	にほん nihon	ふたり **futari**	にまい nimai	にはい nihai	にひき nihiki	にさつ nisatsu
3	さんだい sandai	さんぼん san**bon**	さんにん sannin	さんまい sanmai	さんばい san**bai**	さんびき sanbiki	さんさつ sansatsu
4	よんだい yondai	よんほん yonhon	よにん **yonin**	よんまい yonmai	よんはい yonhai	よんひき yonhiki	よんさつ yonsatsu
5	ごだい godai	ごほん gohon	ごにん gonin	ごまい gomai	ごはい gohai	ごひき gohiki	ごさつ gosatsu
6	ろくだい rokudai	ろっぽん roppon	ろくにん rokunin	ろくまい rokumai	ろっぱい roppai	ろっぴき roppiki	ろくさつ rokusatsu
7	ななだい nanadai	ななほん nanahon	ななにん nananin	ななまい nanamai	ななはい nanahai	ななひき nanahiki	ななさつ nanasatsu
8	はちだい hachidai	はっぽん / はちほん **happon/ hachihon**	はちにん hachinin	はちまい hachimai	はっぱい / はちはい **happai/ hachihai**	はっぴき / はちひき **happiki/ hachihiki**	はっさつ hassatsu
9	きゅうだい kyūdai	きゅうほん kyūhon	きゅうにん kyūnin	きゅうまい kyūmai	きゅうはい kyūhai	きゅうひき kyūhiki	きゅうさつ kyūsatsu
10	じゅうだい jūdai	じゅっぽん jup**pon**	じゅうにん jūnin	じゅうまい jūmai	じゅっぱい juppai	じゅっぴき juppiki	じゅっさつ jussatsu

#	〜ど **do** *1-4 times, Degrees*	〜かい **kai** **kai** *1+ times, Rounds, Floors of a bldg.*	〜こ **ko** *Small Items*	〜さい **sai** *Age*	〜日 **ka** *Days of the Month*	〜時 **ji** *Hours*	〜分 **fun** *Minutes*
1	いちど ichido	いっかい ikkai	いっこ ikko	いっさい issai	ついたち **tsuitachi**	いちじ ichiji	いっぷん ippun
2	にど nido	にかい nikai	にこ niko	にさい nisai	ふつか **futsuka**	にじ niji	にふん nifun
3	さんど sando	さんかい sankai	さんこ sanko	さんさい sansai	みっか **mikka**	さんじ sanji	さんぷん sanpun
4	よんど yondo	よんかい yonkai	よんこ yonko	よんさい yonsai	よっか **yokka**	よじ **yoji**	よんぷん yonpun
5	ごど godo	ごかい gokai	ごこ gogo	ごさい gosai	いつか **itsuka**	ごじ goji	ごふん gofun
6	ろくど rokudo	ろっかい rokkai	ろっこ rokko	ろくさい rokusai	むいか **muika**	ろくじ rokuji	ろっぷん roppun

#	～ど do *1-4 times, Degrees*	～かい **kai** *1+ times, Rounds, Floors of a bldg.*	～こ ko *Small Items*	～さい sai *Age*	～日 ka *Days of the Month*	～時 ji *Hours*	～分 fun *Minutes*
7	ななど **nanado**	ななかい **nanakai**	ななこ **nanako**	ななさい **nanasai**	なのか **nanoka**	しちじ／ ななじ **shichiji/ nanaji**	ななふん **nanafun**
8	はちど **hachido**	はっかい／ はちかい **hakkai/ hachikai**	はっこ／ はちこ **hakko/ hachiko**	はっさい **hassai**	ようか **yōka**	はちじ **hachiji**	はっぷん／ はちふん **happun/ hachifun**
9	きゅうど／くど **kyūdo/kudo**	きゅうかい **kyūkai**	きゅうこ **kyūko**	きゅうさい **kyūsai**	ここのか **kokonoka**	くじ **kuji**	きゅうふん **kyūfun**
10	じゅうど **jūdo**	じゅっかい **jukkai**	じゅっこ **jukko**	じゅっさい **jussai**	とおか **tōka**	じゅうじ **jūji**	じゅっぷん **juppun**

NOTES:

* For counting ages over 10 you only have to add じゅう (10), にじゅう (20), etc. before the counters above.

18 years old = じゅうはっさい **jū-has-sai**

31 years old = さんじゅういっさい **san-jū-is-sai**

One exception is for 20 years old:

20 years old = はたち **hatachi**

** For counting days of the month after the 10th of the month:

Number + 日 **nichi**

<u>EXAMPLE</u>

15th = じゅうごにち **jū-go-nichi**

Except for the following:

14th = じゅうよっか **jū-yokka**

20th = はつか **hatsuka**

24th = にじゅうよっか **ni-jū-yokka**

FORM

> Counter + (の) + object/subject + verb
> Object/subject + counter + verb

EXAMPLES

1. いぬには 四本の あしが あります。
   Inu ni wa yonhon no ashi ga arimasu.
   A dog has four legs.

2. ネクタイを 二つ 買います。
   Nekutai o futatsu kaimasu.
   I'm going to buy two neckties.

3. にまいの はがきを ください。
   Nimai no hagaki o kudasai.
   Two postcards please.

4. もう 一本 ください。
   Mō ippon kudasai.
   Another cylindrical item (e.g. a beer bottle) please.

5. わたしは ２０さいです。
   Watashi wa hatachi desu.
   I'm 20 years old.

6. 今日は ２０日、げつようびです。
   Kyō wa hatsuka, getsuyōbi desu.
   Today is Monday the 20th.

7. 今、１２時４５分です。
   Ima, jūni-ji yonjūgo-fun desu.
   Now, it's 12:45.

WATCH OUT!

There will most likely be at least one question in the 文字 **moji** (vocabulary) section of the exam that covers irregular pronunciations of the counters.

GIVE IT A SHOT!

How do you count the following? Write what you would say in the blank below the pictures.

 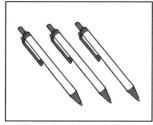 

e.g. <u>いっさつ</u>　　1. _____　　2. _____

3. _____　　4. _____　　5. _____

  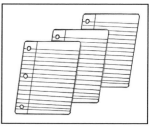

6. _____　　7. _____　　8. _____

ADJECTIVES

What fun would the world be without adjectives? In Japanese you can use three different parts of speech to talk about a noun: い-adjectives, な-adjectives, and nouns.

FORM

いA
なA + な ⎤ + N
N + の

EXAMPLES

1. これは あまい デザートです。
   Kore wa amai dezāto desu.
   This is a sweet dessert.

2. あかるい へやです。
   Akarui heya desu.
   (It)'s a bright room.

3. きたむらさんは きれいな 女の人です。
   Kitamura-san wa kirei na onna no hito desu.
   Ms. Kitamura is a pretty woman.

4. それは ゆうめいな 本です。
   Sore wa yūmei na hon desu.
   That is a famous book.

5. ギターの れんしゅうを します。
   Gitā no renshū o shimasu.
   (I)'m going to practice the guitar.

6. これは せんせいの ぼうしです
   Kore wa sensei no bōshi desu.
   This is the teacher's hat.

*NOTE: You can also use the の particle to refer to a specific kind of thing.

あかいの → (a/the) red one
akai no

げんきなの → (a/the) energetic one
genki na no

日本の → (a/the) Japanese one
Nihon no

WATCH OUT!

Note the following pairs of sentences: the sentences marked with X are incorrect.

X 田中さんには 大きいの いえが あります。
Tanaka-san ni wa ōkii no ie ga arimasu.

→ 田中さんには 大きい いえが あります。
Tanaka-san ni wa ōkii ie ga arimasu.
Mr. Tanaka has a big house.

X さとうさんは ゆうめい いしゃです。
Satō-san wa yūmei isha desu.

→ さとうさんは ゆうめいな いしゃです。
Satō-san wa <u>yūmei na</u> isha desu.
Mr. Sato is a famous doctor.

The following adjectives are all な-adjectives, even though they end with the い sound:

べんり (**benri**, convenient), げんき (**genki**, energetic), きれい (**kirei**, pretty), きらい (**kirai**, hated), すき (**suki**, liked), だいすき (**daisuki**, really liked), ゆうめい (**yūmei**, famous).

GIVE IT A SHOT!

Rearrange the clusters of words to form a correct sentence each, like the example below.

れい) あります / ホテル / 大<small>おお</small>きい / が
→ あそこに <u>大きい ホテルが あります。</u>

1) は / スポーツ / な / すき

→ _____スキーです。

2) たいせつ / かいぎは / の / 今日<small>きょう</small>

→ _____です。

3) は / ビール / 飲<small>の</small>みません / を / わたし / ぬるい

→ _____

4) おもしろい / ダンさん / 人<small>ひと</small> / です / は

→ _____

5) の / あした / は / です / やまださん / たんじょうび

→ _____

6) きれい / です / な / なら / まち / は

→ _____

THE は *wa* AND が *ga* PARTICLES

The は particle is the topic-marking particle in Japanese. It acts as a "box" that the rest of the sentence is placed in, giving it context. The topic can often be dropped from the sentence and it will keep a similar meaning.

- 田中さんは ほそいです。
  Tanaka-san wa hosoi desu.
  Mr. Tanaka is thin.

- いぬは かわいいです。
  Inu wa kawaii desu.
  Dogs are cute.

- X さとうさんは います。 → さとうさんが* います。
  Satō-san wa imasu.   **Satō-san ga imasu.**
                                       (There) is Mr. Sato.

*NOTE: が **ga** is most often used with あります and います, but は **wa** can sometimes be used as well.

The は particle can also be used to show contrast. In this way it can be translated as "as for ~." It can also be combined with other particles like で, へ, and に, but not with some particles like を or が.

- わたしは ビールを 飲みます。
  Watashi wa bīru o nomimasu.
  As for me (in contrast to other people), (I) drink beer.

- 東京へは 電車で 行きます。
  Tōkyō e wa densha de ikimasu.
  As for heading to Tokyo, (I) am going by train.

- X ビールをは 飲みません。 → ビールは 飲みません。
  Biiru o wa nomimasen.   **Biiru wa nomimasen.**
                                        As for beer, (I) don't drink (it).

Note also that the は particle is pronounced '**wa**' and not '**ha.**'

The が particle is the subject-marking particle in Japanese. It often marks the doer in a sentence or it could mark the object when used with certain adjectives like すき (**suki**, to like).

    Unlike the topic-marking particle は, removing the subject marked with the が particle from the sentence will make the sentence confusing or ungrammatical.

- スミスさんが 日本語を べんきょう しています。
  Sumisu-san ga Nihongo o benkyō shite imasu.
  Mr. Smith studies the Japanese language.

- スミスさんは ねこが すきです。
  Sumisu-san wa neko ga suki desu.
  Mr. Smith likes cats.

➡ X 東京へが 電車で 行きます。 → 東京へ 電車で 行きます。

Tōkyō e ga densha de ikimasu.   **Tōkyō e densha de ikimasu.**

(I) am going to Tokyo by train.

TRY IT OUT!

Rearrange the words to form a correct sentence like the example below.

れい）わたし / です / は / ジル

→ <u>わたしは ジルです。</u>

1) できます / 日本語 / は / ミラーさん / が

  → _____

2) エレベーター / あります / が / に / そこ

  → _____

3) その / 読みません / は / ほん

  → _____

4) は / スペイン人 / です / サントスさん

  → _____

5) が / 目 / です / いたい

  → _____

QUESTION WORDS

It would be hard to continue a conversation without asking about details such as name, place, reason, etc.

だれ・どなた **dare donata** *who*	なに・なん **nani nan** *what*	いつ **itsu** *when*	どこ・どちら **doko dochira** *where*
どうして・なぜ **dōshite naze** *why*	なんで・どうやって **nande dōyatte** *how*	どう・いかが **dō ikaga** *how (do you like...)*	どれ・どっち **dore docchi** *which (of)*
どの ＋ Noun **dono** *which noun*	どんな ＋ Noun **donna** *what kind of + noun*	どちら **dochira** *which (polite)*	いくら **ikura** *how much (does it cost)*

FORM

There are two basic structures for questions.

> Question word + verb + か
> Topic + は + Question word + ですか

EXAMPLES

1) A: 日本の ビールは どうですか。
   Nihon no biiru wa dō desu ka.
   How is Japanese beer?

   B: おいしいです。
   Oishii desu.
   (It) is delicious.

2) A: どれが わたしの にもつですか。
   Dore ga watashi no nimotsu desu ka.
   Which is my luggage?

   B: このにもつです。
   Kono nimotsu desu.
   This luggage is.

3) A: どの車を 買いますか。
   Dono kuruma o kaimasu ka.
   Which car are (you) going to buy?

   B: そのあかい車を 買います。
   Sono akai kuruma o kaimasu.
   (I) am going to buy that red car.

4) A: リチャードは どんな人ですか。
   Richādo wa donna hito desu ka.
   What is Richard like?

   B: やさしい人です。
   Yasashii hito desu.
   (He is) a kind person.

5) A: このとけいは いくらですか。
   Kono tokei wa ikura desu ka.
   How much is this watch?

   B: 15000円です。
   Ichi-man go-sen-en desu.
   (It) is 15,000 yen.

One important rule for question words is that the は **wa** particle cannot immediately follow a question word.

X どれは　すきですか。 → どれが　すきですか。
Dore wa suki desu ka.　　**Dore ga suki desu ka.**
Which do you like?

X 何時ですか。　 → 何時ですか。*
Naniji desu ka　　**Nanji desu ka.**
What time is it?

X なまえは　何ですか。 → なまえは　何ですか。**
Namae wa nani desu ka.　　**Namae wa nan desu ka.**
What is (your) name?

NOTE:* When 何 is placed in front of a counter to ask how many (e.g. 何人), the pronunciation of the character is なん.
When 何 is placed in front of **n/t/d sounds, it is also pronounced なん.

GIVE IT A SHOT!

Fill in the spaces with a word from the box, like the example below.

れい)　A:（**どんな**）カレーですか。
　　　B: やさいの　カレーです。

1)　A:（　　　）が　パーティーに　来ます。
　　B: トムが　パーティーに　来ます。

2)　A:（　　　）を　食べますか。
　　B: りんごです。

3)　A: あさって（　　　）に　行きますか。
　　B: おおさかに　行きます。

4)　A: いもうとさんは（　　　）ぼうしを　買いましたか。
　　B: あかいぼうしを　買いました。

5)　A: それは（　　　）ですか。
　　B: これは　えんぴつです。

6)　A: このペンは（　　　）ですか。
　　B: ５００円です。

~~どんな~~　　なに　　だれ　　いくら　　なん　　どこ　　どの

JLPT-Style Questions

Choose the correct word for each blank.

1) アメリカは とても （　　） 国^{くに}です。

   1 大^{おお}きくて　2 大^{おお}きいな　3 大^{おお}きさ　4 大^{おお}きい

2) A:「このカレーは おいしいですか。」

   B:「いいえ、（　　） です。」

   1 おいしいではない　2 おいしかない　3 おいしい　4 おいしくない

3) 田中^{たなか}さんは （　　） 人^{ひと}です。

   1 げんき　2 げんきくない　3 げんきで　4 げんきな

4) A:「コーヒーが きらいですね。」

   B:「はい、そうですね。（　　） ですか。」

   1 すきでは ありません　2 すき　3 すきくない　4 すきな

5) 今日^{きょう} は 天気^{てんき}が （　　） です。

   1 いくない　2 よくない　3 いくてない　4 いいではない

6) （　　） かばんが すきですか。

   1 どこ　2 どちら　3 どんな　4 どれ

7) A:「かいぎは （　　） ですか。」

   B:「らいしゅうの 月^{げつ}よう日^びです。」

   1 いつ　2 だれ　3 何^{なに}　4 どこから

8) A:「りょうりは （　　） ですか。」

   B:「おいしいです。」

   1 どう　2 なぜ　3 どれ　4 いくら

9) A:「それは （　　） の 国^{くに} の 車^{くるま}ですか。」

   B:「アメリカのです。」

   1 どこ　2 何^{なに}　3 だれ　4 どれ

10) A:「いぬと ねこと （　　） が すきですか。」

    B:「いぬが すきです。」

    1 どう　2 どれぐらい　3 どちら　4 どこ

LESSON 3
Hobbies

DIALOGUE

Matt: しゅうまつに 何を しますか。
Shūmatsu ni nani o shimasu ka.
What do you do on weekends?

Yu: 山に のぼります。
Yama ni noborimasu.
I climb mountains.

Matt: せんしゅうまつは どこに 行きましたか。
Senshū-matsu wa doko ni ikimashita ka.
Where did you go last weekend?

Yu: ふじさんに のぼりました。
Fujisan ni noborimashita.
I climbed Mount Fuji.

Matt: さむかったですか。
Samukatta desu ka.
Was it cold?

Yu: いいえ、さむくなかったです。 しゃしんを 見たいですか。
Iie, samuku nakatta desu. Shashin o mitai desu ka.
No, it wasn't cold. Do you want to see a picture?

Matt: はい、見たいです。
Hai, mitai desu.
Yes, I want to see it.

Yu: ここは ふじさんの 上です。
Koko wa fujisan no ue desu.
Here is the top of Mount Fuji.

Matt: ねこと いっしょに のぼりましたか。
Neko to issho ni noborimashita ka.
You went climbing with your cats?

Yu: はい、わたしの ねこは 山が すきです。
Hai, watashi no neko wa yama ga suki desu.
Yes, my cats love mountains.

Can-Do Key Points

➡ Have a simple conversation about hobbies.
➡ Talk about the past.
➡ Talk about what you want and want to do.

POLITE PAST TENSE

To speak politely about the past, it is best to use ました with verbs, and たです or でした with adjectives.

	Affirmative polite past	Negative polite past
verbs	かきました **kakimashita** *wrote*	かきませんでした **kakimasen deshita** *didn't write*
い-*adjectives*	おもしろかったです **omoshirokatta desu** *(it) was fun*	おもしろくありませんでした **omoshiroku arimasen deshita** おもしろくなかったです **omoshiroku nakatta desu** *(it) wasn't fun*
な-*adjectives* *nouns*	べんりでした **benri deshita** べんりだったです **benri datta desu** *(it) was convenient*	べんり［じゃ/では］ありませんでした **benri [ja/dewa] arimasen deshita** べんり［じゃ/では］なかったです **benri [ja/dewa] nakatta desu** *(it) wasn't convenient*
いい *(irregular)*	よかったです **yokatta desu** *(it) was good*	よくなかったです **yoku nakatta desu** よくありませんでした **yoku arimasen deshita** *(it) wasn't good*

<u>EXAMPLES</u>

1) A:「きのう、ともだちに あいましたか。」
   Kinō, tomodachi ni aimashita ka.
   Did (you) meet (your) friend yesterday?

   B:「いいえ、あいませんでした。」
   Iie, aimasen deshita.
   No, (I) didn't meet (my friend).

2) おとといの かいぎは つまらなかったです。
   Ototoi no kaigi wa tsumaranakatta desu.
   The day before yesterday's meeting was boring.

3) このしょうせつは むずかしくなかったです。
   Kono shōsetsu wa muzukashiku nakatta desu.
   This novel wasn't difficult.

4) せんしゅう、わたしは びょうきでした。
   Senshū, watashi wa byōki deshita.
   Last week, I was sick.

5) A:「そのレストランは にぎやかでしたか。」
   Sono resutoran wa nigiyaka deshita ka.
   Was that restaurant lively?

   B:「いいえ、しずかでした。」
   Iie, shizuka deshita.
   No, it was quiet.

WATCH OUT!

Note the following pairs of sentences: the sentences marked with X are incorrect.

A:「きのうのパーティーは どうでしたか。」
Kinō no pātii wa dō deshita ka.
How was yesterday's party?

X　B:「おもしろいです。」　→　「おもしろかったです。」
Omoshiroi desu.　　　　<u>**Omoshirokatta**</u> **desu.**
(It) is fun.　　　　　　　*(It) was fun.*

X　きのう、あついかったです。　→　きのう、あつかったです。
Kinō, atsui katta desu.　　　**Kinō,** <u>**atsukatta**</u> **desu.**
　　　　　　　　　　　　　　It was hot yesterday.

> X　その女の子は　きれかったです。　→　その女の子は　きれいでした。
> **Sono onna no ko wa kire katta desu.**　**Sono onna no ko wa <u>kirei deshita</u>.**
> *That girl was pretty.*

GIVE IT A SHOT!

Write a response for each question like the example below.

れい）　Q: おとといは　つまらなかったですか。（いいえ）
　　　　A: <u>いいえ、つまらなくなかったです。</u>

1)　Q: せんしゅうは　ゆきではなかったですか。（いいえ）
　　A: _____

2)　Q: きのうは　いそがしかったですか。（いいえ）
　　A: _____

3)　Q: せんげつは　りょこうを　しましたか。（いいえ）
　　A: _____

4)　Q: きのう、何を　れんしゅう　しましたか。（日本語）
　　A: _____

5)　Q: せんしゅうまつは　どこに　行きましたか。（京都）
　　A: _____

6)　Q: いつ　ばんごはんを　食べましたか。（7時）
　　A: _____

HOW TO USE ほしい *hoshii* AND たい *tai*

You can use ほしい **hoshii** to talk about something you want, or the たい **tai** ending with the Vstem of a verb to talk about what you want to do.

FORM

> N ＋ が ＋ ほしいです。
> 　　ga　　hoshii desu
> N ＋ は ＋ ほしくないです。*
> 　　wa　　hoshiku nai desu.
> Vstem** ＋ たいです。
> 　　　　　tai desu.

NOTES

* When using the negative form (past or non-past), the は particle is most often used.

** To get the verb stem of a verb, you only have to take the ます **masu** off the end of the polite non-past form of the verb. For example, for 行く , the polite non-past form is 行きます – ます = 行き (Vstem).

EXAMPLES

1. 新しい車が ほしいです。
   Atarashii kuruma ga hoshii desu.
   (I) want a new car.

2. ワインが ほしいですか。
   Wain ga hoshii desu ka.
   (Do you) want wine?

3. ビールを 飲みたいです。
   Bīru o nomitai desu.
   (I) want to drink beer.

4. どこに 行きたいですか。
   Doko ni ikitai desu ka.
   Where do you want to go?

ほしい and the たい ending can be conjugated just like い-adjectives:

	Affirmative Non-past/past	*Negative Non-past/past*
ほしい	ほしいです **hoshii desu** *(I) want*	ほしくないです／ほしくありません **hoshiku nai desu/hoshiku arimasen** *(I) don't want*
	ほしかったです **hoshikatta desu** *(I) wanted*	ほしくなかったです／ほしくありませんでした **hoshiku nakatta desu/hoshiku arimasen deshita** *(I) didn't want*
行きたい	行きたいです **ikitai desu** *(I) want to go*	行きたくないです／行きたくありません **ikitaku nai desu/ikitaku arimasen** *(I) don't want to go*
	行きたかったです **ikitakatta desu** *(I) wanted to go*	行きたくなかったです／行きたくありませんでした **ikitaku nakatta desu/ikitaku arimasen deshita** *(I) didn't want to go*

1. いぬは ほしくないです。
   Inu wa hoshiku nai desu.
   (I) don't want a dog.

2. あかいぼうしが ほしかったです。
   Akai bōshi ga hoshikatta desu.
   (I) wanted a red hat.

3. ぎゅうにゅうを 飲みたくないです。
   Gyūnyū o nomitaku nai desu.
   (I) don't want to drink milk.

4. おおさかに 行きたくなかったです。
   Ōsaka ni ikitaku nakatta desu.
   (I) didn't want to go to Osaka.

The sentences marked with an X are not correct.

X　カレーを　食べるが　ほしいです。　→　わたしは　カレーを　食べたいです。
Karē o taberu ga hoshii desu.　　　　**Watashi wa karē o tabetai desu.**
(I) want the curry eating.　　　　　　*(I) want to eat curry.*

X　田中さま、何を　食べたいですか。*
Tanaka-sama, nani o tabetai desu ka.
Mr. Tanaka, what do you want to eat?

さま **sama** is a very polite way to refer to someone. It's more polite than
さん **san** and is usually used for guests or customers.

X　田中さんが　この本を　読みたいです。
Tanaka-san ga kono hon o yomitai desu.
Mr. Tanaka wants to read this book.

→　田中さんが　この本を　読みがっています。**
Tanaka-san ga kono hon o yomigatte imasu.
It seems like Mr. Tanaka wants to read this book.

* The たい form can be used in questions, but sounds a little too direct in situations that call for more politeness or humbleness.
** Talking about what someone else wants to do can sound too direct in Japanese. At the N4 level, you will learn the structure ~がっています, which means *it seems like someone wants to ~*.

GIVE IT A SHOT!

Complete the responses with your own ideas like the example below.

れい）Q: ペットが　ほしいですか。
　　　A: <u>はい、ペットが　ほしいです。</u>

1)　Q: どんなペットが　ほしいですか。

　　A: _____

2)　Q: たんじょうびに　何<ruby>何<rt>なに</rt></ruby>が　ほしいですか。

　　A: _____

3)　Q: こんしゅうまつは　何を　したいですか。

　　A: _____

4) Q: こんしゅうまつは 何<ruby>なに</ruby>を したくないですか。

   A: _____

5) Q: きょねんの たんじょうびは 何が ほしかったですか。

   A: _____

6) Q: せんしゅうまつは おおさかに 行<ruby>い</ruby>きたかったですか。

   A: _____

こそあど kosoado

In Japanese, there are a series of words that start with こ, そ, あ and ど that refer to a thing's place or a direction of movement.

こ **ko** – object near the speaker, or something the speaker himself/herself has referred to previously.

そ **so** – object near the listener or not close to either speaker or listener but in the same area, or something the listener has referred to previously.

あ **a** – object far away from and not in the same area as both listener and speaker, or something the listener and speaker have common knowledge about.

ど **do** – used to ask which (item), in which direction or where the object is.

Object	これ **kore** *this*	それ **sore** *that*	あれ **are** *that (over there)*	どれ **dore** *which*
Object	この ＋ N **kono + N** *this (noun)*	その ＋ N **sono + N** *that (noun)*	あの ＋ N **ano + N** *that (noun) (over there)*	どの ＋ N **dono + N** *which (noun)*
Object (polite), Direction	こちら **kochira** *this way*	そちら **sochira** *that way*	あちら **achira** *that way**	どちら **dochira** *which way*
Object (polite)	こちらの ＋ N **kochira no + N** *this (noun)*	そちらの ＋ N **sochira no + N** *that (noun)*	あちらの ＋ N **achira no + N** *that (noun) over there*	どちらの ＋ N **dochira no + N** *which (noun)*
Direction (casual)	こっち **kocchi** *this way*	そっち **socchi** *that way*	あっち **acchi** *that way**	どっち **docchi** *which way*
Place	ここ **koko** *here*	そこ **soko** *there*	あそこ **asoko** *over there*	どこ **doko** *where*
Kind of	こんな **konna** *this kind of*	そんな **sonna** *that kind of*	あんな **anna** *that kind of***	どんな **donna** *what kind of thing*
Way (adverb)	こう **kō** *like this*	そう **sō** *like that*	ああ **ā** *like that*	どう **dō** *in what way*

* in a direction away from both the listener and speaker

**referring to someone or something distant from both the speaker and listener

EXAMPLES

A: 「これは わたしの 車です。」
Kore wa watashi no kuruma desu.
This is my car.

B: 「いいえ、これは わたしの
車です。」
Iie, kore wa watashi no kuruma desu.
No, this is my car.

A: 「あれは グリッツホテルですか。」
Are wa Gurittsu hoteru desu ka.
Is that (over there) the Glitz Hotel?

B: 「はい、あれは グリッツホテル
です。」
Hai, are wa Gurittsu hoteru desu.
Yes, that (over there) is the Glitz Hotel.

A: 「あのパンやに 行きましたか。」
Ano pan-ya ni ikimashita ka.
Did you go to that bakery?

B: 「はい、行きました。おいしかったですよ。」
Hai, ikimashita. Oishikatta desu yo.
Yes, I did. It was a good bakery.

A: 「それは だれの 車ですか。」
Sore wa dare no kuruma desu ka.
Whose car is that?

B: 「ああ、それは わたしの 車です。」
Ā, sore wa watashi no kuruma desu.
Aah, that is my car.

こちらは 田中さんです。
Kochira wa Tanaka-san desu.
This is Ms. Tanaka.

こんなパソコンは いらないです。
Konna pasokon wa iranai desu.
(I) don't need this kind of computer.

LANGUAGE TIPS

どっしり：これは ソーダです。
Dosshiri: Kore wa sōda desu.
Plumpy: This is soda.

ぴかぴか：そうですね。
Pikapika: Sō desu ne.
Shiny: Yes, it is.

そう is used in a lot of common phrases that might show up in different parts of the test.

そうですか – Really? / Is that so?

A 「来週 アメリカに 行きます。」
Raishū Amerika ni ikimasu.
(I)'m going to America next week.

B 「ああ、そうですか。ニューヨークに 行きますか。」
Ā, sō desu ka. Nyūyōku ni ikimasu ka.
Is that so? Are (you) going to New York?

そうですよ – I know. I already knew that.

A 「田中さんは 来週 アメリカに 行きます。」
Tanaka-san wa raishū Amerika ni ikimasu.
Mr. Tanaka is going to America next week.

B 「そうですよ。わたしも いっしょに 行きますよ。」
Sō desu yo. Watashi mo issho ni ikimasu yo.
I know. I'm going together (with him), too.

そうですね – I agree. I feel the same way.

A 「今日は あついですね。」
Kyō wa atsui desu ne.
(It) is hot today, isn't it?

B 「そうですね。はるですが とてもあついですね。」
Sō desu ne. Haru desu ga totemo atsui desu ne.
I agree. (It) is spring, but (it) is totally hot, isn't it?

そうです – Yes!

A 「来週 アメリカに 行きますか。」
Raishū Amerika ni ikimasu ka.
Next week, are (you) going to America?

B 「はい、そうです。」
Hai, sō desu.
Yes!

WATCH OUT!

X これ車は やすいです。 → この車は やすいです。
Kore kuruma wa yasui desu. **Kono kuruma wa yasui desu.**
This car is cheap.

X きのう、東京うに 行きました。あそこで かいぎが ありました。
Kinō, Tōkyō ni ikimashita. Asoko de kaigi ga arimashita.
Yesterday, I went to Tokyo. I had a meeting (over) there.

→ そこで かいぎが ありました。
Soko de kaigi ga arimashita.
I had a meeting there.

X アメリカは どんなですか。 → アメリカは どんな国ですか。
Amerika wa donna desu ka. **Amerika wa donna kuni desu ka.**
What kind of is America? *What kind of country is America?*

GIVE IT A SHOT!

Use the こそあど **kosoado** words from the chart on (page 72) to complete the sentences like the example below.

れい) A:「(これ) は、いい 本です。」
B:「ほんとうですか。」

1) A:「( ) は だれの かぎですか。」
B:「( ) は 田中さんの かぎです。」

2) A:「あなたの かばんは ( )
かばんですか。」
B:「しろい かばんです。」

3) A:「トイレは （ 　　 ）に ありますか。」
　 B:「（ 　　 ）です。」

4) A:（ 　　 ）は スミスさんの いえですか。」
　 B:「いいえ、スミスさんの いえは （ 　　 ）
　 　 に あります。」

5) A:（ 　　 ）くつは いくらですか。」
　 B:「15,600 円です。」

6) A:「きのう、 こうべに 行きました。」
　 B:「（ 　　 ）に いいレストランは
　 　 ありますか。」

JLPT-Style Questions

1) A:「だいじょうぶですか。 いしゃを （ 　　 ）。」
　 B:「はい、 いしゃは 来ますよ。」
　 1 よんでか　　 2 よびましたか　　 3 よみましたか　　 4 よびほしいか

2) A:「金よう日は どうでしたか。」
　 B:「（ 　　 ）。」
　 1 おもしろいでした　　　　　　　　 3 おもしろかったです
　 2 おもしろいです　　　　　　　　　 4 おもしろくないです

3) A:「先週まつは あそびましたか。」

　　B:「いいえ、（　　　）。」

　　1 あそびました　　　　　　　　　3 あそびません

　　2 あそびませんでした　　　　　　4 あそびます

4) ゆうべは パーティーに （　　　）。

　　1 行きましたか　　　　　　　　　3 行きませんか

　　2 行きますか　　　　　　　　　　4 行っていますか

5) A:「先月は いそがしかったですか。」

　　B:「いいえ、（　　　）。」

　　1 ひまかったです　　　　　　　　3 ひまです

　　2 ひまでした　　　　　　　　　　4 ひまでは あります

6) わたしは こども （　　　） です。

　　1 がほしい　2 ができたい　3 をほしい　4 がありたい

7) わたしは 白いズボンを （　　　）。

　　1 買いますほしいです　　　　　　3 買いたいです

　　2 買うほしいです　　　　　　　　4 買うがほしいです

8) A:「パーティーで うたいましたか。」

　　B:「いいえ、でも（　　　）。」

　　1 うたいたかったです　　　　　　3 うたいたくなかったです

　　2 うたいました　　　　　　　　　4 うたいたくないです

9) 新しいしごと（　　　） ほしいです。

　　1 は　　　　　　　　2 が　　　　　　　　3 の　　　　　　　　4 を

10) わたしは にくを （　　　）。

　　1 食べたくないです

　　2 食べりたくないです

　　3 食べたいでは ありません

　　4 食べたいでした

LESSON 4
Simple Instructions

DIALOGUE

Yu: さむいです。
Samui desu.
(It) is cold.

Matt: 何か あたたかいものを 飲みたいですか。
Nani ka atatakai mono o nomitai desu ka.
Do you want to drink something hot?

Yu: はい、 おねがいします。
Hai, onegai shimasu.
Yes, please.

Matt: じゃ、 お店に 行って きます。
Ja, omise ni itte kimasu.
Well, (I) will go to the store and come back.

(Matt leaves to get a drink.)
. . .

(Matt hands Yu the drink.)

Matt: はい、どうぞ。ああ、きれい。わたしの　しゃしんを
とってください。
Hai, dōzo. Ā, kirei. Watashi no shashin o totte kudasai.
Yeah, here you go. Ahh, pretty. Please take my picture.

Yu: はい。
Hai.
Okay.

Matt: このカメラで　とって　ください。
Kono kamera de totte kudasai.
Please take (it) with this camera.

(Matt hands his camera to her.)

Yu: はい。じゃ、右へ　行って　ください。右へ… もっと右へ。
Hai. Ja, migi e itte kudasai. Migi e … motto migi e.
Okay. Well, go right please. (Go) right … more right.

(*Splash* *click*)

Yu: わぁ、いいしゃしんです。
Wā, ii shashin desu.
Wow, great picture.

Can-do Key Points

➡ Give simple commands and directions.
➡ Make polite requests.
➡ Talk about locations of actions or objects.

THE て *te* FORM

The て **te** form can be used to link multiple actions together sequentially, or to link actions in a chronological order.

Verbs

Group 1		Group 2	
言う **iu** *to say*	言って **itte** *say*	見る **miru** *to see*	見て **mite** *see*
立つ **tatsu** *to stand*	立って **tatte** *stand*	食べる **taberu** *to eat*	食べて **tabete** *eat*
かえる **kaeru** *to return*	かえって **kaette** *return*	出る **deru** *to leave/appear*	出て **dete** *leave/appear*
読む **yomu** *to read*	読んで **yonde** *read*	ねる **neru** *to go to bed*	ねて **nete** *go to bed*
あそぶ **asobu** *to play*	あそんで **asonde** *play*	おきる **okiru** *to wake up/rise*	おきて **okite** *wake up/rise*
しぬ **shinu** *to die*	しんで **shinde** *die*	（いぬが）いる **(inu ga) iru** *(a dog) exists*	いて **ite** *exist*
書く **kaku** *to write*	書いて **kaite** *write*	Group 3	
ぬぐ **nugu** *to take off (clothes)*	ぬいで **nuide** *take off (clothes)*	来る **kuru** *to come*	来て **kite** *come*
行く **iku** *to go*	行って * **itte** *go*	する **suru** *to do*	して **shite** *do*
話す **hanasu** *to talk*	話して **hanashite** *talk*		

* exception

EXAMPLES

今日、ひるごはんを 食べて がっこうに 行きます。
Kyō, hirugohan o tabete gakkō ni ikimasu.
Today, (I) am going to eat lunch and then go to the school.

毎日、7時に おきて、はを みがいて、あさごはんを 食べます。
Mainichi, shichiji ni okite, ha o migaite, asagohan o tabemasu.
Every day, (I) wake up at 7, brush my teeth, and then eat breakfast.

WATCH OUT!

X ビールを 飲みて、にくを 食べます。
Biiru o nomite, niku o tabemasu.

→ ビールを 飲んで、にくを 食べます。
Biiru o nonde, niku o tabemasu.
(I) drink beer and eat meat.

X プールで およんで、水を 飲みました。
Pūru de oyonde, mizu o nomimashita.

→ プールで およいで、水を 飲みました。
Pūru de oyoide, mizu o nomimashita.
(I) swam in the pool, and drank water.

X 行いて きます。 → 行って きます。
Iite kimasu. **Itte kimasu.**
I'm off to work./I'm going now.

GIVE IT A SHOT!

Use the て-form of verbs to link the sentences together like the example below.

れい） ともだちに あいます。きっさてんに 行きました。
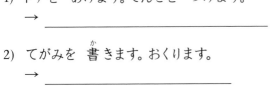
→ ともだちに あって、きっさてんに 行きました。

1) ドアを あけます。でんきを つけます。
→ _____

2) てがみを 書きます。おくります。
→ _____

3) 田中さんは ズボンを はきます。ワイシャツを きます。
→ _____

4) きのう、この本を 読みました。レポートを 書きました。

    → _____

5) いえに つきました。ふくを ぬぎました。シャワーを あびました。ベッド
   で ねました。

    → _____

6) まいばん、ばんごはんを つくります。食べます。テレビを 見ます。

    → _____

THE で *de* PARTICLE

The で **de** particle can be used to mark the location where something takes place.

Form

> N + で **de**

<u>EXAMPLES</u>

■ としょかんで 日本語を べんきょう しました。
  Toshokan de Nihongo o benkyō shimashita.
  (I) studied Japanese at the library.

■ らいしゅう、あのたてもので はたらきます。
  Raishū, ano tatemono de hatarakimasu.
  Next week, (I) am working in that building over there.

WATCH OUT!

X 田中さんは いえで います。
  Tanaka-san wa ie de imasu.

   → 田中さんは いえに います。
     Tanaka-san wa ie ni imasu.
     Mr. Tanaka is at home.

X 日本語の 本は かばんで あります。
  Nihongo no hon wa kaban de arimasu.

   → 日本語の 本は かばんに あります。
     Nihongo no hon wa kaban ni arimasu.
     (My) Japanese book is in (my) bag.

GIVE IT A SHOT!

Rewrite the words into a correct sentence, like the example below.

れい) で / 食べました / を / ひるごはん / スプーン
　　→ スプーンで ひるごはんを 食べました。

1) で / けっこん / こうべ / しました
　　→ きょねん ＿＿＿＿＿＿＿＿＿＿＿＿＿＿

2) します / しゅくだい / ベッド / 日本語 / で / の
　　→ ＿＿＿＿＿＿＿＿＿＿＿＿＿＿＿＿＿

3) と / あそびました / で / いっしょに / こども
　　→ こうえん＿＿＿＿＿＿＿＿＿＿＿＿＿＿＿＿＿＿

4) 買いました / この / を / か / どこ / やさい / で
　　→ ＿＿＿＿＿＿＿＿＿＿＿＿＿＿＿＿＿

5) を / はがき / 買いました / で / ゆうびんきょく
　　→ ＿＿＿＿＿＿＿＿＿＿＿＿＿＿＿＿＿＿＿

The で **de** particle can also be used to mean 'by, with, using' or to mark the cause of something.

Form:

> N + で **de**

<u>EXAMPLES</u>

- スミスさんと 電話で 話しました。
  Sumisu-san to denwa de hanashimashita.
  (I) talked to Mr. Smith on the phone.

- てがみを ペンで 書きました。
  Tegami o pen de kakimashita.
  (I) wrote a letter with a pen.

- りんごは 5つで 1000円です。
  Ringo wa itsutsu de sen-en desu.
  Apples are 1000 yen for 5.

- 山田さんは びょうきで しごとを 休みました。
  Yamada-san wa byōki de shigoto o yasumimashita.
  Mr. Yamada was absent from work because he was sick.

X 東京に でんしゃを のるで 行きます。
Tōkyō ni densha o norude ikimasu.

→ 東京に でんしゃで 行きます。
Tōkyō ni densha de ikimasu.
(I) am going to Tokyo by train.

X 田中さんで ひるごはんを 食べます。
Tanaka-san de hirugohan o tabemasu.

→ 田中さんと ひるごはんを 食べます。
Tanaka-san to hirugohan o tabemasu.
(I) am eating lunch with Mr. Tanaka.

GIVE IT A SHOT!

Rewrite the words into a correct sentence, like the example below.

れい) 行きます / バス / に / えき / で / この
→ <u>このバスで えきに 行きます。</u>

1) を / ケーキ / ナイフ / きります / で
→ _____

2) は / で / えいご / なん / か / です
→「おはようございます」 _____

3) 500円 / その / 3さつ / で / です / 本 / は
→ _____

4) 15分 / 駅 / に / で / つきます。
→ _____

5) その / 1万円 / を / 本 / で / 買いました
→ _____

6) いたい / です / は / スミスさん / で / あたま / かぜ / が
→ _____

THE に *ni* PARTICLE

The に **ni** particle can be used to mark the time or the frequency that something happens.

Form:

> N + に **ni**

EXAMPLES

- まいあさ 8時に おきます。
  Maiasa hachiji ni okimasu.
  Every day, (I) wake up at 8.

- いっしゅうかんに いっかい じゅぎょうが あります。
  Isshū-kan ni ikkai jugyō ga arimasu.
  (I) have class once a week.

WATCH OUT!

X きょねんに いえを 買いました。
Kyonen ni ie o kaimashita.

→ きょねん いえを 買いました。
Kyonen ie o kaimashita.
Last year, (I) bought a house.

X にかいに いっかげつ さんぽを します。
Nikai ni ikkagetsu sanpo o shimasu.

→ いっかげつに にかい さんぽを します。
Ikkagetsu ni nikai sanpo o shimasu.
(I) take a walk twice a month.

The に **ni** particle can also be used to mark a location being traveled to.

EXAMPLES

- いえに かえります。
  Ie ni kaerimasu.
  (I) am going home.

- スミスさんは かいぎに 行きました。
  Sumisu-san wa kaigi ni ikimashita.
  Mr. Smith went to a meeting.

X　わたしは　アパートに　日本語を　れんしゅう　します。
Watashi wa apāto ni Nihongo o renshū shimasu.

→　わたしは　アパートで　日本語を　れんしゅう　します。
Watashi wa apāto de Nihongo o renshū shimasu.
I practice Japanese at (my) apartment.

GIVE IT A SHOT!

Rearrange the words to form a question and answer, making necessary changes to verbs, etc., like the examples below.

れい1)　まいあさ / いえを 出る / 8:00　→
　　　Q: まいあさ 何時に いえを 出ますか。
　　　A: 8時に いえを 出ます。

れい2)　おととい / 行く / きょうと
　　　Q: おととい どこに 行きましたか。
　　　A: きょうとに 行きました。

1)　けさ / おきる / 7:00 →
　　　Q: _____
　　　A: _____

2)　まいばん / ねる / 11:00 →
　　　Q: _____
　　　A: _____

3)　ゆうべ / 電話を する / 8:00 →
　　　Q: _____
　　　A: _____

4)　まいしゅうまつ / ジムに 行く / 2:00 →
　　　Q: _____
　　　A: _____

5)　せんしゅう / 行く / なら
　　　Q: _____
　　　A: _____

6) 毎年（まいとし）ふゆ / 行く（い）/ おきなわ

Q: _____

A: _____

ADDITIONAL LANGUAGE TIPS

あげる、くれる、もらう
ageru, kureru, morau
to give, to give, to receive

All of these verbs can be used to talk about giving and receiving objects. あげ
る and くれる both mean 'to give,' so when do you use which? Well, the
basic answer is that when the receiver is the speaker, you use くれる, but if
the receiver is not the speaker, we would use あげる.

EXAMPLES

■ わたしは 田中さんに プレゼントを あげます。
Watashi wa Tanaka-san ni purezento o agemasu.
I will give a present to Mr. Tanaka.

■ 田中さんは わたしに プレゼントを くれました。
Tanaka-san wa watashi ni purezento o kuremashita.
Mr. Tanaka gave a present to me.

But we can also use くれる in this situation:

■ 田中さんは 父に プレゼントを くれました。
Tanaka-san wa chichi ni purezento o kuremashita.
Mr. Tanaka gave my father a present.

So, why is that? Well, there is a Japanese concept of the 'in-group' (内, **uchi**) and
the 'out-group' (外, **soto**). If the receiver is in the 'out-group' from the viewpoint
of the speaker, we use あげる. If the receiver is in the 'in-group' in respect to the
giver, we use くれる.

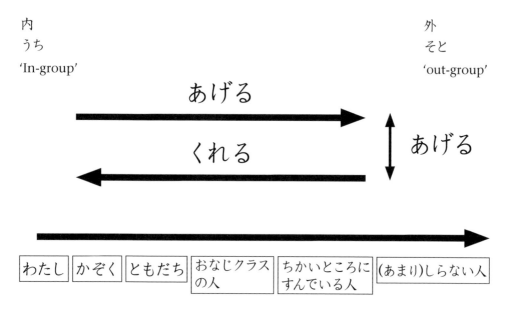

So, let's take a look at that sentence again:

- 田中さんは 父に プレゼントを くれました。
  Tanaka-san wa chichi ni purezento o kuremashita.
  Mr. Tanaka gave my father a present.

田中さん (**Tanaka-san**, Mr. Tanaka) is in a group different from 父 (**chichi**, father). 父 is in the 'in-group' for the speaker, more than 田中さん, so we use くれる.

This is just a general guideline though. Who is in the 'in-group' and who is in the 'out-group' differs, depending on the person and region of Japan. Sometimes friends are included in the 'in-group,' but sometimes they aren't. Generally speaking, the 1st person, the speaker, is always in the 'in-group.' Your immediate family is usually in the 'in-group' too, but beyond that there is nothing really standard. The rule is: anyone you empathize with is in your 'in-group,' which leaves a lot to be interpreted.

もらう is simply 'to receive,' so there is no need to worry about 'in-groups' or 'out-groups' for this verb.

Form:

> (out-group) は・が (in-group) に くれる
> (in-group) は・が (out-group) に あげる
> (out-group) は・が (out-group) に あげる
> (receiver) は・が (giver) に・から もらう

EXAMPLES

- ともだちは 母に プレゼントを くれました。
  Tomodachi wa haha ni purezento o kuremashita.
  My friend gave my mother a present.

- 田中さんは ともだちに プレゼントを くれました/あげました。*
  Tanaka-san wa tomodachi ni purezento o kuremashita/agemashita.
  Mr. Tanaka (somebody I don't know so well) gave my (close) friend a present.

* Both verbs can be used; there are no strict rules when talking about giving to a close
  friend by someone you don't know well.

- ともだちは 田中さんに プレゼントを あげました。
  Tomodachi wa Tanaka-san ni purezento o agemashita.
  My (close) friend gave Mr. Tanaka (somebody I don't know so well) a present.

- 母は ともだちに プレゼントを あげました。
  Haha wa tomodachi ni purezento o agemashita.
  My mother gave my friend a present.

- ともだちは 田中さんに プレゼントを もらいました。
  Tomodachi wa Tanaka-san ni purezento o moraimashita.
  My friend received a present from Mr. Tanaka.

- ともだちは 母から プレゼントを もらいました。
  Tomodachi wa haha kara purezento o moraimashita.
  My friend received a present from my mother.

SOMETHING AND NOTHING

You can add か **ka** to a question word to refer to an unspecified person, place,
thing, etc. (i.e. someone, someplace, something, etc.).

Form

> **Question word +** か **+ (**と*、に*、で*、が**、を、へ**)**
> ka (to*, ni*, de*, ga**, o, e)

Common collocations:

どこか、どこかで、どこかに、どこかへ
doko ka, doko ka de, doko ka ni, doko ka e

何か、何かで、何かに、何かを
nani ka, nani ka de, nani ka ni, nani ka o

だれか、だれかと、だれかに、だれかを、だれかへ
dare ka, dare ka to, dare ka ni, dare ka o, dare ka e

いつか
itsu ka

* Particles と **to**, で **de**, and に **ni** cannot be dropped, but を **o**, and へ **e** are usually dropped.

** The が **ga** particle is rarely used in this structure.

EXAMPLES

1) A:「こんしゅうまつは どこかへ 行きますか。」
    Konshū-matsu wa doko ka e ikimasu ka.
    This weekend, are you going somewhere?

    B:「はい、ほんやへ 行きます。」
    Hai, honya e ikimasu.
    Yes, (I) am going to the bookstore.

2) A:「とうきょうで 何か 買いましたか。」
    Tōkyō de nani ka kaimashita ka.
    Did (you) buy something in Tokyo?

    B:「はい、おいしいおかしを 買いました。」
    Hai, oishii okashi o kaimashita.
    Yes, (I) bought delicious sweets.

3) A:「だれかと プールで およぎましたか。」
    Dare ka to pūru de oyogimashita ka.
    Did (you) swim with someone at the pool?

    B:「にしまきさんと いっしょに およぎました。」
    Nishimaki-san to issho ni oyogimashita.
    (I) swam together with Mr. Nishimaki.

4) だれか ドアを 開けました。
    Dare ka doa o akemashita.
    Somebody opened the door.

You can add も **mo** to a question word with a negative sentence to refer to 'nothing, nowhere, no one,' etc.

Form

> **Question word + (と*、に*、で*、を、へ) + も**
> **(to*, ni*, de*, o, e)   mo**

Common collocations:

どこも、どこでも、どこにも、どこへも
doko mo, doko de mo, doko ni mo, doko e mo

何も、何でも、何にも
nani mo, nani de mo, nani ni mo

だれも、だれでも、だれにも、だれとも
dare mo, dare de mo, dare ni mo, dare to mo

いつも
itsu mo

* Particles と **to**, で **de**, and に **ne** cannot be dropped, but を **o** and へ **e** are usually dropped.

<u>EXAMPLES</u>

1) A:「けさ　何か　食べましたか。」
   Kesa nani ka tabemashita ka.
   Did (you) eat something this morning?

   B:「いいえ、何も　食べませんでした。」
   Iie, nani mo tabemasen deshita.
   No, (I) didn't eat anything.

2) あした　どこへも　行きません。
   Ashita doko e mo ikimasen.
   Tomorrow, (I) am not going anywhere.

3) だれにも　言いませんでした。
   Dare ni mo iimasen deshita.
   (I) didn't tell anyone.

In a positive sentence, this same construction can be used to refer to 'everywhere, every time, always' etc.

4) 田中さんは　いつも　はたらいています。
   Tanaka-san wa itsu mo hataraite imasu.
   Ms. Tanaka is always working.

X　だれは　わかりません。　→　だれも　わかりません
Dare wa wakarimasen.　　　　**Dare mo wakarimasen.**
Nobody knows.

X　このけいたいでんわは　どこもで　つかいます。
Kono keitai denwa wa doko mo de tsukaimasu.

→　このけいたいでんわは　どこでも　つかいます。
Kono keitai denwa wa doko de mo tsukaimasu.
(I) use this cellphone everywhere.

X　だれにか　あいました。　→　だれかに　あいました。
Dare ni ka aimashita.　　　　**Dare ka ni aimashita.**
(I) met somebody.

GIVE IT A SHOT!

Fill in the correct word from the box below like the example below.

れい)(<u>何か</u>) 飲みものを　ください。

1)　わたしの　さいふを (　　　　) 見ましたか。

2)　A:「おなかが　いたいです。」
　　B:「そうなんですか。(　　　　) 食べましたか。」

3)　しゅうまつは (　　　　) 行きたいです。

4)　あしたは (　　　　) あいますか。

5)　(　　　　) えいごを　話しますか。

どこかで	だれか	どこかへ	だれかに	何か

1)　ゆうべは　ともだちは (　　　　) 来ませんでした。

2)　きょうは (　　　　) 行きませんでした。

3)　きのうは (　　　　) 話したくなかったです。

4)　これは (　　　　) あげません。

5)　本には (　　　　) 書きませんでした。

どこへも	何も	だれも	だれにも	だれとも

THE へ e PARTICLE

You can use the へ e particle to mark a location that is being moved to or toward. In a lot of situations, it can be interchanged with に ni, but there is more emphasis on the direction of travel.

Form

N + へ e

EXAMPLES

- わたしは ひこうきで とうきょうへ 行きます。
  Watashi wa hikōki de Tōkyō e ikimasu.
  (I) am going to Tokyo by plane.

- 外国へ 行きたいです。
  Gaikoku e ikitai desu.
  (I) want to go to a foreign country.

WATCH OUT!

X 7時へ かいぎが あります。 → 7時に かいぎが あります。
　Shichiji e kaigi ga arimasu.　　　**Shichiji ni kaigi ga arimasu.**
　　　　　　　　　　　　　　　　There is a meeting at 7.

X ともだちへ あいました。 → ともだちに あいました。
　Tomodachi e aimashita.　　　　**Tomodachi ni aimashita.**
　　　　　　　　　　　　　　　　(I) met (my) friend.

GIVE IT A SHOT!

Use the words to form sentences like the example below.

れい) は / 行きました / か / どこ / お父さん / へ
　　→ お父さんは どこへ 行きましたか。

1) へ / こっち / ください / 来て
　　→ _____

2) 西川さん / へ / は / 毎日 / 行きます / そこ
　　→ _____

3) は / 田中さん / へ / どこ / 行きました / か

→ _____

4) 西 / その / へ / は / 行きました / 車

→ _____

5) を / は / もって / 行きました / へ / はこ / 森下さん / にかい

→ _____

ください kudasai AND くださいませんか kudasaimasenka

You can use ください kudasai for smaller requests or くださいませんか kudasaimasenka for bigger requests or to be very polite.

Form:

> Vte / N を + ください
>   o   kudasai
> Vte / N を + くださいませんか
>   o   kudasaimasen ka

EXAMPLES

■ すわって ください。
Suwatte kudasai
Sit please.

■ ビールを 一つ ください。
Biiru o hitotsu kudasai.
One beer please.

■ 道を おしえて くださいませんか。
Michi o oshiete kudasaimasen ka.
Could you please tell me the way/street?

■ のみものを くださいませんか。
Nomimono o kudasaimasen ka.
Could you please (give me) a drink?

GIVE IT A SHOT!

Fill in each blank with the correct word from the box below to make requests.

れい) (ゆうびんきょくで) <u>きってを</u> ください。

1) まどを ＿＿＿＿ ください。

2) ＿＿＿＿ いっぱい ください。

3) くつを ＿＿＿ くださいませんか。

4) 何か^{なに} ＿＿＿ くださいませんか。

＿＿＿＿＿＿＿＿＿＿＿＿＿＿＿＿＿＿＿＿＿＿＿＿＿＿＿＿
　　水^{みず}　　　~~きって~~　　　しめる　　　しごと　　　ぬぐ
＿＿＿＿＿＿＿＿＿＿＿＿＿＿＿＿＿＿＿＿＿＿＿＿＿＿＿＿

JLPT-Style Questions

1) あさって 東京^{とうきょう}へ 電車^{でんしゃ}（　）行^いきます。
   1 に　　　　　　2 は　　　　　　3 が　　　　　　4 で

2) 一年^{いちねん}（　）3かい 山^{やま}に のぼります。
   1 に　　　　　　2 が　　　　　　3 と　　　　　　4 を

3) あした デパート（　）買^かいものを します。
   1 に　　　　　　2 で　　　　　　3 へ　　　　　　4 が

4) としょかん（　）西村さんに　会いましたか。

    1 を   2 に   3 は   4 で

5) 先週の　日よう日は　どこ（　）出かけなかったですか。

    1 かへ   2 へも   3 へか   4 もへ

6) この　くつしたは　5つ（　）500円です。

    1 が   2 を   3 に   4 で

7) その　本は（　）ありません。

    1 どこも   2 どこに   3 どこにも   4 どこへ

8) 山田さんは　まんねんひつ（　）てがみを　書きます。

    1 で   2 を   3 は   4 に

9) 父は　しごと（　）東京に　行きます。

    1 で   2 に   3 が   4 を

10) この　道を　左（　）まがってください。

    1 が   2 で   3 を   4 へ

それでは、りんごと バナナの アイスクリームを 食べましょうか。
Well, let's eat apple and banana ice cream.

わたしの ねこも 来るでしょう。
My cats are probably coming too.

ねこも 来ますか。
(Your) cats are coming, too?

ええ、ねこも りんごと バナナの アイスクリームが すきですから。
Yeah, because (my) cats also like apple and banana ice cream.

ねこは いつも バナナを 食べています。
My cats are always eating bananas.

LESSON 5
Weekend Plans

Matt: こんしゅうまつは おすしを 食べに 行きませんか。
Konshū-matsu wa osushi o tabe ni ikimasen ka.
Would you like to go and eat sushi this weekend?

Yu: いいですね。 アイスクリームも 食べたいです。
Ii desu ne. Aisu kuriimu mo tabetai desu.
That's a good idea. (I) also want to eat some ice cream.

Matt: わたしも。 どんなアイスクリームが すきですか。
Watashi mo. Donna aisu kuriimu ga suki desu ka.
Me, too. What kind of ice cream do you like?

Yu: りんごと バナナが すきです。
Ringo to banana ga suki desu.
I like apple and banana (ice cream).

Matt: りんごと バナナですか。
Ringo to banana desu ka.
Apple and banana?

Yu: はい、 バニラや チョコレートより おいしいです。
Hai, banira ya chokorēto yori oishii desu.
Yeah, it is more delicious than vanilla, chocolate, etc...

Matt: それでは、りんごと バナナの アイスクリームを 食べましょうか。
Sore de wa, ringo to banana no aisu kuriimu o tabemashō ka.
Well, let's eat apple and banana ice cream.

Yu: わたしの ねこも 来るでしょう。
Watashi no neko mo kuru deshō.
My cats are probably coming too.

Matt: ねこも 来ますか。
Neko mo kimasu ka.
(Your) cats are coming, too?

Yu: ええ、ねこも りんごと バナナの アイスクリームが すきですから。ねこは いつも バナナを 食べています。
Ē, neko mo ringo to banana no aisu kuriimu ga suki desu kara. Neko wa itsumo banana o tabete imasu.
Yeah, because (my) cats also like apple and banana ice cream. My cats are always eating bananas.

Can-Do Key Points

➡ Give options or examples
➡ Make suggestions

THE を *o* PARTICLE

The most common use of the を **o** particle is to mark the object of a sentence.

Form:

> N + を **o**

EXAMPLES

■ りんごを 食べました。
Ringo o tabemashita.
(I) ate an apple.

■ はを みがきました。
Ha o migakimashita.
(I) brushed (my) teeth.

Sometimes を **o** can be replaced with が **ga** if you are talking about something you like or something you want to do:

O りんごが 食べたいです。
Ringo ga tabetai desu.
(I) want to eat an apple.

X りんごが 食べます。
Ringo ga tabemasu.
An apple is going to eat.

The が **ga** particle can also be used when we talk about the state of an object (て ある **te aru**, page 116).

■ かみに メッセージが 書いてあります。
Kami ni messēji ga kaite arimasu.
There is a message written on the paper.

It can also be replaced by は **wa** if it is the topic of the conversation or to use it for contrast.

■ コーヒーは 飲みます。おちゃは 飲みません。
Kōhii wa nomimasu. Ocha wa nomimasen.
As for coffee, (I) drink (it). As for tea, (I) don't drink (it).

WATCH OUT!

X ギターを れんしゅうを します。 → ギターの れんしゅうを します。
Gitā o renshū o shimasu.   **Gitā no renshū o shimasu.**
                                    (I) am going to practice the guitar.

X ビールをは 飲みません。 → ビールは 飲みません。
Biiru o wa nomimasen.   **Biiru wa nomimasen.**
                                (I) don't drink beer.

If the が **ga** particle can be used, write it in the blank. If not, use the を **o** particle.

れい1) わたしは かいぎで 日本語（ **が** ）話したいです。

れい2) わたしは かいぎで 日本語（ **を** ）話します。

1) あしたは おすし（　　）食べたいです。

2) しゃしん（　　）とります。

3) トムの 名前（　　）よびました。

4) 新しい カメラ（　　）買いたいです。

THE と *to*, や *ya*, AND か *ga* PARTICLES

The と **to**, や **ya** and か **ka** particles can link nouns together, but they have different meanings. と **to** links two (or more) nouns together like "and" in English. や **ya** also has a meaning of "and," but や implies that there are more options. か **ka** can be used to mark two (or more) alternatives, like "or" in English.

Form:

> N + と (to) + N
> N + や (ya) + N
> N + か (ka) + N

EXAMPLES

- 田中さんと 西村さんが 来ました。
  Tanaka-san to Nishimura-san ga kimashita.
  Mr. Tanaka and Mr. Nishimura came.

- パスタや おすしが すきです。
  Pasuta ya osushi ga suki desu.
  (I) like pasta, sushi (and something else).

- パスタか ピザを 食べます。
  Pasuta ka piza o tabemasu.
  (I) am going to eat pasta or pizza.

WATCH OUT!

X （レストランで）おちゃや ビールを ください。
(Resutoran de) ocha ya biiru o kudasai.
(At a restaurant) Tea and beer (and something else) please.

→ おちゃと ビールを ください。
Ocha to biiru o kudasai.
Tea and beer please.

X ビールや ワインや 飲みたいです。
Biiru ya wain ya nomitai desu.

→ ビールや ワインを 飲みたいです。
Biiru ya wain o nomitai desu.
(I) want to drink beer and wine (and something else).

GIVE IT A SHOT!

Form a sentence with the words like the example below.

れい）田中さん / 川口さん / 来ます / パーティー / に / が / と
→ 田中さんと 川口さんが パーティーに 来ます。

1) が / や / すきです / いぬ / ねこ
→ _____

2) コーヒー / きって / と / にまい / ください / ふたつ
→ _____
_____

3) か / を / ねこ / 買います / いぬ
→ _____

4) と / にしむらさん / しました / を / テニス
→ _____

5) 月よう日 / 金よう日 / に / はしります / や
→ _____

The と **to** particle can also be used to quote what a person is saying:

■ 「はい。」と 言いました。
「**Hai.**」 **to iimashita.**
(He) said, "Yes."

■ 「これは いくらですか。」と 聞きました。
「**Kore wa ikura desu ka.**」 **to kikimashita.**
(He) asked, "How much is this?"

You will often see this structure being used in the reading section when somebody is telling a story.

THE も *mo* PARTICLE

The も **mo** particle can mean 'too' or 'also' when used with a positive sentence, or 'not either' with a negative sentence.

Form:

> N + も
>   mo
>
> N + で, に, へ + も
>   de ni e   mo

<u>EXAMPLES</u>

- ドイツに 行きました。フランスにも 行きました。
  Doitsu ni ikimashita. Furansu ni mo ikimashita.
  (I) went to Germany. (I) also went to France.

- A:「いぬが すきです。」
  Inu ga suki desu.
  (I) like dogs.
  B:「わたしも すきです。」
  Watashi mo suki desu.
  (I) like (them) too.

- 東京に バスでも 行きます。
  Tōkyō ni basu de mo ikimasu.
  (I) am also taking the bus to Tokyo.

- おてあらいは あそこにも あります。
  Otearai wa asoko ni mo arimasu.
  There is a restroom over there, too.

WATCH OUT!

X わたしもは 来ます。 → わたしも 来ます。
Watashi mo wa kimasu.   **Watashi mo kimasu.**
                              I'm also coming.

X ピザをも つくりました。 → ピザも つくりました。*
Piza o mo tsukurimashita.   **Piza mo tsukurimashita.**
                              (I) also made pizza.

---

* In rare cases, the particles を **o** and も **mo** can be used together to emphasize objects.

GIVE IT A SHOT!

Use the words to form a sentence like the example below.

れい) やさしい / です / も / 神戸^{こうべ} / の / 人^{ひと}

→ 神戸の 食^たべものは おいしいです。

　　そして <u>神戸の 人も やさしいです。</u>

1) も / に / そこ / 新聞^{しんぶん} / は / 本^{ほん} / も / あります

→ _____

2) ざっし / も / あります / 2さつ

→ <u>新聞^{しんぶん}が 2さつ あります。</u>

3) て / おすし / 食^たべます / は / も / で

→ _____

4) も / 月^{げつ}よう日^び / も / 休^{やす}み / 今週^{こんしゅう} / 火^かよう日^び / は / は

→ _____

5) いしゃ / も / 田中^{たなか}さん / 西村^{にしむら}さん / も / です

→ _____

6) に / わたし / ください / おなじ / も / もの / を

→ _____

ましょうか mashō ka AND ませんか masen ka

You can make invitations with ましょうか **mashō ka** and ませんか **masen ka**. ましょうか is used to seek mutual understanding or agreement of something, while ませんか is to ask the listener's opinion.

Form:

> **V-masu + ましょうか**
> 　　　　mashō ka
>
> **V-masu + ませんか**
> 　　　　masen ka

EXAMPLES

- ばんごはんは 何に しましょうか。
  Bangohan wa nani ni shimashō ka.
  What should we do for dinner?

- およぎに 行きませんか。
  Oyogi ni ikimasen ka.
  Would you like to go swimming?

WATCH OUT!

X 何を 食べませんか。
Nani o tabemasen ka.

→ 何か 食べませんか。 / 何を 食べましょうか。
Nani ka tabemasen ka. / Nani o tabemashō ka.
Would you like to eat something?

X スミスさんは 国へ かえりましょうか。
Sumisu-san wa kuni e kaerimashō ka.

→ スミスさんは 国へ かえりますか。
Sumisu-san wa kuni e kaerimasu ka.
Is Mr. Smith going to return to his country?

GIVE IT A SHOT!

Use either ましょうか **mashō ka** or ませんか **masen ka** in your response to each statement like the examples given below.

れい 1) A「くだものを 食べたいです。」

B「わたしも 食べたいです。**食べましょうか。**」   [食べる]

れい 2) A「つぎの 火よう日は スキーに **行きませんか。**」   [行く]

B「いいですね。」

1) A「あした どこで あいますか。」

B「としょかんで ＿＿＿＿＿＿＿」   [あう]

2) A「ばんごはんを 何か ＿＿＿＿＿＿＿」   [食べる]

B「じゃあ、おすしを ＿＿＿＿＿＿＿」   [食べる]

3) A「おつかれました。 しごとは たいへんでしたね。」

B「天気も わるかったです。 ビールを _____」 ［飲む］

4) A「なつ休みは どこか _____」 ［行く］

B「いいえ、どこにも 行きません。」

5) メールの ともだちに _____ ［なる］

に ni + 行く iku

You can use this structure to talk about the reason you are going somewhere.

Form:

> Vstem + に + 行く
>   ni   iku

EXAMPLES

■ きのう、山に のぼりに 行きました。
Kinō, yama ni nobori ni ikimashita.
Yesterday, (I) went and climbed a mountain.

■ 日本を 見に 行きたいです。
Nihon o mi ni ikitai desu.
(I) want to go see Japan.

■ きょうしつに ピアノを れんしゅう(し) に 行きます。*
Kyōshitsu ni piano o renshū(shi) ni ikimasu.
(I) am going to practice piano in a classroom.

* If you are using a compound verb with the form N + する **suru** like べんきょうする
(**benkyō suru**, to study) or そうじする (**sōji suru**, to wash), you can leave out し **shi**,
but it might sound too casual.

Although 行く (**iku**, to go) is the most common verb to be used in this form, you
can also use other verbs of motion like 来る (**kuru**, to come), かえる (**kaeru**, to
return), etc.

■ 日本に 日本語の べんきょうを しに 来ました。
Nihon ni Nihongo no benkyō o shi ni kimashita.
(I) came to Japan to study Japanese.

However, verbs that express the *way* of moving cannot be used, e.g. あるく (**aruku**, to walk), はしる (**hashiru**, to run), or およぐ (**oyogu**, to swim).

X　コンビニに 食べものを 買いに あるきました。
Konbini ni tabemono o kai ni arukimashita.
(I) walked to the convenience store to buy food.

WATCH OUT!

X　としょかんに 日本語を べんきょうを しに 行きます。
Toshokan ni Nihongo o benkyō o shi ni ikimasu.

→ としょかんに 日本語の べんきょうを しに 行きます。
Toshokan ni Nihongo no benkyō o shi ni ikimasu.
(I) am going to the library to study Japanese.

X　きのう、あそんだに 行きました。
Kinō, asonda ni ikimashita.

→ きのう、あそびに 行きました。
Kinō, asobi ni ikimashita.
Yesterday, (I) went out and had fun.

GIVE IT A SHOT!

Fill in the spaces with verbs from the box in their correct form like the example below.

れい) うどんを 食べに 行きたいです。

1) いい天気です。こうえんへ ＿＿＿＿＿ に 行きませんか。

2) おととい、新しいじでんしゃを ＿＿＿＿＿ に 行きました。

3) あしたは プールへ ＿＿＿＿＿ に 行きます。

4) しゅうまつは、駅まで ともだちに ＿＿＿＿＿ に 行きます。

5) 来月、パリへ ＿＿＿＿＿ に 行きます。

6) こどもは そとへ ＿＿＿＿＿ に 行きました。

およぐ　あそぶ　食べる　あう　りょこうする　さんぽする　買う

JLPT-Style Questions

1) ピザを 食べました。そして、ビール（　）飲みました。

    1 か　　　　　　2 も　　　　　　3 や　　　　　　4 と

2) 今日は 田中さん（　）会いました。

    1 にも　　　　　2 をも　　　　　3 で　　　　　　4 を

3) りんごは 3つ あります。バナナ（　）3つ あります。

    1 も　　　　　　2 が　　　　　　3 と　　　　　　4 を

4) ばんごはんは よく 魚や にく（　）食べます。

    1 を　　　　　　2 や　　　　　　3 も　　　　　　4 と

5) あさごはんには ぎゅうにゅう（　）飲みたいです。

    1 が　　　　　　2 も　　　　　　3 と　　　　　　4 に

6) 毎日、日本語の 本（　）読みます。

    1 が　　　　　　2 や　　　　　　3 と　　　　　　4 を

7) りょこうで 名古屋や 東京（　）行きました。

    1 に　　　　　　2 と　　　　　　3 や　　　　　　4 も

8) 田中「西村さんは 先生ですか。」
    山田「いいえ。そして中村さん（　）先生では ありません。」

    1 も　　　　　　2 と　　　　　　3 や　　　　　　4 を

9) わたしは くつしたや スカート（　）ほしいです。

    1 が　　　　　　2 を　　　　　　3 も　　　　　　4 や

10) わたしは ねこ（　）いぬ（　）すきです。

    1 も / も　　　　2 も / が　　　　3 と / と　　　　4 が / と

LESSON 6
Describing Your Room

Dad: もしもし。
Moshi moshi
Hello.

Yu: 今、何を しています か。
Ima, nani o shite imasu ka.
What are (you) doing now?

Dad: テレビを 見ています。
Terebi o mite imasu.
(I)'m watching TV.

Yu: そうですか。もう花に 水を あげましたか。
Sō desu ka. Mō hana ni mizu o agemashita ka.
Oh, okay. Have (you) given the flowers water yet?

Dad: まだ あげていません。すみませんね。
Mada agete imasen. Sumimasen ne.
(I) haven't given (them water) yet. Sorry.

Yu: だいじょうぶですよ。あのう、さいふを わすれました。
Daijōbu desu yo. Anō, saifu o wasuremashita.
That's okay. Ahh, (I) forgot (my) wallet.

Dad:	ああ、たいへん。 どこに ありますか。ベッドの ちかくに ありますか。
	Ā, taihen. Doko ni arimasu ka. Beddo no chikaku ni arimasu ka.
	Oh, that's not good. Where is (it)? Is (it) near the bed?

Yu:	ベッドの ちかくに あるか ないか わかりません。たぶん、 ねこの ほんだなの 中に あります。
	Beddo no chikaku ni aru ka nai ka wakarimasen. Tabun, neko no hondana no naka ni arimasu.
	(I) don't know if it is near the bed or not. Probably, (it) is in the cat bookshelf.

Dad:	いいえ、 ありません。
	Iie, arimasen.
	No, not there.

Yu:	ねこの つくえの 上に ありますか。
	Neko no tsukue no ue ni arimasu ka.
	Is (it) on the cat desk?

Dad:	ああ、 ありました。ねこの 下に ありました。
	Ā, arimashita. Neko no shita ni arimashita.
	Ah, there (it) is. (It) is under (your) cat .

Yu:	ねこは わたしの さいふが すきですから。
	Neko wa watashi no saifu ga suki desu kara.
	(My) cat likes my wallet.

Can-Do Key Points

➡ Talk about what you are doing now.
➡ Talk about complete and incomplete tasks.
➡ Give locations for items in a room.

THE NEGATIVE CASUAL NON-PAST FORM

Usually when speaking to family and friends, it is best to use the casual tense. The casual affirmative form is the same as a verb's dictionary form, but the negative tense is a little more difficult to form.

Form:

Group 1		Group 2	
Affirmative	*Negative*	*Affirmative*	*Negative*
つく **tsuku** *to arrive at*	つかない **tsukanai** *not arrive at*	食べる **taberu** *to eat*	食べない **tabenai** *not eat*
なくす **nakusu** *to lose something*	なくさない **nakusanai** *not lose something*	（学生が）いる **(gakusei ga) iru** *(student) exists*	いない **inai** *not exist*
まつ **matsu** *to wait*	またない **matanai** *not wait*	おりる **oriru** *to get off*	おりない **orinai** *not get off*
しぬ **shinu** *to die*	しなない **shinanai** *not die*	（うわぎを）きる **(uwagi o) kiru** *to wear (a jacket)*	きない **kinai** *not wear*
飲む **nomu** *to drink*	飲まない **nomanai** *not drink*		
のる **noru** *to ride*	のらない **noranai** *not ride*	Group 3	
		Affirmative	*Negative*
言う **iu** *to say*	言わない **iwanai** *not say*	来る **kuru** *to come*	来ない **konai** *not come*
あそぶ **asobu** *to enjoy*	あそばない **asobanai** *not enjoy*	する **suru** *to do/play*	しない **shinai** *not do/play*

You can also use the negative casual non-past tense with the か **ka** particle to talk about whether or not you want to do something.

Sentence Form:

> **Vdict** + か + **Vnai** + か + わかりません
>   ka   ka   wakarimasen

<u>EXAMPLES</u>

- フランスに 行くか 行かないか わかりません。
  Furansu ni iku ka ikanai ka wakarimasen.
  (I) don't know if (I) am going to France or not.

- 新しいパソコンを 買うか 買わないか わかりません。
  Atarashii pasokon o kau ka kawanai ka wakarimasen.
  (I) don't know if (I) am going to buy a new computer or not.

The negative casual non-past form can also be used with て **de** to tell someone not to do something.

Sentence Form:

> **Vnai + て + ください**
>   de   kudasai

- タバコを すわないで ください。
  Tabako o suwanaide kudasai.
  Please don't smoke.

- ビールを 飲まないで ください。
  Biiru o nomanaide kudasai.
  Please don't drink beer.

WATCH OUT!

X 何も 言あないで ください。 → 何も 言わないで ください。
  Nani mo ianaide kudasai.   Nani mo iwanaide kudasai.
                                   Please don't say anything.

X にしむらさんが ここに 来るか くないか わかりません。
  Nishimura-san ga koko ni kuru ka kunai ka wakarimasen.

  → にしむらさんが ここに 来るか 来ないか わかりません。
    Nishimura-san ga koko ni kuru ka konai ka wakarimasen.
    (I) don't know if Mr. Nishimura is coming here or not.

GIVE IT A SHOT!

Choose a suitable verb from the box below and change it to its –nai form, then fill in the blank for each sentence, like the two examples below.

れい 1) そのひこうきに のるか **のらない**か わかりません。

れい 2) そのワインを **飲まないで** ください。

1) テストで 本を ＿＿＿＿＿ で ください。

2)　ともだちに　お金（かね）を　かすか　＿＿＿＿＿　か　わかりません。

3)　そのいけで　＿＿＿＿＿　で　ください。

4)　１２時（じ）です。うちへ　かえるか　＿＿＿＿＿か　わかりません。

5)　今日（きょう）は　さむいです。うわぎを　きるか　＿＿＿＿か　わかりません。

6)　ふじさんに　のぼるか　＿＿＿＿＿　か　わかりません。

7)　今日は　雨（あめ）が　ふっているから、かさを　＿＿＿＿＿　で　ください。

8)　この　おかしを　＿＿＿＿　で　ください。

開（あ）ける　のぼる　およぐ　わすれる　かす　~~飲（の）む~~　食（た）べる　~~のる~~　きる　かえる

THE よ yo, わ wa AND ね ne PARTICLES

You can use the よ yo, わ wa and ね ne particles at the end of sentences. よ and わ are used to point out certain facts or to call someone's attention to something. However, わ is feminine and not used as often. ね is used to confirm information. It is very similar to adding 'isn't it?' to the end of a sentence in English.

Form:

> Sentence + よ **yo**
> Sentence + わ **wa**
> Sentence + ね **ne**

EXAMPLES

- もう　おきる　時間です**よ**。
  Mō okiru jikan desu yo.
  Hey, it's already time to wake up!

- このケーキは　おいしいです**わ**。
  Kono kēki wa oishii desu wa.
  This cake is delicious.

- このテレビは　高いです**ね**。
  Kono terebi wa takai desu ne.
  This TV is expensive, right?

■ でんわばんごうは　５５５−４５６５ですよね。
Denwa bangō wa go-go-go no yon-go-roku-go desu yo ne.
(The) phone number is 555-4565, isn't it?

GIVE IT A SHOT!

Use よ **yo** or ね **ne** to complete each sentence like the examples below.

れい）　A「あしたは　えいがを　見ませんか。」
　　　　B「テストが　ありますよ。」
　　　　A「ああ、そうか。ざんねんです**ね**。」

1) A「田中さんが　日本語を　話しています＿。」
　　B「はい。じょうずです＿。」

2) A「西村さんは　おすしが　きらいです＿。」
　　B「いいえ、西村さんは　おすしが　だいすきです＿。」

3) A「このはなは　うつくしいです＿。」
　　B「はい、うつくしいですね。どこで　買いましたか。」

4) A「もうねる　時間です＿。」
　　B「はい、はい、ねます＿。」

ている *te iru* AND てある *te aru*

To talk about states of being, you can use ている **te iru** and てある **te aru**. ている is used to talk about an action taking place now or a current state of something. てある is used to show the result of something being completed.

Form:

Vて ＋ いる/います
　te　　iru/imasu
Vて ＋ ある/あります
　te　　aru/arimasu

EXAMPLES

■ 今は　雨が　ふっています。
Ima wa ame ga futte imasu.
(It) is raining now.

- ドアが あいています。
  Doa ga aite imasu.
  The door is open.

- わたしは にしむらさんを しんじていません。
  Watashi wa Nishimura-san o shinjite imasen.
  I don't believe in Mr. Nishimura.

- てがみには 何が 書いてありますか。
  Tegami ni wa nani ga kaite arimasu ka.
  What is written on (the) letter?

WATCH OUT!

X あなたの 名前を しっていません。
  Anata no namae o shitte imasen

  → あなたの 名前を しりません。
     Anata no namae o shirimasen.
     (I) don't know your name.

X あなたの 名前を しります。 → あなたの 名前を しっています。
  Anata no namae o shirimasu.　　**Anata no namae o shitte imasu.**
  　　　　　　　　　　　　　　　　　　(I) know your name.

X 今日は くもってあります。 → 今日は くもっています。
  Kyō wa kumotte arimasu.　　**Kyō wa kumotte imasu.**
  　　　　　　　　　　　　　　　　(It) is cloudy today.

GIVE IT A SHOT!

Complete the sentences using the て-form, like the example below.

れい）まいばん、山田さんは ビールを <u>飲んで</u> います。

1) 毎週 まつ わたしは ギターを ＿＿＿＿ います。

2) A「田中さんは 今 何を していますか。」
   B「今、ともだちと ＿＿＿＿ います。」

3) きのうは うたを ＿＿＿＿ いました。

4) 中川さんは 東京に ＿＿＿＿ います。

5) スミスさんは 本を ＿＿＿＿ います。

6) 川口さんは 新しいぼうしを _____ います。

7) 田中さんは うわぎを _____ います。

8) だれが その大きいブーツを _____ いますか。

9) 車は _____ あります。

10) あした ともだちが わたしのいえへ 来ますので ビールが _____ あり
ます。

読む 話す ひく かぶる おぼえる はく みがく ~~飲む~~ きる すむ 買う

もう *mō* AND まだ *mada*

When you talk about a change in state, you can use もう **mō**. In a positive context, もう is similar to "already" in English. In a negative context, もう means "no longer." When you want to talk about a state remaining the same, you can use まだ **mada**. In a positive context, まだ is similar to "still." In a negative context, まだ expresses "not yet."

Form:

もう + past tense affirmative
mō

もう + negative form
mō

まだ + non-past verb
mada

EXAMPLES

- 北村さんは もう 来ました。
  Kitamura-san wa mō kimashita.
  Ms. Kitamura already came.

- タバコは もう すいません。
  Tabako wa mō suimasen.
  (I) don't smoke anymore.

- 今月は まだ 雨が ふっていません。
  Kongetsu wa mada ame ga futte imasen.
  (It) has not rained yet this month.

- 雨が まだ ふっています。
  Ame ga mada futte imasu.
  (It is) still raining.

WATCH OUT!

X まだ シャワーを あびました。 → もう シャワーを あびました。
  Mada shawā o abimashita. **Mō shawā o abimashita.**
  (I) have already showered.

X ひるごはんを まだ 食べませんでした。
  Hirugohan o mada tabemasen deshita.

  → ひるごはんを まだ 食べていません。
  Hirugohan o mada tabete imasen.
  (I) haven't eaten lunch yet.

GIVE IT A SHOT!

Complete the sentences with either もう or まだ like the examples below.

れい1) A「かいぎは もう おわりましたか。」
　　　 B「はい、<u>**もう**</u> おわりました。」

れい2) A「何か 食べたいです。」
　　　 B「くだものが <u>**まだ**</u> あります。」

1) 5月です。しかし、＿＿＿ さむいです。

2) 田中さんは ＿＿＿ いすに すわっています。

3) あしたの しゅくだいは、＿＿＿ ぜんぶ しました。

4) おふろに ＿＿＿ 入りました。

5) 食べものを ＿＿＿ たくさん 食べました。

6) お父さんは ＿＿＿ おきていないです。

7) コーヒーを 飲みました。しかし、＿＿＿ ねむたいです。

8) 田中さんに ＿＿＿ 電話を かけません。

LOCATION WORDS

To talk about where something is, you need to use location words.

Form:

> N + の + location word
>   no

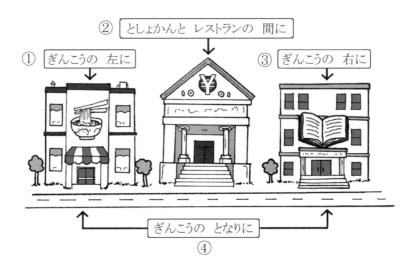

① ぎんこうの　左に
ginkō no migi ni
to the right of the bank

② としょかんと　レストランの　間に
toshokan to resutoran no aida ni
between the library and the restaurant

③ ぎんこうの　左に
ginkō no hidari ni
to the left of the bank

④ ぎんこうの　となりに
ginkō no tonari ni
next to the bank

たなかさんの 左に
Tanaka-san no hidari ni
to the left of Mr. Tanaka

たなかさんの 右に
Tanaka-san no migi ni
to the right of Mr. Tanaka.

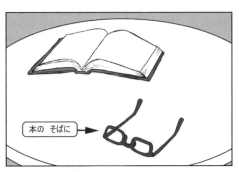

本の そばに
hon no soba ni
near the book

くつの 中に
kutsu no naka ni
in the shoe

はこの 外に
hako no soto ni
outside the box

バスの 前に
basu no mae ni
in front of the bus

バスの 後ろに
basu no ushiro ni
behind the bus

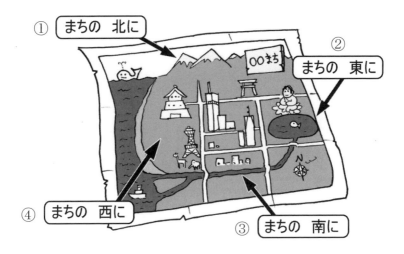

① まちの　北に
machi no kita ni
in/to the north of the city

② まちの　東に
machi no higashi ni
in/to the east of the city

③ まちの　南に
machi no minami ni
in/to the south of the city

④ まちの　西に
machi no nishi ni
in/to the west of the city

このへんに
kono hen ni
in this area

道の　むこうに
michi no mukō ni
across the street

It might be better to think of むこう **mukō** as 'the opposite side.' To use this word, you need to implicitly or explicitly state something on the other side of another thing. むこう is also used when talking about something over there or beyond another thing.

■ ゆうびんきょくは ホテルの むこうに あります。
Yūbinkyoku wa hoteru no mukō ni arimasu.
The post office is on the other side of the hotel.

If you want to talk about something that is facing you, you have to use a different word, むかい **mukai**:

■ わたしは ホテルの むかいに います。
Watashi wa hoteru no mukai ni imasu.
I am across from the hotel, i.e. I am facing the hotel.

つくえの 上に
tsukue no ue ni
on top of the desk

つくえの 下に
tsukue no shita ni
under the desk

駅の ちかくに
eki no chikaku ni
near the station

EXAMPLES

■ このへんに ゆうびんきょくは ありますか。
Kono hen ni yūbinkyoku wa arimasu ka.
Is there a post office in this area?

■ わたしの いえは 川の となりに あります。
Watashi no ie wa kawa no tonari ni arimasu.
My house is next to the river.

- はこの 中に 何が ありますか。
  Hako no naka ni nani ga arimasu ka.
  What is inside the box?

- 北海道は 日本の 北に あります。
  Hokkaidō wa Nihon no kita ni arimasu.
  Hokkaido is in the north of Japan.

WATCH OUT!

X びょういんは ホテルの ちかくに います。
Byōin wa hoteru no chikaku ni imasu.

→ びょういんは ホテルの ちかくに あります。
Byōin wa hoteru no chikaku ni arimasu.
The hospital is near the hotel.

X きたむらさんは わたなべさんの 右に あります。
Kitamura-san wa Watanabe-san no migi ni arimasu.

→ きたむらさんは わたなべさんの 右に います。
Kitamura-san wa Watanabe-san no migi ni imasu.
Mr. Kitamura is to the right of Mr. Watanabe.

GIVE IT A SHOT!

Choose the correct location word for each blank. An example is given.

れい）いぬは いすの（ <u>上</u> ）にいます。
1 前
2 上
3 下
4 後ろ

1) ざっしは 本の（　）に あります。
1 後ろ
2 下
3 上
4 前

2) りんごは はこの（　　）です。

　　1 そと

　　2 そば

　　3 ちかく

　　4 中^{なか}

3) 田中^{たなか}さんは 西村^{にしむら}さんの（　　）
　　に たっています。

　　1 下^{した}

　　2 前^{まえ}

　　3 後^{うし}ろ

　　4 上^{うえ}

西村さん　　田中さん

4) デパートは 駅^{えき}の（　　）です。

　　1 上

　　2 後ろ

　　3 前

　　4 下

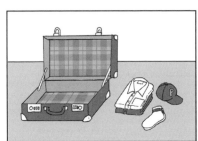

5) ふくは スーツケースの（　　）に
　　あります。

　　1 中

　　2 外^{そと}

　　3 上

　　4 間^{あいだ}

6) 長崎^{ながさき}は 熊本^{くまもと}の（　　）に あります。

　　1 南^{みなみ}

　　2 東^{ひがし}

　　3 西^{にし}

　　4 北^{きた}

ふくおか

おおいた

ながさき

くまもと

かごしま　　みやざき

7) 山田さんは　びょういんの（　　）に
　　います。
　　1 前
　　2 後ろ
　　3 上
　　4 となり

8) いぬは　ほんだなの（　　）にいます。
　　1 となり
　　2 上
　　3 下
　　4 そば

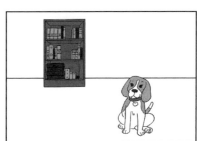

9) フォークは　さらの（　　）に
　　あります。
　　1 後ろ
　　2 前
　　3 となり
　　4 右

10) えんぴつは　本と　ペンの（　　）
　　です。
　　1 そば
　　2 近く
　　3 間
　　4 となり

JLPT-Style Questions

1) ガス（　　）しまっていますか。
　　1 を　　　　2 で　　　　3 は　　　　4 か

2) 田中さんは　赤いぼうしを（　　）。
　　1 もます　　2 もっています　　3 もたています　　4 もちます

3) スミスさんとは（　　）。どんな人ですか。
1 会いません　2 会いました　3 会っています　4 会っていません

4) パーティーで 新しい くつを（　　）わかりません。
1 くるか　こないか　　　　　　3 きるか　きないか
2 はくか　はかないか　　　　　4 かぶるか　かぶらないか

5) A「テストは どうでしたか。」
B「そうです（　　）、かんたんでした。」
1 か　　　　　　2 ね　　　　　　3 わ　　　　　　4 よ

6) A「でんしゃは 9時に 出ます（　　）。」
B「いいえ、8時に 出ます（　　）。」
1 ね / ね　　　　2 よ / ね　　　　3 よ / か　　　　4 ね / よ

7) 西村さんを（　　）よびましたか。
1 どんな　　　　2 まだ　　　　3 あの　　　　4 もう

8) A「父は どこですか。」
B「しりません、（　　）かえっていません。」
1 どこか　　　　2 どこも　　　　3 もう　　　　4 まだ

9) わたしは 来年 大学に 行きたいです。今は お金に（　　）。
1 こまっています　　　　　　3 こまってあります
2 こまります　　　　　　　　4 こまりました

10) 新しい けいたい電話を 買うか（　　）か わかりません。
1 買わない　　　　　　　　　3 買っていない
2 買いません　　　　　　　　4 買いたくない

*うんてんする = to drive

Telling a Simple Story in Chronological Order

DIALOGUE

Yu: りょこうは どうでしたか。
Ryokō wa dō deshita ka.
How was (your) trip?

Matt: おおさかから なごやまでは だいじょうぶでした。なごやに ついた後で、もんだいが ありました。
Ōsaka kara Nagoya made wa daijōbu deshita. Nagoya ni tsuita ato de, mondai ga arimashita.
(It) was fine from Osaka to Nagoya. After (I) arrived in Nagoya, (I) had a problem.

Yu: そうですか。もんだいですか。
Sō desu ka. Mondai desu ka.
Oh, (I) see. A problem?

Matt: はい、なごやで バスが とまりましたから、わたしは 何か 飲みものを 買いに バスを おりました。飲みものを 買って お店を 出ました。けいたい電話を 見ながら バスに はやく かえりました。でも、かおを 上げると バスが ありません。

Hai, Nagoya de basu ga tomarimashita kara, watashi wa nani ka nomimono o kai ni basu o orimashita. Nomimono o katte omise o demashita. Keitai denwa o minagara basu ni hayaku kaerimashita. Demo, kao o ageru to basu ga arimasen.

Yes, the bus stopped at Nagoya, so (I) got off the bus to buy something to drink. (I) bought a drink and left the store. While looking at my cellphone, (I) walked quickly back to the bus. However, when (I) raised (my) head, there was no bus.

Yu: バスが なくなりましたね。たいへんです。
Basu ga naku narimashita ne. Taihen desu.
Huh, the bus disappeared. That's too bad.

Matt: バスを おりる前に じてんしゃが 何か 言いました。
Basu o oriru mae ni jitensha ga nani ka iimashita.
Before (I) got off the bus, the bicycle said something.

Yu: じてんしゃが 何か 言いましたか。
Jitensha ga nani ka iimashita ka.
The bicycle said something?

Matt: はい、そうです。
Hai, sō desu.
Yeah, that's right.

Yu: じてんしゃは 話しませんよ。
Jitensha wa hanashimasen yo.
Bicycles don't talk.

Matt: じてんしゃは バスを うんてんしますね。
Jitensha wa basu o unten shimasu ne.
Bicycles drive a bus, right?

Yu: いいえ、うんてんしゅが バスを うんてんします。
Iie, untenshu ga basu o unten shimasu.
No, drivers drive buses.

Can-Do Key Points

➡ Talk about a trip you took.
➡ Talk about a sequence of events.

から kara, まで made AND より yori

から **kara** can mark a starting point or source. まで **made** can mark an end point. より **yori** has the meaning of 'than' in English and is often used in comparisons.

Form:

> N + から kara
> N + まで made
> N + より yori

EXAMPLES

- きのう、わたしは 大阪から 東京まで 行きました。
  Kinō, watashi wa Ōsaka kara Tōkyō made ikimashita.
  Yesterday, I went to Tokyo from Osaka.

- 9時から 5時まで はたらきます。
  Kuji kara goji made hatarakimasu.
  (I) work 9 to 5.

- 7時から ばんごはんを 食べます。
  Shichiji kara bangohan o tabemasu.
  (We) are eating dinner from 7.

- A「今日、しごとが あります。」
  Kyō, shigoto ga arimasu.
  Today, (I) have work.

  B「何時までですか。」
  Nanji made desu ka.
  Until what time?

- 田中さんは 山田さんより せが 高いです。
  Tanaka-san wa Yamada-san yori se ga takai desu.
  Mr. Tanaka is taller than Mr. Yamada.

WATCH OUT!

X わたしは あにから 2さい わかいです。
Watashi wa ani kara nisai wakai desu.

→ わたしは あにより 2さい わかいです。
Watashi wa ani yori nisai wakai desu.
I am two years younger than my older brother.

X このプレゼントは わたしから おじさんまで 上げました。
Kono purezento wa watashi kara ojisan made agemashita.

→ このプレゼントは わたしから おじさんに 上げました。
Kono purezento wa watashi kara ojisan ni agemashita.
I gave this present to my uncle.

X わたしから ともだちに 本を もらいました。
Watashi kara tomodachi ni hon o moraimashita.

→ わたしは ともだち[から/に] 本を もらいました。
Watashi wa tomodachi [kara/ni] hon o moraimashita.
I received a book from my friend.

GIVE IT A SHOT!

Choose the correct particle for each sentence like the example below.

れい) 田中さんは 名古屋 (より・(から)) 来ました。

1) わたしは この本を 西村さん (から・に) 上げました。

2) わたしは 電車 (から・に) おりました。

3) ６時はんに 電車で 東京に 行きます。６時 (まで・に) まっています。

4) 今日、１２時から ６時まで はたらきます。６時 (から・まで) いそがしい です。

5) アメリカ (から・まで) 来ました。

6) 田中さんは わたし (より・から) はやく はしります。

なる *naru* AND する *suru*

To talk about a change in state, we can use なる **naru** and する **suru**. なる **naru** is used to talk about a change that occurred naturally, while する **suru** can be used to talk about a change somebody makes.

Form:

い adj–い + く なる/する
i   i   ku   naru/suru

な adj/N + に なる/する
na   ni naru/suru

EXAMPLES

■ みじかくして ください。
Mijikaku shite kudasai.
Please make (it) short.

■ ４日から あつくなりました。
Yokka kara atsuku narimashita.
(It) is been hot since the 4th.

- 1年後に しごとは かんたんに なります。
  Ichinen go ni shigoto wa kantan ni narimasu.
  The work will become easier after a year.

- くすりを 飲んだ後に げんきに なりました。
  Kusuri o nonda ato ni genki ni narimashita.
  After (I) took the medicine, (I) felt better.

- このてがみは ちょっと むずかしいので、かんたんにして ください。
  Kono tegami wa chotto muzukashii no de, kantan ni shite kudasai.
  This letter is a little difficult, please make (it) easier.
  (The letter is written with difficult words/kanji, so can you simplify it?)

WATCH OUT!

X このパソコンは 高いです。 やすいして ください。
Kono pasokon wa takai desu. Yasui shite kudasai.

→ このパソコンは 高いです。やすくして ください。
Kono pasokon wa takai desu. Yasuku shite kudasai.
This computer is expensive. Please make (it) cheaper.

X へやが きたないですよ。きれくして ください。
Heya ga kitanai desu yo. Kireku shite kudasai.

→ へやが きたないですよ。きれいにして ください。
Heya ga kitanai desu yo. Kirei ni shite kudasai.
(The) room is in a mess. Clean it up please.

X 田中さんは へやを きれいに なってください。
Tanaka-san wa heya o kirei ni natte kudasai.

→ 田中さんは へやを きれいにして ください。
Tanaka-san wa heya o kirei ni shite kudasai.
Mr. Tanaka, please clean it up.

GIVE IT A SHOT!

Fill in the blanks with words from the box below. Be sure to change the form to match the sentence like the example below.

れい 1) 西村（にしむら）さんは 新（あたら）しいしごとが はじまったので <u>いそがしくなりました</u>。

1) このカレーは つめたいです。＿＿＿＿＿＿ ください。

2) シャーさんが 来（き）た後（あと）、パーティーは ＿＿＿＿＿＿＿＿＿＿。

3) こどもが ねているので、＿＿＿＿＿＿ ください。

4) A「あなたの 日本語は ＿＿＿＿＿＿＿。」

   B「いいえ、いいえ、まだ 下手ですよ。」

5) スーパーができてから このへんが ＿＿＿＿＿＿＿＿。

6) ミラーさんは 本を 書いた後で、＿＿＿＿＿＿＿。

7) わたしの コーヒーは ＿＿＿＿＿ ので、新しいコーヒーを つくりました。

8) わたしの スーツは ＿＿＿＿＿ ので、＿＿＿＿ ください。

にぎやか　　大きい　　~~いそがしい~~　　つめたい　　あつい　　しずか

ゆうめい　　小さい　　おもしろい　　上手

前に mae ni, 後で ato de AND てから te kara

You can use 前に **mae ni** to mean 'before,' and you can use 後で **ato de** and 後に **ato ni** to mean 'after.' 後で **ato de** refers to the time after an event in general, while 後に **ato ni** indicates the specific point in time after an event ended. Moreover, 後 **ato** can often be used without で or に. Vte + から **kara** can mean 'after' as well. It is often used in a sentence that is the speaker's decision or suggestion.

Form:

N + の* + 前に no　　mae ni	N + の* + 後で/後に no　　ato de/ato ni	Vte + から kara
Vdict + 前に mae ni	Vpast + 後で/後に ato de/ato ni	

* The の particle is usually dropped with time periods like 10年前に **jūnen-mae ni**.

EXAMPLES

- いえを 出る前に うわぎを きます。
  Ie o deru mae ni uwagi o kimasu.
  Before (I) leave home, (I) will put on a jacket.

- ゆうしょくを 食べた後で えいがを 見ます。
  Yūshoku o tabeta ato de eiga o mimasu.
  After (I) eat dinner, (I) will watch a movie.

- ４年前に　しごとを　はじめました。
  Yonen-mae ni shigoto o hajimemashita.
  (I) started (my) job 4 years ago.

- しごとの　後で　ビールを　飲みましょう。
  Shigoto no ato de biiru o nomimashō.
  Let's drink beer after work.

- ゆうしょくを　食べてから　ねました。
  Yūshoku o tabete kara nemashita.
  After (I) ate dinner, (I) went to bed.

WATCH OUT!

X　この本は　読む後で　たなかさんに　上げます。
Kono hon wa yomu ato de Tanaka-san ni agemasu.

→　この　本は　読んだ後で　たなかさんに　上げます。
Kono hon wa yonda ato de Tanaka-san ni agemasu.
After (I) read this book, (I) will give (it) to Mr. Tanaka.

X　わたしは　ねた前に　本を　読みました。
Watashi wa neta mae ni hon o yomimashita.

→　わたしは　ねる前に　本を　読みました。
Watashi wa neru mae ni hon o yomimashita.
Before I went to bed, (I) read a book.

X　6時のあとで　ひまです。　→　6時から　ひまです。
Rokuji no ato de hima desu.　　　**Rokuji kara hima desu.**
(I) am free after 6.

GIVE IT A SHOT!

Form one sentence in the past tense with the two events, like the example below. Event ① happened first. Event ② happened next.

れい 1) ②ねる / ①はを　みがく　→　<u>ねる前に　はを　みがきました。</u>

れい 2) ①ばんごはん / ②ともだちに　電話を　する
　　　→　<u>ばんごはんの　後で　ともだちに　電話を　しました。</u>

1) ①ばんごはん/②しゅくだい　する

　→　_____

2) ②りょこう / ①かぜを ひく

→ _____

3) ①3年間 日本語を べんきょうする / ②日本に 行く

→ _____

4) ②いえに つく / ①かぞくが ねる

→ _____

5) ①おきる / ②そうじする

→ _____

6) ①田中さんが 来る / ②にしむらさんに 電話を する

→ _____

7) ①しごと / ②えいがを 見る

→ _____

8) ①ドアを あける / ②へやは さむく なる

→ _____

れい） ベルが なる / ミラーさんは がっこうに つく

　　　→ ベルが なってから ミラーさんは がっこうに つきました。

1) あかるく なる / でかける

→ _____

2) きっぷを 買う / 電車に のる

→ _____

3) がっこうが おわる / およぐ

→ _____

4) 西村さんは 入る / ドアを しめる

→ _____

ながら nagara AND とき toki

You can use ながら **nagara** to talk about two actions taking place at the same time.
とき **toki** is used to talk about the time something took place or will take place.

Form:

> Secondary action (V-stem) + ながら + main action
>   nagara
>
> N + の + とき   い adj + とき
>   no   toki   i   toki
>
> な adj + な + とき   Clause + とき
> na   na   toki   toki

<u>EXAMPLES</u>

- テレビを 見ながら、ばんごはんを 食べます。
  Terebi o minagara, bangohan o tabemasu.
  (I) eat dinner while watching TV.

- わたしは ２５さいのとき けっこんしました。
  Watashi wa nijūgosai no toki kekkon shimashita.
  I got married when I was 25.

- ひまなとき 何を していますか。
  Hima na toki nani o shite imasu ka.
  When (you) are free, what will (you) be doing?

- おねえさんは わかいとき、うつくしかったです。
  Onēsan wa wakai toki, utsukushikatta desu.
  When my older sister was young, she was beautiful.

- とうきょうに 来るとき 電話を ください。
  Tōkyō ni kuru toki denwa o kudasai.
  Please call (me) when (you) come to Tokyo.

WATCH OUT!

    A「そうじは 終わりましたか。」
      Sōji wa owarimashita ka.
      Are (you) finished cleaning?

X B「はい、そうじを しながら テレビを 見ました。」
      Hai, sōji o shinagara terebi o mimashita.

→ B「はい、テレビを 見ながら そうじを しました。」
      Hai, terebi o minagara sōji o shimashita.
      (I) cleaned while watching TV.

X わたしは そうじを しながら お兄さんは せんたくしていました。
Watashi wa sōji o shinagara oniisan wa sentaku shite imashita.

→ わたしが そうじを していたとき お兄さんは せんたくしていました。
Watashi ga sōji o shiteita toki oniisan wa sentaku shite imashita.
When I was cleaning, my older brother was doing the laundry.

X よるのとき、ときどき ビールを 飲みに 行きます。
Yoru no toki, tokidoki biiru o nomi ni ikimasu.

→ よるに ときどき ビールを 飲みに 行きます。
Yoru ni tokidoki biiru o nomi ni ikimasu.
(I) sometimes go and drink at night.

GIVE IT A SHOT!

Form sentences with the sentence fragments below like the examples. Be sure to change verb forms if necessary.

れい 1) いつも きぶんが わるい / いつも くすりを 飲む

　　　→ きぶんが わるいとき いつも くすりを 飲みます。

れい 2) ときどき うたを うたう / そうじする。

　　　→ ときどき うたを うたいながら そうじします。

1) わたしは ビールを 飲む / お父さんは テレビで スポーツを 見る

　→ _____

2) ともだちと あるく / 話す

　→ _____

3) コーヒーでも 飲む / まちましょうか。

　→ _____

4) いもうとは なく / いえに かえる

　→ _____

5) あるく / スマホを つかわないで ください。

　→ _____

6) わたしは こども / 上手に およぐ

　→ _____

7) おとうとは 学生 / 毎日 べんきょうする
   _{がくせい} _{まいにち}

   → _____

8) しずか / 本を 読みたい
   _{ほん} _よ

   → _____

9) 天気が いい / 山に のぼる
   _{てんき} _{やま}

   → _____

10) いえに 入る / くつを ぬいでください
    _{はい}

   → _____

ADVERBS

Adverbs can be used to describe how an action takes place. You can form adverbs from both な- and い-adjectives.

Form:

な adj + に + verb	い adj - い + く + verb
na ni	i i ku

EXAMPLES

■ 母は はやく はしります。
Haha wa hayaku hashirimasu.
Mom runs fast.

■ にしむらさんは いつも おそく おきます。
Nishimura-san wa itsumo osoku okimasu.
Mr. Nishimura always wakes up late.

■ 父は かんたんに 木に のぼります。
Chichi wa kantan ni ki ni noborimasu.
Dad climbs trees easily.

■ その女の人は しずかに 話します。
Sono onna no hito wa shizuka ni hanashimasu.
That woman speaks quietly.

WATCH OUT!

X　いすを　まっすぐで　ならべてください。
Isu o massugu de narabete kudasai.

→　いすを　まっすぐに　ならべてください。
Isu o massugu ni narabete kudasai.
Please line the chairs up straight.

X　おばさんは　うつくしいに　うたいます。
Obasan wa utsukushii ni utaimasu.

→　おばさんは　うつくしく　うたいます。
Obasan wa utsukushiku utaimasu.
My aunt sings beautifully.

X　わたしは　日本語を　わるく　話します。
Watashi wa Nihongo o waruku hanashimasu.

→　わたしの　日本語は　下手です。
Watashi no Nihongo wa heta desu.
My Japanese is terrible/unskillful.

GIVE IT A SHOT!

Fill in the blanks with adjectives from the box like the example below. Be sure to change the adjectives to the proper form.

れい）　だいすきな　うたを　いつも　**げんきに**　うたいます。

1)　この本は　古いですから、＿＿＿＿＿＿＿　読んで　ください。

2)　こどもが　ねているので、＿＿＿＿　して　ください。

3)　いもうとは　ピアノを　＿＿＿＿　ひきます。

4)　わたしの　あねを　＿＿＿＿　言わないで　ください。

5)　田中さんは　てがみに　わたしの　名前を　＿＿＿＿　書きました。

6)　今日は　かぜが　＿＿＿＿　ふきます。

つよい　　上手　　たいせつ　　大きい　　しずか　　わるい　　~~げんき~~

The following groups of adverbs are essential to know for the grammar section of the exam:

ADVERBS OF CONDITIONS

1) もっとゆっくり 話してくださいませんか。
Motto yukkuri hanashite kudasaimasen ka.
*Could (you) please speak more **slowly**?*

2) ゆっくり 食べて ください。
Yukkuri tabete kudasai.
*Please eat **slowly**.*

3) 田中さんも いっしょに 来ますか。
Tanaka-san mo **isshoni** kimasu ka.
*Is Mr. Tanaka coming **together (with us)**, too?*

4) 駅まで いっしょに 行きますか。
Eki made **isshoni** ikimasu ka.
*Are (you) coming **together (with me)** to the station?*

5) ちょうど今は いそがしいです。
Chōdo ima wa isogashii desu.
*(I) am busy **just** now.*

6) ちょうどいいです。
Chōdo ii desu.
*(It) is **just** right.*

7) にしむらさんの むすこは だんだん せが 高くなっていますね。
Nishimura-san no musuko wa **dandan** se ga takaku natte imasu ne.
*Mr. Nishimura's son is **gradually** getting taller, isn't he?*

8) おとは だんだん 大きくなっています。
Oto wa **dandan** ōkiku natte imasu.
*(The) sound is getting **gradually** louder.*

9) 父は まっすぐ 立っていました。
Chichi wa **massugu** tatte imashita.
*Father was standing **straight**.*

10) わたしは まっすぐ いえに かえりました。
Watashi wa **massugu** ie ni kaerimashita.
*I returned **straight** home.*

11) なつは ぎゅうにゅうが すぐに わるく なります。
Natsu wa gyūnyū ga **sugu ni** waruku narimasu.
*In summer, milk becomes bad **right away**.*

12) 母は いえに かえって すぐに ねました。
Haha wa ie ni kaette **sugu ni** nemashita.
*Mom returned home and went to bed **immediately**.*

ADVERBS OF FREQUENCY

1) わたしは　あねに　**ときどき**　てがみを　書きました。
   Watashi wa ane ni tokidoki tegami o kakimashita.
   *I **sometimes** wrote letters to my older sister.*

2) **ときどき**　田中さんに　あいます。
   Tokidoki Tanaka-san ni aimasu.
   *(I) **sometimes** meet Mr. Tanaka.*

3) わたしは　5時に　**たいてい**　おきます。
   Watashi wa goji ni taitei okimasu.
   *I **almost always** wake up at 5.*

4) わたしは　**たいてい**　ねる前に　おふろに　入ります。
   Watashi wa taitei neru mae ni ofuro ni hairimasu.
   *I **almost always** take a bath before I go to bed.*

5) ばんごはんは　**いつも**　何を　食べていますか。
   Bangohan wa itsumo nani o tabete imasu ka.
   *What are (you) **always** eating for dinner?*

6) ミラーさんは　**いつも**　えいごを　話します。
   Mirā-san wa itsumo Eigo o hanashimasu.
   *Mr. Miller **always** speaks English.*

7) ここに　**よく**来ますか。
   Koko ni yoku kimasu ka.
   *Do (you) come here **often**?*

8) わたしの　むすめは　**よく**　なきます。
   Watashi no musume wa yoku nakimasu.
   *My daughter cries **often**.*

9) **また**　ゆきが　ふっていますか。
   Mata yuki ga futte imasu ka.
   *Is it snowing **again**? (lit., Is the snow falling **again**?)*

10) **また**　来て　ください。
   Mata kite kudasai.
   *Please come **again**.*

11) きのうは　ばんごはんを　**はじめて**　つくりました。
   Kinō wa bangohan o hajimete tsukurimashita.
   *Yesterday, (I) made dinner **for the first time**.*

12) きょねん　**はじめて**　日本に　行きました。
   Kyonen hajimete Nihon ni ikimashita.
   *Last year, (I) went to Japan **for the first time**.*

13) おじいさんは　テレビを　**あまり**　見ません。
Ojiisan wa terebi o amari mimasen.
Grandpa doesn't watch TV so much.

14) 母は　えいごを　**あまり**　話しません。
Haha wa Eigo o amari hanashimasen.
Mother doesn't speak English so much.

ADVERBS OF QUANTITY

1) この食べものは　おいしいので　**たくさん**食べました。
Kono tabemono wa oishii no de takusan tabemashita.
This food is delicious, so (I) ate a lot.

2) シャーさんは　ともだちが　**たくさん**　います。
Shā-san wa tomodachi ga takusan imasu.
Mr. Shah has a lot of friends.

3) 山に　のぼったので　**すこし**　つかれました。
Yama ni nobotta no de sukoshi tsukaremashita.
(I) climbed a mountain, so (I) am a little tired.

4) お金を　**すこし**　もっています。
Okane o sukoshi motte imasu.
(I) have a little money.

5) **ちょっと**　出かけて　きます。
Chotto dekakete kimasu.
(I) am going out for a little bit (and coming back).

6) もう　**ちょっと**　ねたいです。
Mō chotto netai desu.
(I) want to sleep somewhat more.

7) **ちょっと**…
Chotto...
Ah, well... (a way of politely refusing an invitation)

8) 日本には　外国人が　**おおぜい**　いますか。*
Nihon ni wa gaikokujin ga ōzei imasu ka.
Are there many foreigners in Japan?

9) このレストランは　いつも　人が　**おおぜい**　いますよ。*
Kono resutoran wa itsumo hito ga ōzei imasu yo.
This restaurant always has a lot of people.

10) もう一つ　ください。
Mō hitotsu kudasai.
One more please.

11) そのうたを もういちど 聞きたいです。
Sono uta o mō ichido kikitai desu.
*(I) want to listen to that song one **more** time.*

12) その本を ぜんぶ 読みました。
Sono hon o zenbu yomimashita.
*(I) read that **whole** book.*

13) この店の ものは ぜんぶ たかいです。
Kono mise no mono wa zenbu takai desu.
*The things at this store are **all expensive**.*

* おおぜい **ōzei** is only used for people.

ADVERBS OF DEGREE

1) 北村さんの むすめは けっこう かわいいです。
Kitamura-san no musume wa kekkō kawaii desu.
*Ms. Kitamura's daughter is **quite** pretty.*

2) けっこうです。
Kekkō desu.
No, thanks.

3) このカメラは ちょっと 高いです。 もっと やすくなりますか。
Kono kamera wa chotto takai desu. Motto yasuku narimasu ka.
*This camera is a little expensive. Will (you) make (it) **cheaper**?*

4) ビールが もっと ほしいですか。
Biiru ga motto hoshii desu ka.
*Do (you) want **more** beer?*

5) あなたの けいたい電話は ほんとうに 小さいです。
Anata no keitai denwa wa hontō ni chiisai desu.
*Your cellphone is **really** small.*

6) 田中さんの ねこは ほんとうに あたまが いいです。
Tanaka-san no neko wa hontō ni atama ga ii desu.
*Mr. Tanaka's cat is **really** smart.*

7) 父は 毎日 とても いそがしいです。
Chichi wa mainichi totemo isogashii desu.
*Dad is **very** busy every day.*

8) おじいさんの いえは とても ひろいです。
Ojiisan no ie wa totemo hiroi desu.
*Grandpa's house is **very** large (spacious).*

9) コーヒーは いろいろ あります。
Kōhii wa iroiro arimasu.
There is a variety of coffee.

10) 西村先生は わたしに いろいろ おしえてくれました。
Nishimura-sensei wa watashi ni iroiro oshiete kuremashita.
Nishimura-sensei has taught me a variety of (things).

11) わたしの アパートは たいへん 小さいです。
Watashi no apāto wa taihen chiisai desu.
My apartment is terribly small.

12) きのうの よるは たいへん しずかでした。
Kinō no yoru wa taihen shizuka deshita.
Last night was terribly quiet.

13) さとうさんは 毎日 よくはたらきます。
Satō-san wa mainichi yoku hatarakimasu.
Mr. Sato works well every day.

14) きのうの よるは よくねました。
Kinō no yoru wa yoku nemashita.
(I) slept well last night.

15) 森下さんは たぶん ねています。
Morishita-san wa tabun nete imasu.
Mr. Morishita is probably sleeping.

16) 山中さんは たぶん ゆうめいに なります。
Yamanaka-san wa tabun yūmei ni narimasu.
Mr. Yamanaka is probably going to become famous.

CONJUNCTIONS

Conjunctions can link together sentences by showing contrasts or by calling attention to how the two sentences are related.

Form:

> Clause + conjunction + clause

が as a conjunction

One of the more common conjunctions is が **ga**, which can mean 'but' in English.

EXAMPLES

- 何か 食べたいですが、お金が ありません。
  Nani ka tabetai desu ga, okane ga arimasen.
  *(I) want to eat something, **but** (I) don't have money.*

- お酒を 飲みませんでしたが、きぶんが わるいです。
  Osake o nomimasen deshita ga, kibun ga warui desu.
  *(I) didn't drink alcohol, **but** (I) feel bad.*

が **ga** can also simply show a weak connection between the two clauses of a sentence:

- ビールを 飲みますが、あなたは 飲みますか。
  Biiru o nomimasu ga, anata wa nomimasu ka.
  (I) am going to drink beer, are you drinking?

- りょこうを したいですが、どこが いいですか。
  Ryokō o shitai desu ga, doko ga ii desu ka.
  (I) want to take a trip, where is good?

Here are a few more useful conjunctions that will most likely come up in the grammar section of the exam:

To Show Contrast: しかし, でも

しかし **shikashi** and でも **demo** can both be used to mean 'but.' しかし is considered to be more formal.

EXAMPLES

1) しゅくだいは ぜんぶ しました。しかし、まだ よく わかりません。
   Shukudai wa zenbu shimashita. Shikashi, mada yoku wakarimasen.
   (I) did all the homework. However, (I) still don't understand.

2) 日本語は むずかしいです。しかし、おもしろいですよ。
   Nihongo wa muzukashii desu. Shikashi, omoshiroi desu yo.
   Japanese is difficult. However, (it) is fun.

3) フランスに 行きたいです。でも、ちょっと とおいです。
   Furansu ni ikitai desu. Demo, chotto tōi desu.
   (I) want to go to France, but it is a little far.

4) いぬは すきです。でも、ねこは すきじゃないです。
   Inu wa suki desu. Demo, neko wa suki ja nai desu.
   (I) like dogs. But, (I) don't like cats.

To Show Reason: から

から **kara** can be used in the same sentence to state the reason for something. だから **dakara** is often used when the reason for something is more detailed and requires a separate sentence or the speaker wants to place more emphasis on the reason. だから **dakara** is then used to refer to the previous sentence to state the reason.

5) しごとが たくさん あるから、今日の よるは ねません。
   Shigoto ga takusan aru kara, kyō no yoru wa nemasen.
   (I) have a lot of work, so (I) am not going to sleep tonight.

6) わるい食べものを たくさん 食べているから、ふとく なりました。
   Warui tabemono o takusan tabete iru kara, futoku narimashita.
   (I) am eating a lot of bad food, so (I) have gained weight.

7) さむいですよ。だから、今日は 出かけたくないです。
   Samui desu yo. Dakara, kyō wa dekaketaku nai desu.
   *(It) is cold. **That's why** (I) don't want to go out today.*

8) わたしは 新しい車を 買いました。その車は とても 高かったです。だから、お金が あまり ありません。
   Watashi wa atarashii kuruma o kaimashita. Sono kuruma wa totemo takakatta desu. Dakara, okane ga amari arimasen.
   *I bought a new car. That car was very expensive. **That's why** I don't have much money.*

To Link Two Ideas: そして, それから, それに, では, それでは

そして **soshite** can link two sentences together even if the topics are different. It has the meaning of 'and' in English. それから **sore kara** is used to link two sentences chronologically and has the meaning of 'and then' in English. それに **sore ni** can link two sentences that have the same topic. では **de wa** and それでは **sore de wa** are used at the start of a sentence as a conjunction leading in from the previous statement, like 'well,' 'so,' or 'well then' in English.

9) おとうとは せが 高いです。そして、あたまが いい人ですよ。
   Otōto wa se ga takai desu. Soshite, atama ga ii hito desu yo.
   My younger brother is tall. And, (he) is a smart person.

10) 田中さんは かいしゃを つくりました。 そして、本を さんさつ 書きました。
    Tanaka-san wa kaisha o tsukurimashita. Soshite, hon o sansatsu kakimashita.
    Ms. Tanaka created a company. And (she) wrote three books.

11) 左に まがって、それから まっすぐ 行って ください。

Hidari ni magatte, sore kara massugu itte kudasai.

*Turn left, **and then** go straight please.*

12) 駅に 行きました。それから、ともだちに あって ひるごはんを 食べました。

Eki ni ikimashita. Sore kara, tomodachi ni atte hirugohan o tabemashita.

*(I) went to the station. **And then** (I) met my friend and ate lunch.*

13) それでは、かいぎが はじまります。

Sore de wa, kaigi ga hajimarimasu.

***Well then**, the meeting is starting.*

14) それでは、飲みに 行きましょうか。

Sore de wa, nomi ni ikimashō ka.

***Well then**, let's go drinking.*

15) では、しごとの 後に えいがかんで あいましょう。

De wa, shigoto no ato ni eigakan de aimashō.

***Well**, after work let's meet at the movie theater.*

16) では、シャワーを あびます。

De wa, shawā o abimasu.

***Well**, (I) am going to take a shower.*

17) 北村さんは 日本語と えいごを 話します。それに スペイン語も 話します。

Kitamura-san wa Nihongo to Eigo o hanashimasu. **Sore ni** Supeingo mo hanashimasu.

*Ms. Kitamura speaks Japanese and English. **Moreover**, (she) speaks Spanish, too.*

18) 今日は、しごとを して 日本語を べんきょうしました。それに せんたくを して そうじを しました。

Kyō wa shigoto o shite Nihongo o benkyō shimashita. **Sore ni** sentaku o shite sōji o shimashita.

*Today, (I) did work and studied Japanese. **Moreover**, (I) did the laundry and cleaned.*

JLPT-Style Questions

1) かいぎは （　　） 六時に おわりました。

   1 まっすぐ　　　　2 だんだん　　　　3 ちょうど　　　　4 ちょっと

2) かみを （　　） つかいました。

   1 ぜんぶ　　　　　2 たいへん　　　　3 あまり　　　　　4 とても

3) しゅうまつは （　　） ゴルフを します。

   1 ときどき　　　　2 もう　　　　　　3 だんだん　　　　4 たいへん

4) 車に お金を （　　） かけます。

   1 おおぜい　　　　2 たくさん　　　　3 たいへん　　　　4 あまり

5) 中川さんは （　　） 来ないでしょう。

   1 とても　　　　　2 ちょうど　　　　3 たぶん　　　　　4 たいへん

6) A「ゆうべは こどもが ないていたので、ひとばん 中 おきていました」

   B「それは （　　） でしたね。」

   1 けっこう　　　　2 たいへん　　　　3 ぜんぶ　　　　　4 ちょっと

7) わたしは （　　） にかい テストが あります。

   1 ちょっと　　　　2 もう　　　　　　3 とても　　　　　4 もっと

8) わたしは ロンドンに りょこうしたいです。（　　）、ともだちは ロンドン
   が きらいです。

   1 それに　　　　　2 でも　　　　　　3 それでは　　　　4 だから

9) かいぎは ちょうど 1時に はじまります。（　　）、山下さんは まだ
   ひるごはんを 食べていません。

   1 そして　　　　　2 から　　　　　　3 それから　　　　4 しかし

10) おなかが いたい （　　） あまり 食べませんでした。

   1 しかし　　　　　2 が　　　　　　　3 だから　　　　　4 から

11) 今日は、6時に おきて 山に のぼって 4時に かえって 8時に
おさけを 飲みました。(　　)つかれました。
1 それに　　　　　　2 から　　　　　　3 だから　　　　　　4 しかし

12) A「今日は 何を しましたか。」
B「わたしは せんたくをしました。(　　)、あねは そうじをしました。
1 それに　　　　　2 それでは　　　　3 だから　　　　　4 そして

13) A「京都は どうでしたか。」
B「たのしかったです。おちゃを 飲みました。(　　)、四条へ
買いものに 行きました。」
1 では　　　　　　2 しかし　　　　　3 から　　　　　　4 それから

14) A「なぜ 気分が わるいですか。」
B「ええと、今日は、ピザ 二つと ハンバーグ 一つを 食べました。
(　　)、ケーキ 二つを 食べました。」
1 それでは　　　　2 だから　　　　　3 でも　　　　　　4 それに

15) コーヒーを 飲みました (　　)、おちゃは 飲みませんでした。
1 それから　　　　2 それに　　　　　3 だから　　　　　4 が

16) はる (　　) ふゆが 来ます。
1 の前に　　　　　2 の後で　　　　　3 前に　　　　　　4 後で

17) このうわぎを きる (　　) せんたくして ください。
1 前に　　　　　　2 後で　　　　　　3 の後で　　　　　4 の前に

18) かいぎ (　　) いえに かえります。
1 に後で　　　　　2 の後で　　　　　3 後で　　　　　　4 な後で

19) (　　) げんきに なりますよ。
1 ねる後で　　　　2 ねる前に　　　　3 ねた後で　　　　4 ねた前に

20) りょこうは 何日（なにいち）（　　） はじまりますか。

1 まで 　　　　2 にも 　　　　　　　3 から 　　　　　　　4 では

21) スミスさんは アメリカ（　　） 来（き）ました。

1 にへ 　　　　2 までに 　　　　　　3 では 　　　　　　　4 から

22) 駅（えき）（　　） いっしょに 行（い）きませんか。

1 もへ 　　　　2 では 　　　　　　　3 だけ 　　　　　　　4 まで

23) 今（いま）（　　） どこに いましたか。

1 に 　　　　　2 から 　　　　　　　3 まで 　　　　　　　4 の前（まえ）に

24) わたしは（　　）、本（ほん）を 読（よ）みました。

1 ねたとき 　2 ねているとき 　　　　3 ねるながら 　　　4 ねながら

25) 16さい（　　） あなたは どんな子（こ） でしたか。

1 の前（まえ）に 　2 のとき 　　　　　3 とき 　　　　　　4 前（まえ）に

LESSON 8
Describing a Place

DIALOGUE

Yu: あついですね。
Atsui desu ne.
Hot, isn't it?

Matt: あついですね。つめたくて あまいものを 食べたいです。
Atsui desu ne. Tsumetakute amai mono o tabetai desu.
Yeah, it's hot. I want to eat something cool and sweet.

Yu: こうえんに アイスクリームを うっている店が ありますが、行きませんか。
Kōen ni aisu kuriimu o utte iru mise ga arimasu ga, ikimasen ka.
There is a shop that is selling ice cream in the park. Do you want to go?

Matt: こうえんは きれいですか。
Kōen wa kirei desu ka.
Is the park clean?

Yu: はい、 うつくしい木が たくさん あって いつも 人が あまり いません。それに いろいろな はなが あります。ときどき そのこうえんで ひるごはんを 食べたり わたしの ねこと いっしょに あるいたりします。

Hai, utsukushii ki ga takusan atte itsumo hito ga amari imasen. Sore ni iroiro na hana ga arimasu. Tokidoki sono kōen de hirugohan o tabetari watashi no neko to isshoni aruitari shimasu.

Yes, it has many beautiful trees, and there are always not so many people. Moreover, there is a variety of flowers. Sometimes, I eat lunch in that park, walk with my cats and do stuff like that.

Matt: いいですね。 こうえんまで どれぐらい かかりますか。

Ii desu ne. Kōen made dore gurai kakarimasu ka.

Sounds nice, huh? How far is it to the park?

Yu: にじゅっぷんぐらいです。 行きましょう。

Nijuppun gurai desu. Ikimashō.

About twenty minutes. Let's go.

（アイスクリームの 店で。）
(Aisu kuriimu no mise de.)
(At the ice cream stand.)

Matt: さかなの アイスクリームは ねこしか 食べないでしょう。何に しますか。わたしは たぶん まっちゃに します。

Sakana no aisu kuriimu wa neko shika tabenai deshō. Nani ni shimasu ka. Watashi wa tabun maccha ni shimasu.

No one would eat fish ice cream except for cats. What are you having? I am probably getting macha.

Yu: わたしは…

Watashi wa …

I …

（バチッ！）

Store staff: ええ、 ちょっと まって。 すみません、 さかなの アイスクリームだけを うっています。

Ē, chotto matte. Sumimasen, sakana no aisu kuriimu dake o utte imasu.

Ah, wait a minute. Sorry, (we) are only selling fish ice cream.

Can-Do Key Points

➡ Describe places and things in more detail.
➡ Talk about approximate amounts.

LINKING ADJECTIVES

Previously, we learned about how to link together a sequence of events with the て-form of a verb. We can also link two or more adjectives together with くて kute or で de to describe something or someone.

Form:

> い adj – い + くて + い adj + N
> i   i   kute   i
>
> な adj + で + な adj + な + N
> na   de   na   na

EXAMPLES

■ きのうは くらくて さむかったです。
Kinō wa kurakute samukatta desu.
Yesterday, (it) was dark and cold.

■ 西村さんは せが たかくて ほそいです。
Nishimura-san wa se ga takakute hosoi desu.
Mr. Nishimura is tall and thin.

■ そのホテルは りっぱで 大きいです。
Sono hoteru wa rippa de ōkii desu.
That hotel is splendid and large.

■ シャーさんは げんきで おもしろい人です。
Shā-san wa genki de omoshiroi hito desu.
Mr. Shah is a cheerful and funny person.

Another common usage of the て-form is to show the cause or reason for something.

■ 北村さんは やさしくて すきです。
Kitamura-san wa yasashikute suki desu.
Ms. Kitamura is nice, so (I) like (her).

X わたしは 白くて あおい ネクタイを 買いました。
Watashi wa shirokute aoi nekutai o kaimashita.
I bought a whitish blue necktie.

→ わたしは 白と あおの ネクタイを 買いました。
Watashi wa shiro to ao no nekutai o kaimashita.
I bought a white and blue necktie.

X そのかいぎは ながくて おもしろかったです。
Sono kaigi wa nagakute omoshirokatta desu.
That meeting was long and fun.

→ そのかいぎは ながかったですが、おもしろかったです。
Sono kaigi wa nagakatta desu ga, omoshirokatta desu.
That meeting was long and fun.

GIVE IT A SHOT!

Link the two adjectives together like the example below.

れい）そのじどうしゃは（はやい／やすい）です。

→ そのじどうしゃは はやくて やすいです。

1) 田中さんの アパートは（きれい／ちかい）です。
   たなか
   → _____

2) おとうとは（しずか／やさしい）です。
   → _____

3) このレストランの りょうりは（からい／おいしい）です。
   → _____

4) このへやは（あかるい／ひろい）です。
   → _____

5) このケーキは（まずい／たかい）です。
   → _____

どのくらい *dono kurai* AND どれくらい *dore kurai*

You can use どのくらい **dono kurai** and どれくらい **dore kurai** to ask about degree, amount or extent (e.g. how much, how many, etc.) of something. どのぐらい **dono gurai** and どれぐらい **dore gurai** can also be used in the same way.

Form:

> Topic + は + どのくらい + adj + ですか。
>   wa   dono kurai   desu ka.
>
> Topic + は + どのくらい + Vます + か。
>   wa   dono kurai   Vmasu ka

EXAMPLES

- この川は　どのくらい　ふかいですか。
  Kono kawa wa dono kurai fukai desu ka.
  How deep is this river?

- その山は　どれくらい　高いですか。
  Sono yama wa dore kurai takai desu ka.
  How tall is that mountain?

- 毎月　どれくらい　本を　読みますか。
  Maitsuki dore kurai hon o yomimasu ka.
  How many books do (you) read every month?

- 駅まで　どのくらい　かかりますか。
  Eki made dono kurai kakarimasu ka.
  How long does it take to get to the station?

WATCH OUT!

X　このくつは　どれくらいですか。
   Kono kutsu wa dore kurai desu ka.

   →　このくつは　いくらですか。
      Kono kutsu wa ikura desu ka.
      How much are these shoes?

X　となりの　まちまで　どのとおいですか。
   Tonari no machi made dono tōi desu ka.

   →　となりの　まちまで　どのくらいですか。
      Tonari no machi made dono kurai desu ka.
      How far is it to the next city?

GIVE IT A SHOT!

Write a question about each picture, using the words from the box, like the example below.

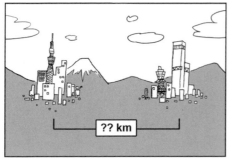

れい) <u>どのくらい　とおいですか。</u>

1) _____

2) _____

3) _____

4) _____

5) _____

りんごを　食^たべる　一^いか月^{げつ}に／ゴルフに　行^いく　　まっている
ながい　　かぜ／つよい　　とおい

ぐらい gurai vs. ごろ goro

You can use ごろ **goro** to talk about approximate times, whereas ぐらい **gurai** is used to talk about approximate amounts.

Form:

Point in time + ごろ (に) goro (ni)	Amount of something + ぐらい gurai

EXAMPLES

- 東京まで 電車で 2時間ぐらい かかります。
  Tōkyō made densha de ni jikan gurai kakarimasu.
  It takes about 2 hours to get to Tokyo by train.

- 田中さんは 30さいぐらいです。
  Tanaka-san wa sanjūsai gurai desu.
  Ms. Tanaka is about 30 years old.

- 3時ごろ あいましょう。
  San ji goro aimashō.
  Let's meet around 3.

- 今日は 何時ごろ おきましたか。
  Kyō wa nanji goro okimashita ka.
  About when did you wake up today?

WATCH OUT!

X 6時ぐらい おきました。 → 6時ごろ おきました。
Roku ji gurai okimashita. **Roku ji goro okimashita.**
(I) woke up around 6.

X 8時間ごろ ねました。 → 8時間ぐらい ねました。
Hachi jikan goro nemashita. **Hachi jikan gurai nemashita.**
(I) slept for about 8 hours.

GIVE IT A SHOT!

Circle the correct particle for each sentence like the example below.

れい）8時（ごろ・ぐらい）に しごとに つきます。

1) ひこうきの チケットは 20,000えん（ごろ・ぐらい）かかります。

2) らいねんの 8月（ごろ・ぐらい）日本に 行きます。

3) この（ごろ・ぐらい）いそがしいです。

4) 2年間（ごろ・ぐらい）京都に すんでいます。

5) パーティーに 20人（ごろ・ぐらい）来ました。

6) よっか（ごろ・ぐらい）に かいぎが あります。

USING しか *shika* IN NEGATIVE SENTENCES

When you want to exclude something from a negative sentence, you can use
しか **shika**.

Form:

> N + (に・で・と・へ・まで) + しか + Vneg
>   ni de to e made   shika
>
> **Counter or numbers** + しか + Vneg
>   shika

EXAMPLES:

- 土よう日しか ひまじゃありません。
  Doyōbi shika hima ja arimasen.
  (I) am not free except Saturday.

- 10えんしか お金が ありません。
  Jūen shika okane ga arimasen.
  (I) have no money except 10 yen.

- 東京にしか 行きませんでした。
  Tōkyō ni shika ikimasen deshita.
  (I) didn't go anywhere but Tokyo.

- 水しか 飲みません。
  Mizu shika nomimasen.
  (I) didn't drink anything but water.

X 西村さんは 五百円しか もっています。
Nishimura-san wa gohyaku-en shika motte imasu.
Mr. Nishimura has money except 500 yen.

→ 西村さんは 五百円しか もっていません。
Nishimura-san wa gohyaku-en shika motte imasen.
Mr. Nishimura has no money except 500 yen.

X パーティーに 2人しかが 来ました。
Pātii ni futari shika ga kimashita.

→ パーティーに 2人しか 来ませんでした。
Pātii ni futari shika kimasen deshita.
Nobody came to the party except two people.

GIVE IT A SHOT!

Rearrange the words to form sentences using しか like the example below.

れい) ない / です。/ 北村さん / あいたく / しか / に

→ <u>北村さんに しか あいたくないです。</u>

1) 30分 / が / が / しか / おおぜい / いました / でした / 人 / まっていません

→ _____

2) A「毎日 はしりますか。」

に / はしりません / よっか / しか / 一週間

→ B「いいえ、_____」

3) しか / で / 東京 / 行きません / に / バス / は

→ _____

4) へ / 3日間 / しか / は / 行きません / 大阪 / でした

→ _____

5) 30人 / でした / しか / 買いません / 本 / の / わたし / を

→ _____

6) しか / 行きません / 京都 / 車 / で / に / は

→ _____

だけ dake FOR 'ONLY'

You can use だけ **dake** to mean 'only.'

Form:

> N + (に/と) + だけ + (に/と/が/は/を/で)
>   ni /to   dake   ni/to/ga/wa/o/de
>
> Vdict + だけ
>   dake
>
> な adj + な + だけ
> na   na   dake

EXAMPLES

- どうして わたしにだけ あいたいですか。
  Dōshite watashi ni dake aitai desu ka.
  Why do (you) want to meet only me?

- わたしだけが えいがを 見に 行きました。
  Watashi dake ga eiga o mi ni ikimashita.
  Only I went to see the movie.

- 女の人の 名前は わすれましたが、かおだけは おぼえています。
  Onna no hito no namae wa wasuremashita ga, kao dake wa oboete imasu.
  (I) forgot (the) woman's name. (I) only remember her face.

- らいしゅうまつは いえで 本を たくさん 読むだけです。
  Raishū-matsu wa ie de hon o takusan yomu dake desu.
  Next weekend, (I) am just going to read books at home.

- あなたに 会いたかっただけです。
  Anata ni aitakatta dake desu.
  (I) just wanted to see you.

WATCH OUT!

X ねこのだけ いますよ。　→　ねこだけ(が) いますよ。
Neko no dake imasu yo.　　　**Neko dake (ga) imasu yo.**
　　　　　　　　　　　　　　　There is only a cat.

X にくをだけ 食べます。　→　にくだけ(を) 食べます。
Niku o dake tabemasu.　　　**Niku dake (o) tabemasu.**
　　　　　　　　　　　　　　　(I) eat meat only.

GIVE IT A SHOT!

Rearrange the words into a sentence using だけ like the example below.

れい) 山田さん / が / です / だけ / カレー / すき

　　→ 山田さんだけ カレーが すきです。

1) だけ / この人 / と / は / わたし / したい / けっこん / です

　　→ _____

2) は / を / していました / なつやすみ / しごと / だけ

　　→ _____

3) だけ / 好き / ください / 食べて / な

　　→ _____

4) バス / を / で / りょこう / は / つかいます / だけ

　　→ _____

5) お店 / です / 見たい / 中 / の / を / だけ

　　→ _____

6) でした / 見た / を / です / が / しゅくだい / テレビ / だけ / を / したかった

　　→ _____

～たり～たり　する ~tari~tari suru FOR A LIST OF THINGS/ACTIVITIES

You can use ～たり～たり　する **~tari~tari suru** to give examples of activities.

Form:

> Vpast + り + (Vpast + り +) する
> 　　　ri　　　　　　 ri　　 suru

EXAMPLES

■ しゅうまつは 本を 読んだり えいがを 見たり します。
Shū-matsu wa hon o yondari eiga o mitari shimasu.
On weekends, (I) read books and watch movies (and do stuff like that).

- びょういんで タバコを すったり、おさけを 飲んだり しないで ください。
  Byōin de tabako o suttari, osake o nondari shinaide kudasai.
  Please don't smoke cigarettes or drink alcohol (or do stuff like that) in the hospital.

- あした、大阪で すしを 食べたり、買いものを したり します。
  Ashita, Ōsaka de sushi o tabetari, kaimono o shitari shimasu.
  Tomorrow, (I) am going to eat sushi, go shopping (and do stuff like that) in Osaka.

WATCH OUT!

X 手を あらいたり ばんごはんを 食べたり しました。
Te o araitari bangohan o tabetari shimashita.
→ 手を あらって ばんごはんを 食べました。
Te o aratte bangohan o tabemashita.
(I) washed my hands and ate dinner.

X しゅうまつは お母さんが おさらを あらいたり せんたく します。
Shū-matsu wa okāsan ga osara o araitari sentaku shimasu.
→ しゅうまつは お母さんが おさらを あらったり せんたく したり します。
Shū-matsu wa okāsan ga osara o arattari sentaku shitari shimasu.
On weekends, my mom washes dishes and does laundry (and stuff like that).

GIVE IT A SHOT!

Fill in the blanks with a verbs from the box like the example below. Be sure to change the form of the verb to match the sentence.

れい) 休みの 日は ときどき テニスを (<u>したり</u>)、としょかんに
(<u>行ったり</u>) します。

1) きのう、神戸で ケーキを (　　　　)、おちゃを (　　　　) しました。
2) としょかんで 本を (　　　　)、てがみを (　　　　) します。
3) 沖縄で しゃしんを (　　　　)、うみで (　　　　) したいです。
4) 今日の よるは ギターを (　　　　)、うたを (　　　　) します。
5) 毎日 日本語の うたを (　　　　)、まんがを (　　　　) します。
6) しゅうまつは ビールを 飲みに (　　　　)、べんきょうを (　　　　)
   します。

┌───┐
　読む　飲む　聞く　~~行く~~　とる　行く　およぐ　食べる　読む
　うたう　~~する~~　する　ひく　書く
└───┘

CLAUSES

You can use clauses before a noun to modify it, like relative clauses in English.

Form

> **Subject of clause + が/の + Vplain + N**
> ga/no
>
> **Subject of clause + が/の + な adj + な + N**
> ga/no na

Clauses will almost always use a verb in the casual or dictionary form. We went over the negative casual form in lesson 6 (page 111). But, we didn't go over how to make the past tense of verbs, which can be a little trickier.

Group 1

Affirmative		Negative	
non-past/dictionary	*past*	*non-past/dictionary*	*past*
書く **kaku** *to write*	書いた **kaita** *wrote*	書かない **kakanai** *not write*	書かなかった **kakanakatta** *didn't write*
話す **hanasu** *to speak*	話した **hanashita** *spoke*	話さない **hanasanai** *not speak*	話さなかった **hanasanakatta** *didn't speak*
立つ **tatsu** *to stand*	立った **tatta** *stood*	立たない **tatanai** *not stand*	立たなかった **tatanakatta** *didn't stand*
しぬ **shinu** *to die*	しんだ **shinda** *died*	しなない **shinanai** *not die*	しななかった **shinanakatta** *didn't die*
とぶ **tobu** *to fly*	とんだ **tonda** *flew*	とばない **tobanai** *not fly*	とばなかった **tobanakatta** *didn't fly*
飲む **nomu** *to drink*	飲んだ **nonda** *drank*	飲まない **nomanai** *not drink*	飲まなかった **nomanakatta** *didn't drink*
かえる **kaeru** *to return*	かえった **kaetta** *returned*	かえらない **kaeranai** *not return*	かえらなかった **kaeranakatta** *didn't return*
言う **iu** *to say*	言った **itta** *said*	言わない **iwanai** *not say*	言わなかった **iwanakatta** *didn't say*

Group 2 and irregular

Affirmative		Negative	
non-past/dictionary	*past*	*non-past/dictionary*	*past*
食べる **taberu** *to eat (group 2)*	食べた **tabeta** *ate*	食べない **tabenai** *not eat*	食べなかった **tabenakatta** *didn't eat*
する **suru** *to do*	した **shita** *did*	しない **shinai** *not do*	しなかった **shinakatta** *didn't do*
来る **kuru** *to come*	来た **kita** *came*	来ない **konai** *not come*	来なかった **konakatta** *didn't come*
行く **iku** *to go*	行った **itta** *went*	行かない **ikanai** *not go*	行かなかった **ikanakatta** *didn't go*

Adjectives

Affirmative		Negative	
non-past/dictionary	*past*	*non-past/dictionary*	*past*
おもしろい **omoshiroi** *interesting* (い -*adjective*)	おもしろかった **omoshirokatta** *was interesting*	おもしろくない **omoshirokunai** *not interesting*	おもしろくなかった **omoshirokunakatta** *wasn't interesting*
べんり **benri** *convenient* (な -*adjective*)	べんりだった **benridatta** *was convenient*	べんりではない **benri dewa nai** *not convenient*	べんりではなかった **benri dewanakatta** *wasn't convenient*
いい **ii** *good* *(irregular)*	よかった **yokatta** *was good*	よくない **yokunai** *not good*	よくなかった **yokunakatta** *wasn't good*

EXAMPLES

- きのう わたしが 買ったDVDを 見ます。
  Kinō watashi ga katta diibuidii o mimasu.
  (I) am going to watch the DVD I bought yesterday.

- 行きたいところは どこですか。
  Ikitai tokoro wa doko desu ka.
  Where is the place (you) want to go?

- おとうとが はたらいている店へ 買いものに 行きました。
  Otōto ga hataraite iru mise e kaimono ni ikimashita.
  (I) went shopping to the store where my younger brother works.

- 毎日 わたしは 日本語が かんたんな 本を 読みます。
  Mainichi watashi wa Nihongo ga kantan na hon o yomimasu.
  Every day, I read books whose Japanese is easy.

WATCH OUT!

X わたしが 母は 書いたてがみを もらいました。
Watashi ga haha wa kaita tegami o moraimashita.

→ わたしは 母が 書いたてがみを もらいました。*
Watashi wa haha ga kaita tegami o moraimashita.
I received a letter written by my mom.

X きのう わたしが 見ましたえいがは おもしろかったです。
Kinō watashi ga mimashita eiga wa omoshirokatta desu.

→ きのう わたしが 見たえいがは おもしろかったです。
Kinō watashi ga mita eiga wa omoshirokatta desu.
The movie that I saw yesterday was fun.

---

* The が **ga** particle is usually used to mark the subject of a clause, whereas the は **wa** particle marks the topic of the whole sentence.

GIVE IT A SHOT!

Combine the two sentences using a clause like the example below.

れい) きっさてんが ゆうびんきょくの そばに あります。そのきっさてんに 行きました。

→ <u>ゆうびんきょくの そばに ある きっさてんに 行きました。</u>

1) わたしは 北海道で さかなを 食べました。そのさかなは おいしかった です。

→ _____

2) いえの にわが きれいです。わたしは そのいえに すんでいます。

→ _____

3) ソンさんは 日本語が 上手です。ソンさんは わたしの 会社で はたら
いています。

→ _____

4) ミラーさんは 本を 書きました。その本は おもしろいです。

→ _____

5) 西川さんは ぼうしを かぶります。そのぼうしは 大きいです。

→ _____

6) わたしは 男の人と かいぎが ありました。その男の人は 大きなこえで
話します。

→ _____

JLPT-Style Questions

1) わたしは ともだちから（　）ネクタイを しています。

   1 もらう　　　　　2 もらった　　　　　3 もらい　　　　　4 もらって

2) 毎日 2時間（　）日本語を べんきょうします。

   1 しか　　　　　　2 ぐらい　　　　　　3 ごろ　　　　　　4 に

3) お金は 100円（　）ありません。

   1 あまり　　　　　2 ぐらい　　　　　　3 しか　　　　　　4 だけ

4) きのう、このネクタイを 買いました。これは、父に（　）プレゼントです。

   1 もらった　　　　2 もらう　　　　　　3 あげった　　　　4 あげる

5) それを あなた（　）言いたくなかったです。

   1 とだけは　　　　2 にだけが　　　　　3 だけも　　　　　4 にだけは

6) 西村_{にしむら}さんが（　　）会社_{かいしゃ}は　東京_{とうきょう}に　あります。

1 はたらきました　　　　　　　　　3 はたらいて
2 はたらきな　　　　　　　　　　　4 はたらいている

7) ねむたいです。ゆうべは　5時間_{じかん}しか（　　）。

1 ねていました　　　　　　　　　3 ねませんでした
2 ねます　　　　　　　　　　　　4 ねました

8) A「あしたは　いつ　出_でかけますか。」
B「8時_じ（　　）出_でかけます。」

1 で　　　　　　　2 だけ　　　　　　3 ぐらい　　　　　　4 ごろ

9) A「（　　）しごとを　休_{やす}みましたか。」
B「6日間_{むいかかん}ぐらいです。」

1 どのくらい　　　2 いつ　　　　　　3 何　　　　　　　4 なぜ

10) A「きれいですね。あなたと　あなたのお父_{とう}さんが　いえの　そうじを
しましたか。」
B「いいえ、わたし（　　）そうじを　しました。」

1 だけが　　　　　2 がだけ　　　　　3 はだけ　　　　　4 だけは

LESSON 9
Other Grammar Points

Can-Do Key Points

➡ Use transitive and intransitive verbs
➡ Understand sentence structure

TRANSITIVE vs. INTRANSITIVE VERBS

In Japanese, it's important to be aware of the transitive and intransitive forms of some verbs.

Meaning	Transitive	Intransitive
To open	あける akeru	あく aku
To raise	あげる ageru	あがる agaru
To close	しめる shimeru	しまる shimaru
To turn on	つける tsukeru	つく tsuku
To line up	ならべる naraberu	ならぶ narabu
To stop	とめる tomeru	とまる tomaru
To start	はじめる hajimeru	はじまる hajimaru

FORM:

Object + を (o) + transitive verb
Subject + が (ga) + intransitive verb

EXAMPLES

■ ドアを しめます。
Doa o shimemasu.
(I) will close the door.

■ ドアが しまります。
Doa ga shimarimasu.
(The) door will close.

- 電気を つけました。
  Denki o tsukemashita.
  (I) will turn on the lights.

- 電気が つきました。
  Denki ga tsukimashita.
  (The) lights turned on.

WATCH OUT!

X おさらが ならべました。 → おさらを ならべました。
Osara ga narabemashita. **Osara o narabemashita.**
(I) arranged the plates.

X ドアを あきました。 → ドアを あけました。
Doa o akimashita. **Doa o akemashita.**
(I) opened the door.

JLPT-Style Questions

1) ここで 車を (　) ください。

　1 とまて　　　　　2 とめ　　　　　3 とめて　　　　　4 とまって

2) テレビを (　) ごはんを つくります。

　1 つって　　　　　2 つきて　　　　　3 ついて　　　　　4 つけて

3) 電車を まっているとき、みなさんは (　)。

　1 ならびましょう　　　　　　　3 ならんでいました
　2 ならべていました　　　　　　4 ならべました

4) 電車が 京都駅に (　) とき、田中さんは おりました。

　1 とまって　　　　　2 とめた　　　　　3 とまった　　　　　4 とめて

5) えいがが (　) 前に 電気を けしました。

　1 はじまている　　　　　　　3 はじまる
　2 はじめる　　　　　　　　　4 はじめている

SUFFIXES

You can use suffixes to modify nouns.

Form:

> N + ずつ/たち/がた/すぎ/中
> **zutsu/tachi/gata/sugi/[chū, jū]**

EXAMPLES

- ぺんは 一人 一本ずつ です。
  Pen wa hitori ippon-zutsu desu.
  There is one pen for each person.

- わたしたちは 駅に 行きますよ。
  Watashi-tachi wa eki ni ikimasu yo.
  We are going to the station.

- あなたがたは きょうのよるに 何を していますか。
  Anata-gata wa kyō no yoru ni nani o shite imasu ka.
  What are you (all) doing tonight?

- 3時すぎに バスが 出ますよ。
  Sanji-sugi ni basu ga demasu yo.
  The bus leaves after 3 o'clock.

- 西村さんは 午前中に 来ます。
  Nishimura-san wa gozen-chū ni kimasu.*
  Mr. Nishimura is coming in the morning.

- ひとばん中 日本語を べんきょう しました。
  Hitoban-jū Nihongo o benkyō shimashita.*
  (I) studied Japanese all night.

* The kanji 中 is often pronounced **chū** when referring to a one-time action that happened during a certain time period. On the other hand, it's often pronounced **jū** when referring to something continuing for a period of time or to the whole extent of a certain period, area or organization.

WATCH OUT!

> X りんごは 一つずつ 300えんです。
> **Ringo wa hitotsu-zutsu sanbyaku-en desu.**
>
> → りんごは 一つ 300えんです。*
> **Ringo wa hitotsu sanbyaku-en desu.**
> *Apples are 300 yen each.*

> X 田中さんは いちにちちゅう けいたい電話で ゲームを していました。
> **Tanaka-san wa ichinichi-chū keitai denwa de gēmu o shite imashita.**
>
> → 田中さんは いちにちじゅう けいたい電話で ゲームを していました。
> **Tanaka-san wa ichinichi-jū keitai denwa de gēmu o shite imashita.**
> *Mr. Tanaka was playing video games with his cellphone all day.*

* ずつ indicates an equal distribution of quantity. When talking about prices, we are not distributing or connecting the money to each item.

JLPT-Style Questions

1) わたし（　）は 来月 けっこんします。

   1 すぎ　　　　　　　2 たち　　　　　　　3 中　　　　　　　4 ずつ

2) バスが 3時30分に 来ます。今、3時3分すぎですから、あと（　）まちましょう。

   1 27分　　　　　　2 17分　　　　　　3 33分　　　　　　4 23分

3) A「北村さんは どこですか。」
   B「午前（　）ぎんこうに 行って、まだかえっていません。」

   1 すぎ　　　　　　　2 ちゅう　　　　　　3 じゅう　　　　　　4 ずつ

4) A「きのうは たいへんでしたね。」
   B「そうですよ。一日（　）かいぎでした。」

   1 ずつ　　　　　　　2 じゅう　　　　　　3 ちゅう　　　　　　4 すぎ

5) バナナを（　）食べました。

   1 ずつ一つ　　　　　　　　　　　3 一つのずつ
   2 一つずつ　　　　　　　　　　　4 ずつの一つ

SENTENTIAL GRAMMAR 2 (SENTENCE COMPOSITION)

The second set of questions in the grammar section of the exam involves rearranging scrambled up sentences. You will see a sentence with four blanks. To answer the question, you need to place the answers 1 through 4 in the blanks and then write the number of the answer that fits in the blank with the star.

Before this set of questions you will see a sample question like this explaining how to answer the questions:

(もんだいれい) Question Example

A「_____ __★__ _____ _____ か。」

B「えんぴつです。」

1 です 　　　　 2 これ 　　　　 3 は 　　　　 4 何^{なん}

(こたえかた) How to Answer

1. ただしい 文^{ぶん}を つくります。

Rearrange the answers to make a correct sentence.

> A「_____ __★__ _____ _____ か。」
>
> 1 これ 　　　　 2 は 　　　　 3 何^{なん} 　　　　 4 です
>
> B「えんぴつです。」

2. __★__ に 入^{はい}る ばんごうを くろく ぬります。

Shade the number of the answer that is represented by the star.

(かいとうようし) 　| (れい) | ① ② ● ④

The aim of these questions is to test your understanding of Japanese grammar structure. These questions will mostly target how to put together clauses (page 165), use conjunctions (page 145), link adjectives together (page 155), how to form questions (page 61), and the て-form (page 81). Reviewing grammar, and writing down and testing out some of those structures will be a huge help for this section.

In general, this is a very odd way of thinking about the grammar, and something you will have to get used to doing. Try to look for ways the different answers can link to each other. Also, this section typically has two-line conversations that should give you a good amount of context. Use this to help you figure out what kind of answer goes in the blanks.

You might even want to try to visualize what you would write in the blanks before you take a look at the answers in order to more easily sort out the different parts. You can write in the test booklet, so use this to quickly sort out where to put each answer. Just remember to mark it on your answer sheet!

1) A「きのうは　こうえんに　行きました。」

　　B「わたしは　このしゅうまつ ＿＿＿＿ ＿＿＿＿ ＿★＿ ＿＿＿＿ 行きま
　　せんでした。」

　　1 どこ　　　　　2 は　　　　　　　　3 も　　　　　　　4 へ

2) A「えいがは　どうでしたか。」

　　B「＿＿＿＿ ＿＿＿＿ ＿★＿ ＿＿＿＿ かえりました。」

　　1 話し　　　　　2 つまらなくて　　　3 はやく　　　　　4 が

3) A「今日は　電話が　ありましたか。」

　　B「はい、＿＿＿＿ ＿＿＿＿ ＿★＿ ＿＿＿＿ ありました。」

　　1 一本　　　　　2 電話　　　　　　　3 だけ　　　　　　4 が

4) A「今日は　何も　しませんでしたか。」

　　B「いいえ、わたしは ＿＿＿＿ ＿＿＿＿ ＿★＿ ＿＿＿＿ しました。」

　　1 の　　　　　　2 を　　　　　　　　3 へや　　　　　　4 そうじ

5) A「＿＿＿＿ ＿★＿ ＿＿＿＿ ＿＿＿＿ ください。」

　　B「でも、いそがしいんですよ。」

　　1 クラス　　　　2 来て　　　　　　　3 に　　　　　　　4 あさって

6) A「このまちは　いつも　にぎやかですね。」

　　B「はい、でも、＿＿＿＿ ＿＿＿＿ ＿★＿ ＿＿＿＿ は　しずかでした。」

　　1 わかい　　　　2 が　　　　　　　　3 わたし　　　　　4 とき

7) A「ゆうべは　何を　しましたか。」

　　B「きのう ＿＿＿＿ ＿＿＿＿ ＿★＿ ＿＿＿＿ ねました。」

　　1 買った　　　　2 見た　　　　　　　3 後で　　　　　　4 DVDを

8) A「こうえん ＿＿＿＿ ＿★＿ ＿＿＿＿ ＿＿＿＿ きます。」

　　B「いってらっしゃい」

　　1 行って　　　　2 あそび　　　　　　3 に　　　　　　　4 へ

9) A「わたしの いえは 4000万円 かかりました。」

   B「日本 _____ _____ ★ _____ 高いですね。」

   1 は   2 いえ   3 は   4 で

10) A「ビールを 飲みますか。」

   B「いいえ、ぎゅうにゅう _____ _____ ★ _____ 飲みます。」

   1 を   2 水   3 と   4 だけ

11) A「そのえいがを 見ましたか。」

   B「田中先生が _____ ★ _____ _____ 後で 見ました。」

   1 行った   2 おしえている   3 大学   4 に

12) A「今日は _____ _____ ★ _____。」

   B「さんぽを しませんか。」

   1 天気です   2 いい   3 すずしくて   4 ね

13) A「この本は どこに おきますか。」

   B「わたし _____ _____ ★ _____ おかないで ください。」

   1 の   2 に   3 つくえ   4 は

14) A「その本は いくらですか。」

   B「この _____ _____ ★ _____ です。」

   1 本は   2 100円   3 にさつ   4 で

15) A「りょこうで パリへ 行きましたか。」

   B「ええ、_____ _____ ★ _____ 行きました。」

   1 そして   2 も   3 ローマ   4 へ

16) A「田中さんは おすしが すきですか。」

   B「いいえ、何でも _____ _____ ★ _____ 食べません。」

   1 だけ   2 は   3 食べますが   4 おすし

17) A「じゅぎょうは　いつですか。」

　　B「じゅぎょうは ＿＿＿＿ ＿★＿ ＿＿＿＿ ＿＿＿＿ です。」

　　１ ９時　　　　　　　２ １１時　　　３ まで　　　　　　４ から

18) 日本語を ＿＿＿＿ ＿＿＿＿ ＿★＿ ＿＿＿＿ います。

　　１ しながら　　　　　２ して　　　　３ りょうりを　　　４ れんしゅう

19) A「大きい　にわですね。」

　　B「そうですね。それに、ここは ＿＿＿＿ ＿＿＿＿ ＿★＿ ＿＿＿＿ です。」

　　１ しずか　　　　　　２ まち　　　３ で　　　　　４ いい

20) A「MONY で　はたらいていますか。」

　　B「いいえ、田中さん ＿＿＿＿ ＿＿＿＿ ＿★＿ ＿＿＿＿ つとめています。」

　　１ はたらいていた　　２ に　　　３ 会社　　　　４ が

TEXT GRAMMAR (USING GRAMMAR IN CONTEXT)

The third set of questions in the grammar section involves choosing the correct grammar point to go into a text. You are given a text with numbered blanks and then, typically on the opposite page, you will see numbers corresponding to those blanks. Choose the most appropriate answer and mark it on the answer sheet.

This section usually covers grammar points that require some context. The text is typically 200 to 250 characters in length (about 2 good-sized paragraphs). You will most likely see at least 1 question about particles, 1 or 2 questions about conjunctions (page 145), and then 2 or 3 questions about forms (past tense on page 66, て いる form on page 116, expressing desire on page 68, etc.).

The paragraphs are typically about everyday activities like self-introductions, everyday habits, a typical weekend, places you want to go, a favorite shop, journal entries, a happy moment, New Year cards, or about one's family.

Passage 1

日本で　べんきょうして　いる　学生が　「毎日　あさに　する　こと」の　ぶんしょうを　書きました。

6時に おきて シャワーを ［1］ メールを 読みます。それから、はを みがいて あさごはんを 食べます。いつも あさごはん ［2］ パンを 食べます。7時に いえを 出ます。ときどき 7時5分ごろに 家を 出て 駅まで はしります。プラットホームで 電車を まちます。ふゆの あさは ［3］ たいへんです。7時15分の 電車に のります。毎日 人が たくさん ［4］ しごとの 駅で おりるときには もう つかれています。だから、ときどき お店で コーヒーを 買います。そして、そのコーヒーを ［5］ しごとへ あるいていきます。

［1］
1 あびるから　　2 あびてから　　　　3 あびる後で　　　4 あびて後で

［2］
1 を　　　　　　2 に　　　　　　　　3 とき　　　　　　4 が

［3］
1 さむいで　　　2 さむく　　　　　　3 さむい　　　　　4 さむくて

［4］
1 あるから　　　2 のっていますから　3 のりましたから　4 あったから

［5］
1 飲むとき　　　2 飲んだとき　　　　3 飲みながら　　　4 飲んだから

Passage 2

日本で べんきょうして いる 学生が 「かぞく」の ぶんしょうを 書きました。

父は 今55さい ［1］ パンやを しています。母も ときどき そのパンやで はたらいています。パンやで はたらく 前は 父は 20年間 えいご ［2］ 先生を していました。今でも、上手に えいごを 話します。子どものときに 毎日 学校の 後で 父と いっしょに えいごを べんきょう ［3］。しかし、兄は あまり べんきょう しませんでした。兄は 大学へは ［4］ 父と パンやで はたらいています。そして、父は しごと 中 えいごだけを 話します。兄のしごとは ［5］ たいへんです。

[1]
1 に 　　　　　2 より 　　　　　3 へ 　　　　　4 で

[2]
1 が 　　　　　2 で 　　　　　3 の 　　　　　4 を

[3]
1 します 　　　2 していました 　　3 しています 　　4 したいです

[4]
1 行かないで 　2 行く 　　　　　3 行かない 　　　4 行きたくて

[5]
1 やさしくて 　2 かんたんで 　　3 たのしくて 　　4 むずかしくて

Passage 3

日本で べんきょうして いる 学生が「日本語を べんきょうする」の ぶん
しょうを 書きました。

ことばを たくさん [1]。 きょねんは 日本の えいがを たくさん 見ま
した。 いろいろな ことばを ききました。 でも、 そのことばを あまり
[2]。 えいがの ことばは むずかしいです。 だから、 今年は 日本語の
本を [3]。 おととい、 ほんやで [4]を 買いました。 その本は かん
じを あまり [5] やさしいです。 その本の 中の ことばを べんきょう
した後で 新しいそのことばを つかって 日本人と 話したいです。

---

[1]
1 しっていました 　　　　　　3 しりたいです
2 しりたくないです 　　　　　4 しります

[2]
1 おぼえていません 　　　　　3 おぼえます
2 おぼえました 　　　　　　　4 おぼえています

[3]
1 読みます 　　　　　　　　　3 読みたくないです
2 読みました 　　　　　　　　4 読んでいました

[4]

1 こどもは 読みます本　　　　　3 こどもが 読みます本

2 こどもが 読む本　　　　　　　4 こどもは 読む本

[5]

1 つかってから　　　　　　　　　3 つかっていないので

2 つかって　　　　　　　　　　　4 つかう

Passage 4

日本で べんきょうして いる 学生が「いちばん わるかった 日」の ぶん
しょうを 書きました。

> 　4年[1]、ともだちから プレゼントに 12本の 花を もらいました。
> その花を げんかんの かびんに [2] だいどころに 行きました。パン
> を トースターに 入れたとき 何か おとを [3]、げんかんに 行きまし
> た。わたしの いぬが その花を [4]。げんかんを そうじした後で だ
> いどころに 行きました。パンは くろく なっていました。その日は し
> ごとに [5]。だから、いえを 出ないで テレビを 見て ねていました。

[1]

1 ごろ　　　　　　2 ぐらい　　　　　3 前に　　　　　4 後で

[2]

1 入れてから　　　2 入れる前に　　　3 入ってから　　　4 入れる後で

[3]

1 しましたので　　2 聞いていたので　3 したので　　　　4 聞いたので

[4]

1 食べたいです　　　　　　　　　3 食べています

2 食べていました　　　　　　　　4 食べたくないです

[5]

1 行っていました　　　　　　　　3 行きたかったです

2 行きました　　　　　　　　　　4 行きたくなかったです

Part Three

Vocabulary and Kanji

LESSON 1
Kanji Reading

This first part of the vocabulary section of the test, formally called 言語知識(文字・語彙) (language knowledge, [characters • vocabulary]), tests you on the reading of the kanji. First, you will see a Japanese sentence with one or more kanji underlined. Four possible readings for the kanji are given. You must choose one which you think is the correct reading for that kanji.

If you have a regular habit of going over your flashcards for this level, this section should not be a problem. Keep in mind that the list included in this book is a best guess, and the real JLPT might have a few words that are not on the list. That's why in addition to a good daily vocabulary review habit, it is a good idea to study with a variety of materials so that you can get more exposure to kanji.

Also be aware of the small details in the answers. Some answers will only differ by a voicing mark ˚ on one of the hiragana, like つ and づ. Be sure to read all the answers carefully and look for differences between them before marking your best choice.

1) きのう、 りんごを 五つ かいました。
    1 ここのつ   2 ごつ   3 いつつ   4 よっつ

2) これは 何百円ですか。
    1 なにびゃくえん   2 なんびゃくえん
    3 なんひゃくえん   4 なにひゃくえん

3) とりは 空を とびました。
    1 く   2 ぞら   3 そら   4 くう

4) 今週は なにを していますか。
    1 いましゅう   2 こんしゅう   3 きしゅう   4 このしゅう

5) ろくがつは あめの ひが 多いです。
    1 おおい   2 おおぜい   3 たかい   4 おおきい

6) せんせいは しゅくだいを 出しました。
    1 でしました   2 だしました   3 しつしました   4 しゅつしました

7) もりしたさんの　こどもは　学生です。
  1 こせい　　　　　2 がくせい　　　　3 がくしょう　　　4 がっしょう

8) いしかわさんは　足が　ながいです。
  1 そく　　　　　　2 あし　　　　　　3 たり　　　　　　4 うで

9) まいにち　川で　およいでいます。
  1 うみ　　　　　　2 やま　　　　　　3 かわ　　　　　　4 いけ

10) いえを　でた時に　となりの　ひとを　みました。
  1 とき　　　　　　2 どき　　　　　　3 と　　　　　　　4 じ

11) その白いぼうしが　ほしいです。
  1 きいろい　　　　2 しろい　　　　　3 あかい　　　　　4 くろい

12) そのおとこの　ひとの　名前は　しりません。
  1 なまえ　　　　　2 めいまえ　　　　3 なぜん　　　　　4 めいぜん

13) わたしは　りょうりが　下手です。
  1 じょうず　　　　2 したて　　　　　3 へた　　　　　　4 したしゅ

14) わたしの　いえは　小さいですが、えきから　ちかいです。
  1 ちさい　　　　　2 ちいさい　　　　3 しょうさい　　　4 ちっさい

15) にほんごの　先生に　なりたいです。
  1 さきせい　　　　2 せんせい　　　　3 せんしょう　　　4 さきしょう

16) 毎月　どのくらいビールを　のみますか。
  1 まいづき　　　　2 めいづき　　　　3 めいつき　　　　4 まいつき

17) くるまを　かったので　お金が　ありません。
  1 おぎん　　　　　2 おがね　　　　　3 おかね　　　　　4 おきん

18) 四時に　かいぎが　はじまります。
  1 しじ　　　　　　2 よっじ　　　　　3 よじ　　　　　　4 よんじ

19) このかわは　にほんで　いちばん　長いです。
  1 とおい　　　　　2 ながい　　　　　3 ふかい　　　　　4 ひろい

20) たなかさんは　四月に　アメリカに　いきます。
  1 しがつ　　　　　2 よんがつ　　　　3 しちがつ　　　　4 よっがつ

LESSON 2
Orthography

In the second part of the vocabulary section, you will be tested on which kanji matches the reading, which is underlined in the sentence. You must select the answer that uses the correct kanji for the reading.

Here again, a regular habit of drilling N5 words will help you move through this section quickly. With the time you save here, you will have more time to think through the more difficult questions that come later.

In this section, the kanji in the answer will either look similar, or they will have a similar reading. Being familiar with kanji, even kanji that isn't N5 level, will give you a huge boost in this area. Be aware that on the JLPT, they may have 'fake' kanji that are missing a stroke or are in some other way different from the kanji that are normally used in Japanese.

1)　いま、なにかを　<u>いいたい</u>です。
　　1 語いたい　　　2 言いたい　　　3 読いたい　　　4 話いたい

2)　じゅぎょうで　よく<u>きいて</u>　ください。
　　1 聞いて　　　2 着いて　　　3 間いて　　　4 来いて

3)　そのおんなの　ひとは　<u>め</u>が　ちゃいろです。
　　1 日　　　　　2 目　　　　　3 百　　　　　4 白

4)　6じに　ふねは　<u>でます</u>よ。
　　1 入ます　　　2 山ます　　　3 行ます　　　4 出ます

5)　わたしに　みずを　<u>すこし</u>ください。
　　1 多し　　　　2 小し　　　　3 少し　　　　4 大し

6)　そのおとこの　ひとは　わたしの　<u>くに</u>で　ゆうめいです。
　　1 図　　　　　2 固　　　　　3 国　　　　　4 四

7)　たなかさんの　おとうさんを　<u>しりません</u>。
　　1 扣りません　　2 知りません　　3 如りません　　4 矢りません

8) わたしたちは ひの ちかくに すわって はなしていました。

1 父　　　　　　2 火　　　　　　3 人　　　　　　4 水

9) しちじに あいましょうか。

1 十一時　　　2 七時　　　　3 九時　　　　4 四時

10) わたしの ねこは いつも いすの うえで ねています。

1 後　　　　　　2 前　　　　　　3 上　　　　　　4 下

11) わたしは くにへ かえります。

1 四　　　　　　2 王　　　　　　3 国　　　　　　4 玉

12) ときどき ともだちに あいます。

1 含います　　2 会います　　3 合います　　4 企います

13) このでんしゃは きたへ いきます。

1 東　　　　　　2 南　　　　　　3 西　　　　　　4 北

14) ゆうびんきょくは えきの まえに あります。

1 南　　　　　　2 前　　　　　　3 間　　　　　　4 後

15) ごご8じに いえに かえります。

1 午後　　　　2 千後　　　　3 千前　　　　4 午前

16) みぎへ まがって ください。

1 友　　　　　　2 左　　　　　　3 右　　　　　　4 石

17) くろいずぼんは わたしのです。

1 ヅバン　　　2 ヅボン　　　3 ズバン　　　4 ズボン

18) まいにち にじかん てれびを みます。

1 タラビ　　　2 テラビ　　　3 テレビ　　　4 タレビ

19) いま、つよいあめが ふっています。

1 飴　　　　　　2 雨　　　　　　3 雪　　　　　　4 電

20) きょうは いいてんきですね。

1 矢汽　　　　2 天気　　　　3 矢気　　　　4 天汽

LESSON 3
Contextually-Defined Expressions

This is the third part of the vocabulary section and the objective here is to choose the correct word to be used in each sentence. The sentences are relatively short, but will probably have some kind of verb or noun that will point you toward the word that best fits inside the space.

This is where knowing common collocations (two or more words that are commonly used together) can really pay off. For example, here are a few of the common ones you might see:

かいしゃに つとめる
Kaisha ni tsutomeru
to serve at a company

でんきを けす
Denki o kesu
to switch off the lights

かいしゃで はたらく
Kaisha de hataraku
to work at a company

シャワーを あびる
Shawā o abiru
to take a shower

かさを さす
Kasa o sasu
to open an umbrella

おふろに はいる
Ofuro ni hairu
to take a bath

でんしゃに のる
Densha ni noru
to ride a train

ゆきが ふっている
Yuki ga futte iru
snow is falling, i.e. it's snowing

でんしゃを おりる
Densha o oriru
to get off a train

かぜが ふいている
Kaze ga fuite iru
the wind is blowing

でんきを つける
Denki o tsukeru
to turn on the lights

This section is also a place where counters for different objects might come up. Be sure to review the chart on page 53 because there will definitely be a question on the test about counters.

There will also be a few questions possibly toward the end that use illustrations to show locations of objects (page 120) or a particular situation that is hard to describe. Spend a little extra time drilling location words and counters so that you can easily tell the difference between them.

1) スーパーで 5（　）の りんごを かいました。
   1 はい　　　　2 えん　　　　3 こ　　　　4 ほん

2) にほんごで（　）ください。
   1 つかって　　2 わたして　　3 つくって　　4 こたえて

3) そのぎんこうに（　）います。
   1 はたらいて　2 おいて　　　3 つとめて　　4 しごとして

4) わたしの（　）では よく さかなを たべます。
   1 はし　　　　2 たてもの　　3 かてい　　4 かぞく

5) （　）が いちにちじゅう ないています。
   1 れいぞうこ　2 いぬ　　　　3 おんがく　　4 でんき

6) テレビを（　）ください。
   1 やすんで　　2 おりて　　　3 けして　　4 ねて

7) いつも いっしゅうかんに（　）の ほんを よみます。
   1 さんさつ　　2 さんぼん　　3 さんまい　　4 さんぱい

8) げつようびに テストが ありますが、あまり べんきょう
   していませんので（　）。
   1 ならっています　　　　　2 つとめています
   3 できています　　　　　4 こまっています

9) きたむらさんは 4（　）の くるまを もっていますよ。
   1 ばん　　　　2 だい　　　　3 かい　　4 はい

10) かいぎの ひは （　　）に かいて ください。
　　1 シール　　　　　2 ハンカチ　　　3 テープ　　　　　4 カレンダー

11) おふろが （　　）なりましたよ。あつくして ください。
　　1 うすく　　　　　2 ほそく　　　　3 あつく　　　　　4 ぬるく

12) きょうは さむいので （　　）うわぎを きましょう。
　　1 せまい　　　　　2 あつい　　　　3 おおい　　　　　4 ふとい

13) わたしの コーヒーは たなかさんのより （　　）です。
　　1 ほそい　　　　　2 せまい　　　　3 うすい　　　　　4 ふとい

14) いつ その うわぎを （　　）か。
　　1 かえします　　2 みがきます　　3 かえります　　4 かぶります

15) しがつごろに このはなは （　　）。
　　1 あきます　　　2 さきます　　　3 さします　　　4 ふります

16) たなかさんは （　　）を おりました。
　　1 スリッパ　　　2 プール　　　　3 エレベーター　4 トイレ

17) くつやは みちの （　　）に あり
　　ます。
　　1 うしろ
　　2 むこう
　　3 まえ
　　4 がわ

18) もりしたさんは たなかさんと
    にしむらさんの（　　）に います。

    1 まえ

    2 ところ

    3 あいだ

    4 ひだり

たなかさん　　もりしたさん　　にしむらさん

19) にしむらさんは（　　）を
    のぼっています。

    1 げんかん

    2 だいどころ

    3 かいだん

    4 ろうか

20) そのほんは いしかわさんの
    （　　）の うえに あります。

    1 つくえ

    2 テーブル

    3 いす

    4 ほんだな

LESSON 4
Paraphrasing

This is the fourth and final part of the vocabulary section. Here, you are given a sentence and must choose a sentence from the four given, that most closely matches the given sentence in meaning (i.e. a paraphrase of the original). Very often, the exam paper will use one word in the given sentence, and then a version with a word having the opposite meaning + a negative word in the correct answer. For example, the following two sentences have very similar meanings:

そのホテルは　ちかいです。
Sono hoteru wa chikai desu.
That hotel is close.

そのホテルは　とおくないです。
Sono hoteru wa tōkunai desu.
That hotel is not far.

A lot of the questions in this part will be in this form. Other questions might test you on rewordings of words like the following two sentences:

おじいさんは　おおさかに　すんでいます。
Ojiisan wa Ōsaka ni sunde imasu.
My grandpa lives in Osaka.

おとうさんの　おとうさんは　おおさかに　すんでいます。
Otōsan no otōsan wa Ōsaka ni sunde imasu.
My father's father lives in Osaka.

It's okay to spend a little extra time to review these questions and double-check the meaning of all the possible answers before choosing the closest match.

1) おばさんは　カレーが　すきです。

　1 おかあさんの　おかあさんは　カレーが　すきです。

　2 おとうさんの　あねは　カレーが　すきです。

　3 おとうさんの　おとうさんは　カレーが　すきです。

　4 おかあさんの　おとうとは　カレーが　すきです。

2) わたしは ともだちが すくないです。
　　1 わたしは ともだちが たくさん いません。
　　2 わたしは ともだちが ちいさいです。
　　3 わたしの ともだちは いいひとです。
　　4 わたしは ともだちが おおぜいです。

3) どようび いちにちじゅう くもりでした。
　　1 どようび いちにちじゅう ゆきが ふっていました。
　　2 どようび いちにちじゅう あかるかったです。
　　3 どようび いちにちじゅう はれていませんでした。
　　4 どようび いちにちじゅう あめが ふっていました。

4) わたしの おじいさんは とうきょうに すんでいます。
　　1 わたしの おとうさんの あには とうきょうに すんでいます。
　　2 わたしの おとうさんの いもうとは とうきょうに すんでいます。
　　3 わたしの おかあさんの おかあさんは とうきょうに すんでいます。
　　4 わたしの おかあさんの おとうさんは とうきょうに すんでいます。

5) わたしは カレーが だいすきです。
　　1 わたしは カレーを たべたくないです。
　　2 わたしは カレーを たくさん たべたいです。
　　3 わたしは カレーが きらいです。
　　4 わたしは カレーを つくります。

6) いいてんきだから、こうえんを あるきましょう。
　　1 いいてんきだから、こうえんを さんぽ しましょう。
　　2 いいてんきだから、こうえんを きれいに しましょう。
　　3 いいてんきだから、こうえんで あそびましょう。
　　4 いいてんきだから、こうえんを はしりましょう。

7) あなたの へやは あかるいですね。
　1 あなたの へやは やすいですね。
　2 あなたの へやは きれいですね。
　3 あなたの へやは ひろいですね。
　4 あなたの へやは くらくないですね。

8) せんしゅうは あつかったです。
　1 せんしゅうは たのしかったです。
　2 せんしゅうは さむかったです。
　3 せんしゅうは おもしろかったです。
　4 せんしゅうは すずしくなかったです。

9) えきの ひとに きっぷを わたしました。
　1 きっぷは わたしが もっています。
　2 きっぷは えきの ひとが もっています。
　3 きっぷは こうばんに あります。
　4 きっぷは でんしゃの なかに あります。

10) ケーキは れいぞうこに はいっています。
　1 ケーキは れいぞうこに はっていました。
　2 ケーキを れいぞうこから だしました。
　3 ケーキは れいぞうこの なかに おいています。
　4 ケーキは れいぞうこの そとに あります。

Part Four

Reading Comprehension

LESSON 1
How to Improve Your Reading Comprehension

Do you understand the *when, where, who, what, why* and *how* of the passage?

Whenever you do any kind of reading practice, you should focus on the details of the passage. Almost all questions in reading passages can be narrowed down to 6 simple questions—*who, what, when, where, why*, and *how*. Keep in mind that the answers to some of these questions might have to be inferred from the reading—they are not directly stated.

Read the following passage.

わたしは 先週の 土よう日 ともだちが けっこんしましたから 金よう日に 電車で 東京に 行きました。東京で ともだちに あって ビールを 飲みました。

Now, answer the questions below:

1) だれ (**dare,** who)?　　　　　　（わたしと ともだち／わたし）

2) 何 (**nani,** what)?　　　　　　（けっこんしました／東京に 行きました）

3) いつ (**itsu,** when)?　　　　　　（金よう日／土よう日）

4) どこ (**doko,** where)?　　　　　　（東京／大阪）

5) どうして (**dōshite,** why)?　　　（けっこんしました／りょこうしました）

6) どのように(**dono yō ni,** how)?　（車／電車）

ANSWERS

1. わたし　　　　　　　　3. 金よう日　　　　　　　5. けっこんしました
2. 東京に 行きました　　4. 東京　　　　　　　　　6. 電車

GIVE IT A SHOT!

Now, let's look at a few passages where you will have to infer something from the passage.

1) ともだちからの　てがみです。

> マットさん
>
> ５月17日の　よるに　東京に　行きます。　19日の　あさに　かえり
> ます。　そして、　18日の　あさは　かいぎです。　ひまですか。　会いた
> いです。
>
> アラン

アランさんは　いつ　ひまですか。

a. 18日の　よる

b. 17日の　あさ

Nowhere in the passage does it specifically say that "Alan" is free on the night of the 18th, but you can infer it from what is written. He comes to Tokyo on the night of the 17th, has a meeting the morning of the 18th, and goes back home on the morning of the 19th. The only time he doesn't have something scheduled is the night of the 18th.

2) 田中さんからの　メールです。

> 石川さん
>
> あしたは　かいぎです。　かいぎの　前に　水を　かってきてください。
> それから、　その前に　かいぎの　へやも　そうじして　ください。

石川さんは　はじめに　何を　しますか

a. 水を　買います。

b. かいぎの　へやを　そうじします。

In this passage, the sequence of events is important. The question is asking specifically what Mr. Ishikawa has to do *first*, which is to clean the meeting room. Pay attention to keywords that can hint at what the question is really asking for.

3) わたしは　おととい　新しいゲームを　買いました。その日は　いそがし
かったので　ゲームを　しませんでした。きのう　おとうとは
そのゲームを　しました。まだ　おとうとは　わたしに　それを
かえしていません。

だれが　ゲームを　しましたか。

a. おとうと

b. おとうとと　「わたし」

In this passage you have to keep track of who had the game and what they did with it. Notice the keyword in the last sentence, まだ (**mada**, yet). This lets us know that the poor author still hasn't gotten his game back, and he didn't have a chance to play it earlier. So, the only person that played it was his younger brother.

Break Down Sentences to Improve Your Comprehension

Sentences can get quite long in Japanese, so it's helpful to break them down in order to understand them better. Here are some simple rules to keep in mind:

Rule 1: The subject of a clause is marked by either the が **ga** particle or the の **no** particle.

Rule 2: The topic of the whole sentence is marked with は **wa**.

If you remember from Grammar Lesson 2, the は particle frames the conversation around a particular topic, while the が particle marks the subject. In other words, the topic is kind of like the subject for the whole sentence.

Take a look at the following sentence:

石川さんは、ともだちが　家に　来た後で　母のくれたDVDを　いっしょに
見ました。

Ishikawa-san wa, tomodachi ga ie ni kita ato de haha no kureta diibuidii o issho ni mimashita.

Can you answer these questions?

1) だれが　来ましたか。　　　　→　ともだち / 石川さん / 母
   Dare ga kimashita ka.　　　　　　tomodachi Ishikawa-san haha

2) だれが　DVDを　くれましたか。　→　ともだち / 石川さん / 母
   Dare ga diibuidii o kuremashita ka.　　tomodachi Ishikawa-san haha

3) だれが DVD を 見ましたか。
Dare ga diibuidii o mimashita ka
→ 石川さん / ともだち / 石川さんと ともだち
Ishikawa-san tomodachi Ishikawa-san to tomodachi

Let's break that sentence down:

石川さんは、 ①ともだちが 家に 来た後で
Ishikawa-san wa, tomodachi ga ie ni kita ato de
②母の くれた DVD を いっしょに 見ました。
haha no kureta diibuidii o issho ni mimashita.

① and ② are clauses. If you take those out, you have the main sentence:
石川さんは、 DVD を いっしょに 見ました。
Ishikawa-san wa, diibuidii o issho ni mimashita.

Clause ① tells us when they watched the DVD:
ともだちが 家に 来た後で
tomodachi ga ie ni kita ato de

And clause ② gives us more information about the DVD:
母 [の/が] くれた DVD
haha [no/ga] kureta diibuidii

When you break the sentence down, you can see that it is actually quite simple. The clauses simply add more detail to the main sentence.

Answers
1) ともだち 2) 母 3) 石川さんと ともだち

GIVE IT A SHOT!
1) わたしは、姉が つくったスカートを はいて いえを 出ました。
   a. だれが スカートを はいて いえを 出ましたか。
      → わたし ／ 姉
   b. だれが スカートを つくりましたか。
      → わたし ／ 姉

Taking it apart, you have only one clause in this sentence:

わたしは、姉が つくったスカートを はいて いえを 出ました。

Removing it, we have the main clause:

わたしは、スカートを　はいて　いえを　出ました。

So, 「わたし」 or 'I' wore the skirt and left the house. So the answer to a. is わたし. Now, let's look at the clause:

姉が　つくった

This describes the skirt. The skirt was made by "my" older sister. So the answer to b. is 姉.

2)　兄は、わたしが　弟から　かりた本を　読みました。
　　 a. だれが　本を　読みましたか。　　→　兄／わたし／弟
　　 b. だれが　本を　かりましたか。　　→　兄／わたし／弟
　　 c. だれから　本を　かりましたか。　→　兄／わたし／弟

This sentence is a little more complicated. There is still only one clause, but it is a little more involved:

兄は、<u>わたしが　弟から　かりた</u>本を　読みました。

If we remove that complicated clause we have the main sentence:

兄は、本を　読みました。

So, the person that read the book is あに. Question a. is あに. Let's look at the much more complicated clause:

わたしが　弟から　かりた

This describes the book. "I" borrowed the book from "my" younger brother. So, the answer to b. is わたし　and the answer to c. (who from?) is おとうと.

3)　太郎さんは　わたしが　あげたネクタイを　していましたが、
　　今は　かすみさんから　もらったネクタイを　しています。

　　 a. だれが　ネクタイを　していますか。
　　　　→　わたし／太郎さん／かすみさん
　　 b. だれが　ネクタイを　あげましたか。
　　　　→　わたし／かすみさん／わたしと　かすみさん

c. 太郎さんが 今 しているネクタイを、太郎さんに あげましたか。
→ わたし／かすみさん／わたしと かすみさん

This final sentence has two clauses in it:

太郎さんは ①わたしが あげたネクタイを していましたが、今
②かすみさんから もらったネクタイを しています。

If you take out the two clauses, you get the main sentence:

太郎さんは ネクタイを していましたが、今 ネクタイを しています。

This main sentence doesn't actually make much sense without the clauses. But, you can see that the person wearing the necktie is 太郎さん, so the answer to a. is 太郎さん.

Now, let's look at the first clause:

わたしが あげた

This describes the necktie Taro was wearing. So the person that gave Taro the first necktie he was wearing is わたし.

Let's take a look at the second clause:

かすみさんから もらった

This describes the necktie Taro is wearing now. He received it from Kasumi. So, each of the two people gave him a necktie. That makes the answer to b., わたし と かすみさん. However, the necktie Taro is wearing now is from Kasumi, so the answer to c. is かすみさん.

　Be sure to read the questions carefully and don't assume what they are asking. Sometimes the use of one particle can completely change the answer.

Understanding Conjunctions to Understand Flow

We covered the three main categories of conjunctions in Grammar Lesson 7 (page 145) that you will see at the N5 level—those that link two ideas, those that show contrast, and those that show reason. Searching these out in a passage and marking them, when you are skimming over it, can help give you an idea of how the passage flows.

そして・それから・それに
Conjunctions used to link similar ideas

そして (**soshite**, and), それから (**sore kara**, and then), and それに (**sore ni**, in addition) can all be used to link two ideas together.

そして can be used to link two ideas:

姉は テニスを します。**そして、** 妹 は ゴルフを します。
Ane wa tenisu o shimasu. Soshite, imōto wa gorufu o shimasu.
*My older sister plays tennis. **And**, my younger sister plays golf.*

それから can link two events that happen in sequence:

姉は テニスを しました。**それから、** いえに かえりました。
Ane wa tenisu o shimashita. Sore kara, ie ni kaerimashita.
*My older sister played tennis. **And then**, (she) returned home.*

そして can also be used in this way:

姉は テニスを しました。**そして、** いえに かえりました。
Ane wa tenisu o shimashita. Soshite, ie ni kaerimashita.
*My older sister played tennis. **And**, (she) returned home.*

それに can be used to link similar ideas together:

姉は テニスを しました。**それに、** ゴルフにも 行きました。
Ane wa tenisu o shimashita. Sore ni, gorufu ni mo ikimashita.
*My older sister played tennis. **In addition**, (she) played golf.*

から・だから
Conjunctions used to show reason

から (**kara**, so) marks the reason for something to occur. だから/ですから (**dakara/desu kara**, therefore or so) can also be used to mark reasons.

から is often used mid-sentence to show reason:

雨が ふるから、 いえに かえりましょう。
Ame ga furu kara, ie ni kaerimashō.
(It) is raining, so let's return home.

だから can be used at the beginning of a sentence to link it to the previous sentence:

お金が ありません。 だから、新しい 車を 買いたくないです。
Okane ga arimasen. Dakara, atarashii kuruma o kaitakunai desu.
*(I) don't have money. **That's why,** (I) don't want to buy a new car.*

でも・しかし・が
Conjunctions used to show contrast

でも (**demo**, but), しかし (**shikashi**, however), and が (**ga**, but) can show a contrast between two clauses. And mark a change in the direction of the conversation.

でも is most often used in casual situations:

毎日、べんきょうを していました。でも、テストは むずかしかった です。
Mainichi, benkyō o shite imashita. Demo, tesuto wa muzukashikatta desu.
Every day, (I) was studying. **But,** the test was difficult.

しかし is more often used in formal situations and writing:

こうえんに 行きたかった です。しかし、今 雨が ふっています。
Kōen ni ikitakatta desu. Shikashi, ima ame ga futte imasu.
*(I) wanted to go to the park. **However,** (it) is raining now.*

Using が marks a weaker contrast in the same sentence:

お店に 行きましたが、しまっていました。
Omise ni ikimashita ga, shimatte imashita.
*(I) went to the store, **but** it was closed.*

GIVE IT A SHOT!

1) この土よう日に パーティーが あります。食べものと 飲みものを たくさん 買いました。ビールと ワインも 買いました。田中さんは いいぎゅうにくを もってきます。それに、やさいも もって 来ます。

　だれが やさいを もって 来ますか。

a.「わたし」
b. 田中さん

It's very easy to lose track of the subject in Japanese, so you really need to focus on context. Here, we are looking for who is bringing the vegetables. But there is no subject in the following sentence:

それに、やさいも もって 来^きます。

But, there is one in the sentence before it— 田中^{たなか}さん . The それに (in addition) links the two sentences together, so we know that Mr. Tanaka is the one bringing the vegetables.

2)　あしたは ともだちの たんじょうびです。 ともだちは いぬが すきです から いぬのえのさらを 買^かいました。 あした、 ともだちに あげます。

　　なぜ 「わたし」 は いぬのえのさらを 買^かいましたか。

　　a.「わたし」 は いぬが すきだから。

　　b. いぬが すきな ともだちに あげるから。

The question is asking why, so this should help you understand what you are looking for. You need to find the reason why「わたし」bought the plate with dogs (on it). Notice that the correct answer, b, isn't as straightforward as you might think. It mentions the reason marked with the から particle, but gives a little longer answer. Try to think of the passage as a whole when answering questions. The JLPT rarely 'hands' you the answer. You usually have to use a few of the sentences in a passage to make your conclusions.

3)　きのう おいしいケーキを 買^かいました。 今日^{きょう} そのケーキを 食^たべたかっ たです。 しかし、兄^{あに}が ケーキを ぜんぶ 食^たべました。

　　だれが ケーキを 食^たべましたか。

　　a.「わたし」

　　b. あに

If you were reading this passage a little too fast, you might think that the writer, 「わたし」, ate the cake, but you have to pay attention to the しかし. This signals a turn in the passage, and oftentimes this is where you can find the answer to questions in the reading comprehension section of the test. The answer to the question is actually 兄, b.

Understanding Pronouns

こそあど words (e.g. これ, それ, and あれ) can refer to a thing's physical location in a room. But, they can also refer to previously made statements, or even things that you will mention next.

これ can be used to refer to things just previously mentioned or something that will be referred to later:

きょねん、あかいくつを 買いました。でも、ちょっと 小さかったです。
先月 新しく みどりの くつを 買いました。これは いいくつです。

Kyonen, akai kutsu o kaimashita. Demo, chotto chisakatta desu. Sengetsu atarashiku midori no kutsu o kaimashita. Kore wa ii kutsu desu.

Last year, (I) bought red shoes. But, (they) were a little small. Last month, (I) bought new green shoes. These are good shoes.

「これ」は どの くつ ですか。　→　あかいくつ/みどりの くつ
「Kore」wa dono kutsu desu ka.　　　akai kutsu/midori no kutsu
Which shoes are "these"?　　　　　　*red shoes/green shoes*

Correct Answer is みどりの くつ
　　　　　　　　midori no kutsu
　　　　　　　　green shoes

While ここ can refer to a place that was previously mentioned or even something mentioned later:

いつも 休みの 日には ここに すわって ちかくの カフェで 買った
コーヒーを 飲みます。この こうえんは しずか ですね。

Itsumo yasumi no hi ni wa koko ni suwatte chikaku no kafe de katta kōhii o nomimasu. Kono kōen wa shizuka desu ne.

On my days off, (I) always sit here and drink coffee that (I) bought from the nearby cafe. This park is quiet, isn't it?

「ここ」は どこですか。　→　こうえん/カフェ
「Koko」wa doko desu ka.　　kōen　kafe
Where is "here"?　　　　　　*park*　*cafe*

Correct Answer is こうえん
　　　　　　　　kōen
　　　　　　　　park

While こんな can refer to a certain kind of something:

きのうは 10時まで はたらいていましたから、あさ おそくに おきました。
こんな時は コーヒーを 飲みます。

Kinō wa jū-ji made hataraite imashita kara, asa osoku ni okimashita. Konna toki wa kōhii o nomimasu.

Because (I) worked until 10 yesterday, (I) woke up late in the morning. At this kind of time, (I) drink coffee.

「こんな時」は　どんな　時ですか。
Konna toki wa　donna　toki desu ka.
What kind of time is "this kind of time"?

    a. 10時まで　はたらいた時。
       Jū-ji made　hataraita toki
       The time (I) worked until 10.
    b. おそく　おきた時。
       Osoku　okita toki.
       The time (I) wake up late.

The correct answer is b:　おそく　おきた時
                    Osoku　okita toki
                    The time (I) wake up late.

GIVE IT A SHOT!

1)
本が　だいすきです。「マックといういぬ」がすきです。なんども　読みました。先週の　金よう日に　「マックといういぬ」の　えいがを　見ました。これは　とても　おもしろかったです。

「これ」は　どれですか。
a. 本

b. えいが

Although most of the passage is about the author's favorite book, he talks about the movie in the sentence just before using これ. So, これ refers to the movie, and the correct answer is b.

2)
大阪で　うまれました。しかし、5年前に　東京で　しごとを　はじめました。大阪に　すみたいですが、ここには　おもしろいしごとが　あります。

「ここ」は　どこですか。
a. 大阪
b. 東京

The author says she wants to live in Osaka, but finishes the clause with が which marks a contrast. We can infer from this that the author is not in Osaka, but still in Tokyo, so the answer is **b**.

3)
> 今日は 6時に おきて 7時に いえを 出ました。8時から 6時 まで しごとしました。7時に じゅぎょうに 行きました。9時に いえに かえって ばんごはんを 食べて おふろに はいって 11時 に ねました。こんな日は たいへんですよ。

「こんな日」は どんな日ですか。
a. 11時に ねた日
b. 一日中 いそがしい日。
c. 6時に おきた日。

こんな日 is referring to an entire day, so the best answer is one that refers to the whole day, not just a part of it. That makes answer **b** the best.

ゆう

げんきですか。
おそくに れんらく
して、すみません。
*How are you? Sorry
for contacting you
so late.*

22:50

マットは いちばん やさしい人で
すね。とても あいたいです。でも、
今は きぶんが わるいから…
*Matt is the sweetest person, and
I really want to see you. But, I'm
not feeling well now, so...*

あのう、わたしの いえに さかなを
もってきて くださいませんか。
さかなが だいすきです。いえの
前に おいてください。
*So, could you possibly bring some
fish to my house? I love fish.
Please put it in front of my house.*

すぐに おねがいします。
ありがとうね。
Please do it quickly. Thank you.

LESSON 2
Reading Short Passages

もんだい　つぎの　（1）から　（20）の　ぶんしょうを　読んで、しつもん　に　こたえて　ください。こたえは、1・2・3・4から　いちばん　いい　ものを　一つ　えらんで　ください。

Mondai　**Tsugi no (1) kara (20) no bunshō o yonde, shitsumon ni kotaete kudasai.**
Kotae wa, 1 / 2 / 3 / 4 kara ichiban ii mono o hitotsu erande kudasai.

Question　Read the next passages from (1) to (20) to answer the questions. Choose the best answer from 1 / 2 / 3 / 4.

(1)　お店の　まどに　はってある　かみです。

今日　シャツを　ぜんぶ　やすく　うっています。

あかいテーブルの　上に　あるシャツは　1まい　1000円です！

あおいテーブルの　上に　あるシャツは　1まい　750円です！
→　それに　3まい　買った　人には、2250円を　2000円に　します。

白いテーブルの　上に　あるシャツは　1まい　500円です！
→　それに　5まい　買った　人には、500円　ひきます。

---

[1] シャツを　あかいテーブルから　1まい　とって、あおいテーブルから　4まい　とって、白いテーブルから　5まい　とった人は　いくら　はらいますか。

1 5750円　　　2 6000円　　　3 6250円　　　4 6500円

(2)　このしゃしんの　わたしの　右は　姉です。姉の　となりは　弟　です。姉の　後ろは　りょうしんです。

[2] しゃしんは　どれですか。

(3) 姉は 東京に すんでいます。わたしの ともだちが 東京に 行くの
で、わたしも そこへ 行きます。そして、姉に 会いたいです。でも、姉
は ちょっと いそがしいので、ともだちと ビールを 飲みに 行きます。

[3]「わたし」は 何を しますか。

1 姉に 会います。
2 ともだちと 東京で あそびます。
3 姉と ともだちと ビールを 飲みます。
4 ともだちだけ 東京に 行きます。

(4) なつ休みは ともだちと いっしょに りょこうに 行きたいです。ともだ
ちの 一人は うみへ およぎに 行きたいです。わたしは 山へ のぼり
に 行きたいです。しかし、どのともだちも 車が ないので、わたした
ちは どこかへ 電車で 行きます。

[4]「わたし」は 何を しますか。

1 りょこうへ 車で 行きます。   3 山を のぼります。
2 りょこうへ 電車で 行きます。   4 うみで およぎます。

(5) 先週、フランスへ りょこうしました。そこで 買いものに 行きました。
きれいな はがきと けしゴムを 買いました。それを りょうしんに あげ
ます。そして、フランスの ふくは かわいいです。姉は いつも わたし
に 何か くれるので、くつしたと うわぎを 買いました。でも、うわぎ
は ちょっと 小さかったので、わたしが つかっています。

[5] 姉は 何を もらいましたか。

1 けしゴム 　　　　2 くつした 　　　　3 うわぎ 　　　　4 はがき

(6) これは、会社の だいどころに ある ポスターです。

> みなさん、
> ・しごとに もどる 前に てを あらって ください。
> ・白いおさらを つかってください、つかった後は あらって ください。
> ・あおいおさらを つかわないで ください。
> ・あたたかい飲みものには かみコップを つかわないで ください。

* もどる - かえる

[6] ポスターと あうものは、どれですか。

1 ホットコーヒーを 飲むときに かみコップを つかいます。
2 おさらは 何色でも つかいます。
3 しごとに もどる前に つかったおさらは あらいます。
4 しごとの 後で てを あらいます。

(7) あした りょうしんが 弟の いえに 来るので、今、弟は そうじを
しています。おばさんも 来ます。しかし、しごとが あるから よるに
つきます。みんなは りょうりが きらいなので わたしが します。

[7]「わたし」は 何を しますか

1 りょうりを します。　　　　3 しごとを します。
2 そうじを します。　　　　　4 よるに つきます。

(8) ねこが すきです。ねこは いえで 一日中(いちにちじゅう) ねています。わたしも そう したいですね。いぬは ときどき なきます。でも ねこは あまり なきません。そして、ねこは あたたかいです。ときどき さむい 日(ひ)に わたしの 上(うえ)に ねています。わたしも あたたかいです。

[8] なぜ「わたし」は ねこが すきですか。

1 ねこが ないています。

2 ねこは あまり ねていません。

3 ねこが あたたかく なりたいです。

4 ねこと ねるとき 「わたし」は さむくなく なります。

(9) 会社(かいしゃ)の 出口(でぐち)の ドアに はってあるかみです。

ちょっとまってください！

• パソコンを けしましたか。

• つくえの ひきだしの かぎを かけましたか。

※ 月(げつ)よう日、火(か)よう日、木(もく)よう日は、7時(じ)20分(ぷん)までに へやを 出(で)てください。7時半(じはん)に ドアのかぎが かかります。水(すい)よう日、金(きん)よう日は 午後(ごご)6時(じ)50分(ぷん)までに へやを 出(で)てください。午後(ごご)7時(じ)に ドアの かぎが かかります。ながい 時間(じかん) しごとを するときは 川口(かわぐち)さんに 電話(でんわ)してください。

[9] 上(うえ)と ちがうものは どれですか。

1 水(すい)よう日と 金(きん)よう日、午後(ごご)6時(じ)50分(ぷん)まで 会社(かいしゃ)に います。

2 火(か)よう日、午後(ごご)7時(じ)に へやを 出(で)ます。

3 月(げつ)よう日、火(か)よう日、木(もく)よう日は 7時(じ)40分(ぷん)にへやを 出(で)ます。

4 水(すい)よう日と 金(きん)よう日、午後(ごご)7時(じ)から へやに 入(はい)れません。

(10) これは、日本語の べんきょうの へやに はってある ポスターです。

> ・かえるとき、電気を けして ください。
> ・しゅうまつは このへやで 食べたり 飲んだり しないで ください。
> ・水よう日は、休みです。

[10] ポスターと あっていないものは、どれですか。

1 月よう日に おかしを 食べます。
2 木よう日に 水を 飲みます。
3 毎日 へやを つかいます。
4 いつも、へやを 出るとき 電気を けして ください。

(11) 新しいアパートは ちょっと 小さいです。でも、ちょうどいいですよ。ほんだなは ドアのちかくに あります。わたしが 買ったえは まどの となりに かけました。いつも ドアのむかいに あるいすに すわって、本を 読んでいます。あかるくて いいところですよ。

[11] アパートは どれですか。

1

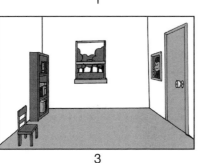

2

3

4

(12) いえに ついた後で シャワーを あびました。シャワーの 後で、ばん
ごはんを 食べながら テレビを 見ました。食べた後で 日本語を べ
んきょうしました。それから、12時に ねました。

[12] ただしいものは どれですか。

1 シャワーを あびてから ばんごはんを 食べました。
2 ばんごはんを 食べながら 日本語を べんきょうしました。
3 ばんごはんの 後で テレビを 見ました。
4 テレビを 見る前に 日本語を べんきょうしました。

(13) せんげつ、新しい アパートに 入りました。わたしの へやは 2かい
です。となりには、おじいさんが すんでいます。1かいの人は、まだ
どんな人か しりません。3かいには、おばあさんと スペイン語の
先生が すんでいます。

[13] この 人の アパートは どれですか。

1

2

3

4

(14) 石川 さんは 西村 さんに メールを おくりました。

西村 さん

こんにちは。

わたしは、あさっての よる 7時に 駅に つきます。駅の きっさてんの 前で まっています。わたしは、ぼうしを かぶっています。かみは ながいです。かばんを もっています。

よろしくおねがいします。

石川

[14] 石川 さんは、どれですか。

1   2   3   4

(15) ともだちへの てがみです

きのう、父は りんごを たくさん 買って わたしに くれました。とても おいしいです。けさ そのりんごで おかしを つくりました。あしたは ひまですか。おちゃを 飲みながら そのおかしを 食べませんか。おいしいですよ。

[15] 今日、「わたし」は 何を しましたか。

1 りんごを もらいました。　　　3 おかしを つくりました。

2 りんごを 食べました。　　　　4 おかしを 食べました。

(16) 来週 ホームパーティーが あります。じゅんこさんが かなさんに おくっ
たメールです。

かなさん

来週の パーティーの れんらくを します。

からいカレーを たくさん つくります。みなさんは やさいを もってき
ます。かなさんは 何か もってきますか。ぶたにくを 食べたかったで
すが、姉が ぎゅうにくを くれたので、これを つかいます。
そして、お花が ほしいです。お店で 花を 買って きてください。
では、よろしく おねがいします。

じゅんこ

[16] かなさんは、何を しますか。

1 やさいを もって、じゅんこの にわで 花を とります。

2 じぶんの にわで 花を とって じゅんこのいえに 行きます。

3 じゅんこのいえに 花を もっていきます。

4 じゅんこのいえに ぶたにくを もって、花を 買っていきます。

(17) 石川さんから 西村さんに メールが きました。

西村さん

来月の 5日から 8日まで しごとで 東京へ 行きます。いっしょ
に ビールを 飲みませんか。5日は たぶん つかれています。わたし
は 6日は 一日中、そして 7日の あさは かいぎが あります。
しかし、その後は ひまです。そのときは どうですか。

石川

[17] 石川さんは いつ 時間が ありますか。

1 5日の よる　　2 6日の ひる　　3 6日の よる　　4 7日の よる

(18) ひるごはんを 食べる へやは 一つの テーブルと 4つの いすが あり
ます。しかし、本は あまり ありません。みなさんは そうじが きらい
です。いつも ちょっと きたないです。

[18] ひるごはんを 食べるへやは どれですか。

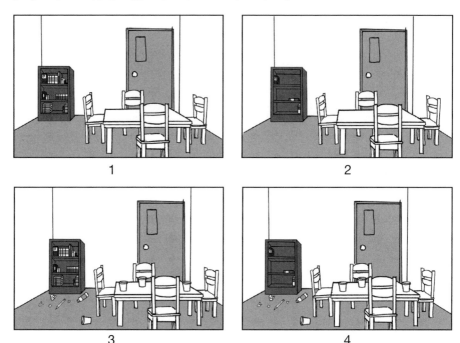

(19) 学生の みなさんに おくったメールです。

新しい日本語の クラスが あります。火よう日の 午前、木よう
日の 午前と 午後が あります。火よう日の 午前は かんじの ク
ラスです。かんじを あまり しらない人には このクラスが いいで
す。水よう日の午前の クラスは 金よう日の クラスより むずかし
いです。木よう日の クラスは ぶんぽうを れんしゅうします。はじ
めての 人の クラスは 木よう日の 午前です。

[19] 日本語の かんじを はじめて ならいます。どの クラスが いいですか。
1 火よう日の 午前　　　　3 木よう日の 午前
2 木よう日の 午前　　　　4 木よう日の 午後

(20) 西村さんの つくえの 上に、ふうとうが あります。ふうとうの 中に
田中さんの メモと しゃしんが あります。

これは りょこうの しゃしんです。いちまいは 50円です。ほしい
しゃしんを とって お金は ふうとうに 入れて ください。ふうとうは、
石川さんに わたしますから、わたしの つくえの 上に おいてくださ
い。金よう日までに かえして ください。

田中

[20] 西村さんは ほしいしゃしんが あります。どうしますか。

1 ほしいしゃしんが 入ったふうとうを 石川さんに わたします。

2 お金を 入れたふうとうを 石川さんに わたします。

3 ほしいしゃしんが 入ったふうとうを 田中さんの つくえの 上に
おきます。

4 お金を 入れたふうとうを 田中さんの つくえの 上に おきます。

LESSON 3
Reading Mid-Length Passages

もんだい つぎの （1）から（10）の ぶんしょうを 読んで、しつもんに
こたえて ください。こたえは、1・2・3・4から いちばん いい
ものを 一つ えらんで ください。

Mondai Tsugi no (1) kara (10) no bunshō o yonde, shitsumon ni kotaete kudasai.
Kotae wa, 1 / 2 / 3 / 4 kara ichiban ii mono o hitotsu erande kudasai.

Question Read the next passages from (1) to (10) to answer the questions.
Choose the best answer from 1 / 2 / 3 / 4.

(1) せんしゅうは 山に のぼりました。はやくおきて、電車で 山へ 行き
ました。しかし、おべんとうを わすれましたので、店で おべんとう
を 買いたかったです。しかし、山の ちかくの 駅に べんとうやや パ
ンやなどが ありませんでした。とても たいへんでした。

それから、食べものを もたないで 山に のぼりました。4時間ぐら
い のぼって とても つかれました。そのとき 雨が ふりました。さむ
かったですから、はやく駅に 帰りました。いえの ちかくの 駅に 行っ
て レストランで あたたかい ばんごはんを たくさん 食べました。

[1] どうして 「たいへん」でしたか。

1 店が ありませんでした。
2 店が とおいからです。
3 山が 高かったからです。
4 食べものを もっているからです。

[2] どこで ばんごはんを 食べましたか。

1 いえの ちかくのところで
2 いえに 行っている 電車で
3 山の 上のところで
4 山の ちかくの 駅のところで

(2) わたしが わかいとき 父は わたしの ゴルフの 先生でした。毎日ねる前に いっしょに ゴルフを れんしゅう しました。そして、しゅうまつは ゴルフを していました。むずかしかったですよ。しかし、どんどん 上手に なりました。なつりょこうに 行くときも ゴルフを していました。

今は 父の からだが よわく なったから いっしょに ゴルフを あまり しません。わたしは まだ ゴルフを しています。一人でも たのしいです。こどもが うまれた後で、こどもと いっしょに したいです。父に「ありがとう。」と 言いたいです。

[3] わかいときに いつ「わたし」は ゴルフを しましたか。

1 まいばん、しゅうまつ

2 まいばん、しゅうまつ、なつ休み

3 毎日、休み

4 しゅうまつ、休み

[4] どうして 「わたし」は 父に 「ありがとう。」と 言いたいですか。

1 こどもと ゴルフの れんしゅうを したからです。

2 今でも いっしょに ゴルフを するからです。

3 父は 一人でも たのしかったからです。

4 わたしに ゴルフを おしえたからです。

(3) ねこは うるさくて 人が あまり すきじゃないと おもいますから、わたしは ねこが きらいです。ときどき ねこは 外の ごみの はこを あけて 中の ごみを 食べます。ごみの はこの あたりを きたなくします。

おととい ねこが ごみを 食べながら とても うるさく ないていましたから、わたしは おきました。外に でて 「つかまえるよ。」と 大きいこえで 言いましたが、ねこは 小さい子ねこと いっしょに いました。その子ねこは まだ 目が あかない 小さい子ねこで ないていました。それから、いえに ぎゅうにゅうを とりに かえって そのねこたちに あげました。

今日は スーパーで えさを 買って そのねこたちに あげます。ほか
の ねこは まだ きらいです。しかし、そのねこたちは すきです。

* えさ - どうぶつの 食べもの
* あたり - へん
* つかまえる - とる
* 子ねこ - こどもの ねこ

[5] どうして 「わたし」は ねこが きらいですか。
1 ねこは きたないからです。
2 ねこは ごみを 食べるからです。
3 ねこは うるさくなくて、人が すきじゃないからです。
4 ねこは 人が きらいで、しずかじゃないからです。

[6]「わたし」は 何を しましたか。
1 ねこを いえに もってきました。
2 ねこの えさを 買いました。
3 ねこを 外に おきました。
4 ねこに 飲みものを あげました。

(4) フランスから 来たわたしのともだちは マーティンさんと 言います。マー
ティンさんと いっしょに 日本語の 学校に 行っています。毎日 わた
しは べんとうを じぶんで つくります。先週、マーティンさんは 「あ
なたの べんとうは なかみが すくないですね。」と 言いました。わたし
は「おべんとうを かんたんに つくって、みじかい 時間で 食べたいです。」
と 言いました。

マーティンさんは いつも べんとうを うつくしく つくります。たぶん、
毎日 30分 ぐらいで つくります。「ひるごはんは うつくしく つくった
ものを たくさん 食べたいです。そして しごとを たくさんします。いえ
で いっしょに りょうりを しませんか。」と、マーティンさんは 言いました。
土よう日は マーティンさんのいえに 行きます。

* なかみ - 中に 入っているもの

[7] どうして マーティンさんは 「わたし」の べんとうが あまり すきじゃ
　　ないですか。

1 べんとうを みじかい時間で 食べるからです。

2 べんとうには いろいろな なかみが あるからです。

3 べんとうの なかみを すくなく かんたんに つくるからです。

4 べんとうが ちょっと 小さいからです。

[8] 土よう日、「わたし」は 何を しますか。

1 うつくしい食べものを 見ます。

2 うつくしいべんとうを つくります。

3 マーティンさんが つくったりょうりを 食べます。

4 べんとうを かんたんに つくります。

(5) 先週、新しい 会社の しごとが はじまりました。会社は べんり
な ところに あります。そばに やすくて おいしいレストランが ありま
す。駅から あるいて5分です。駅の ちかくに パンやが あります。こ
の会社に 入る前は パンを あまり 買いませんでした。しかし、
今は いつも パンを 買います。それから、会社と おいしいレストラン
の あいだに コーヒーの 店が あります。まいあさ コーヒーも 買い
ます。大きなもんだいですよ。

スーツが ふるくなったので、新しいスーツを 買いたいです。しかし、
今は お金が ありません。パンと コーヒーを いつも たくさん 買う
からです。

[9] つぎの 中で、「わたし」の 会社から いちばん ちかい店は どれ
　　ですか。

1 スーツの 店

2 おいしいレストラン

3 コーヒーの 店

4 パンや

[10] なぜ 「大きなもんだいですよ。」 ですか。

1 しごとを している からです。

2 お金が なくなる からです。

3 会社へ あるきながら、 コーヒーを 飲む からです。

4 駅は 会社から とおい からです。

(6) 日本語が すきです。 アメリカに すんでいますが、 毎日、 日本語を べんきょうしています。 日本語の おんがくを 聞きながら せんたくをして、 しごとの後で 日本語のクラスに 行って、 ねる前に 日本語の 本を 読みます。 つぎは、 かんじの れんしゅうを はじめます。

わたしは 日本語を はやく 上手に なりたいですが、 時間が あまり ありません。 先週から いっしょに はたらいている 日本人の ともだちと 日本語を 話しています。 しかし、 ともだちは ながく アメリカに すんでいますから、 ときどき ただしい 日本語が わかりません。

[11] 「わたし」は どうやって 日本語の べんきょうを していないですか。

1 ともだちと 話します。

2 クラスに 行きます。

3 かんじの れんしゅうを します。

4 おんがくを 聞きます。

[12] ともだちは なぜ 日本語が あまり 上手ではないですか。

1 かんじを おぼえません。

2 ながい 間 日本に いません。

3 あまり べんきょうしません。

4 ともだちは アメリカ人です。

(7) けいさんと いっしょに しごとを しています。 2月14日 けいさんから おかしを もらいました。 そのおかしは とてもおいしかったですから、 デパートに 行って いちばん 高い おかしを 買いました。 それから 3月14日に けいさんの つくえに おきました。

3月15日　いっしょに　しごとしているあきこさんは　「ありがとうござい
ます。しかし　わたしは　あなたに　せんげつ　おかしを　あげませんでし
た。」と　言いました。

わたしは「わたしも。」と　言いました。

「ちょっとまってください。　あなたのつくえは　どこですか。」とききました。

「田中さんと　西村さんのあいだです。」

「けいさんは。」

「北村さんのとなりですよ。」

[13] なぜ　高い　おかしを　買いましたか。

1　デパートは　高いものだけ　うっていたからです。

2　けいさんが　だいすきだからです。

3　もらったおかしは　おいしかったからです。

4　いいおかしが　だいすきだからです。

[14] なぜ　あきこさんは　おかしを　もらいましたか。

1　けいさんが　あきこさんに　あげたからです。

2　「わたし」は　あきこさんが　だいすきだからです。

3　あきこさんは　けいさんの　おかしを　とったからです。

4　「わたし」は　ちがうつくえに　おかしを　おいたからです。

(8)　先月　新しいいえに　入りました。だいどころは　きれいにそうじしたの
で、あかるくて　きれいです。一つの　へやには　大きいテレビを　おきま
した。このへやで　いつも　えいがを　見たり　ゲームを　したり　します。
とても　たのしいです。

となりの人は　花が　だいすきです。いえの　にわに　いろいろな　花
が　たくさん　あります。わたしの　こどもは　いつも　その花を　とりたい
ですが、となりの人は　「とらないで　ください。」と　言っています。だから、
わたしも　にわに　花を　おきたいです。あした、花を　買いたいです。

[15] 何が たのしいですか。

1 にわで はなを とること。

2 テレビを おいたへやで ゲームを すること。

3 あかるい だいどころで りょうりを すること。

4 新しい いえに すんでいること。

[16] なぜ あした 花を 買いたいですか。

1 となりの 人に あげたいからです。

2 たくさん花が ほしいからです。

3 こどもが 花を すきだからです。

4 こどもが となりの人の 花を とったからです。

(9)　先週の 土よう日に こうえんで ひるごはんを 食べました。その日の前に みなさんに「おさらと 食べものを もってきてください。」と 言いました。 おすしは ようこさんと あきこさんが もってきました。 やきとりは ようこさんと たかひろさんが もってきました。 サラダは ゆみさんと ようこさんが もってきました。 食べものが たくさん ありました。

しかし、ミラーさんは おさらだけを もってきました。 わたしは「どうして おさらだけを もってきましたか。」と 聞きました。

ミラーさんは「あなたは『おさらを もってきてください。』と 言いましたよ。」とこたえたので、

「ちょっとちがいますよ。」とわたしは 言いました。

[17] ようこさんは 何を ひるごはんに もってきましたか。

1 やきとりと おすし

2 やきとりと おすしと サラダ

3 サラダ

4 おすしと サラダ

[18] なぜ ちょっとちがいますか。

1 おさらを たくさん もってきました。

2 ちがうこうえんに 行きました。

3 ミラーさんは 食べものを もってきませんでした。

4 ぎゅうにくを もってきました。

(10) ふゆは いえから あまり 出かけません。外は さむくて、いつも テレビを 見たり 本を 読んだり します。はるは ときどき こうえんで 花を 見ながら ひるごはんを 食べて ビールを 飲みます。しかし、今年のはるは 天気が わるかった ですから、いえで 本を たくさん 読みました。

なつは プールに 行きたいです。7月と 8月だけ あいていますが、たのしいです。ともだちに あって いっしょに およぎます。毎日 おそくまで かえりません。あきは どこも うつくしくなります。学校へ あるきながら きれいな いろの 木を 見ます。天気は いつも すずしいですから、外に 出かけます。

[19] このはるに 「わたし」は 何を しましたか。

1 こうえんに よく 行きました。

2 あまり いえから 出ませんでした。

3 テレビを 見ました。

4 ビールを 飲みました。

[20] なつに 「わたし」は 何を しますか。

1 一日中 いえに います。

2 ともだちと あそびます。

3 6月しか プールに 行きません。

4 きれいな いろの 木を 見ます。

LESSON 4
Information Retrieval

もんだい　ページの下の　表と　ぶんしょうを　見て、しつもんに　こたえて
　　　　くださいい。こたえは、1・2・3・4から　いちばん　いい　ものを
　　　　一つ　えらんで　ください。

Mondai　Pēji no shita no hyō to bunshō o mite, shita no shitsumon ni kotaete
kudasai. Kotae wa, 1 / 2 / 3 / 4 kara ichiban ii mono o hitotsu erande
kudasai.

Question　Look at the tables and passages at the bottom of each page to answer
the questions. Choose the best answer from 1 / 2 / 3 / 4.

(1)

[1] じしょと　うわぎを　うりたいです。いつ　どこに　行きますか。

　　1 月よう日　おおやま町に　行って　火よう日　さくら町に　行きます。
　　2 火よう日　さくら町と　みどり町に　行きます。
　　3 火よう日　おおやま町に　行って　月よう日　さくら町に　行きます。
　　4 月よう日　にしがわ町と　おおやま町に　行きます。

パンダリサイクル店 やすく　ものを　買いましょう！　ふるいものは　うりましょう！ 大阪に　4店　あります！	
さくら町	本、CD、DVD
みどり町	スポーツ
にしがわ町	CD、DVD
おおやま町	ふく、スポーツ

※ さくら町と　みどり町の　店は　月よう日が　休みです。にしがわ町と
　おおやま町の　店は　火よう日が　休みです。

(2)

[2] シャーさんは 毎週 水よう日と 土よう日に 北村ジムに 行きたいです。でも、土よう日 あまり 行きません。やすいほうが いいです。どのプランが いいですか。

1 4かい フレックス

2 10かい フレックス

3 毎日6時から

4 へいじつ5時まで

プランの 名前	時間	料金
北村ジム 今年は けんこうに なりましょう！		
4かい フレックス	一ヶ月に 4かいで 午前6時から 午後12時まで	4,000円
10かい フレックス	一ヶ月に 10かいで 午前6時から 午後12時まで	9,000円
毎日6時から	毎日 午後6時から	12,000円
へいじつ5時まで	月よう日から 金よう日まで 午前6時から 午後5時まで	6,000円

＊けんこう‐げんきな からだ

(3)

[3] スミスさんと ヤンさんは いつ あやこさんに 会いますか。

　　1 火よう日と 木よう日
　　2 水よう日と 木よう日
　　3 火よう日と 木よう日と 金よう日
　　4 木よう日と 金よう日

ヤンさん

月 - 　9:00 ～ 14:00 じゅぎょう　17:00 ～ 22:00 しごと
火 - 　9:00 ～ 11:00 じゅぎょう　13:00 ～ 18:00 しごと
水 - 14:00 - 19:00 しごと
木 - 10:00 ～ 16:00 しごと
金 - やすみ

スミスさん

月 - 12:00 - 17:00 しごと
火 - 11:00 - 16:00 じゅぎょう
水 - 　9:00 - 15:00 しごと
木 - 19:00 - 22:00 しごと
金 - 11:00 - 16:00 じゅぎょう

今、あやこさんは びょういんに います。スミスさんと ヤンさんは あやこさんに 会いたいです。びょういんの めんかい時間は 毎日 午後５時から 午後８時までです。びょういんまで 1時間が かかります。金よう日 あやこさんは いえに かえります。

*めんかい時間 - ともだちと かぞくが びょういんに いる人に 会う時間

(4)
[4] 高村さんと 北村さんと 田中さんは しぶやから 大村さんに 会いに 行きます。大村さんの 会社は おおてまちに あります。しかし、いけぶくろで 会って ゆうごはんを 食べたいです。大村さんは 午後5時まで しごとします。しゅうまつは やすみだから 会いたくないです。

高村さんと 北村さんと 田中さんは ぜんぶで いくら はらいますか。

1　420円
2　450円
3　465円
4　570円

電車の きっぷが やすいですよ!

しぶやから

	いけぶくろ	きたせんじゅ	おおてまち	ぎんざ
月よう日～金よう日 (午前7時から 午後5時まで)	185円	240円	190円	200円
月よう日～金よう日 (午後5時から)	155円	220円	160円	170円
土よう日、日よう日	140円	190円	140円	150円

※ 2まい 買った人は 10円 ひきます。3まい 買った人は 15円 ひきます。

(5)

[5] あおいテーブルから　1,000円と　1,500円の　シャツを　買って
あかいテーブルから　1,500円と　2,000円の　シャツを　買います。
どうしますか。

1　4,750円を　はらいます。

2　4,750円を　はらって、コーヒーを　もらいます。

3　5,400円を　はらいます。

4　5,400円を　はらって、コーヒーを　もらいます。

スーパーしまかわ
シャツの　クーポン

- 1まい　買った人は　250円を　ひきます。
- 2まい　買った人は　600円を　ひきます。
- 3まい　買った人は　1,000円を　ひきます。
- 4まい　買った人は　1,250円を　ひきます。　そして　プレゼント。

このクーポンを　つかったみなさんに、ホットコーヒーを　あげます！

※あかいテーブルの上の　ふくだけ　このクーポンを　つかってください。

(6)

[6] サントスさんは ふるいくつを うりたいですが ぼうしを 買いたいです。
いつ 学校に 行きますか。

1 木よう日と 金よう日
2 月よう日と 水よう日と 木よう日と 金よう日
3 月よう日と 木よう日と 金よう日
4 火よう日と 金よう日

学校の フリーマーケット

学校で、つかわないものを うりましょう。毎日、ちがうものが ありま
すので 毎日 来てくださいね！

火よう日―きるものを うります！
水よう日―はくものを うります！
木よう日―かぶるものを うります！
金よう日―なんでも うります！

※うりたいものは 月よう日の 午前9時から 午前1時までに 学校
にもって 来てください。よろしくおねがいします。

---

(7)

[7] スミスさんは 日本語を 読むじゅぎょうの せいとです。つぎの じゅぎょうは いつですか。

1　18日の　12：00からです。
2　22日の　14：00からです。
3　15日の　16：00からです。
4　22日の　15：30からです。

学校からの てがみ です。

> 3月15日　20XX
>
> 西川先生は、かぜで 今日は 休みです。
>
> 日本語1　8：00〜9：30　　→　10：00〜11：30※1
> 日本語2　10：00〜11：30　→　18日(土)12：00〜13：30
> かんじ1　13：00〜13：50　→　16：00〜16：50※1
> 日本語を 読む　14：00〜15：30※2
>
> ※1 田中先生が おしえますので　204のへやに 行ってください。
> ※2 来週の じゅぎょうの後 あります。

(8)

[8] みどり町に すんでいる西村さんは 5さいの こどもと いっしょに どうぶつの こうえんに 行きました。それに、アメリカから きた 21さいのともだち ふたりも いっしょに 行きました。こどもと 西村さんは 電車を 2かい のりました。ぜんぶで いくらですか。

1 2,700円
2 2,900円
3 3,000円
4 3,200円

みどり町 どうぶつの こうえん

時間： 午前9時から 午後5時まで

休みの日： 月よう日

料金： みどり町に すんでいる人：4さい～11さい 200円

　　　　　　　　　　　　　　　　 12さい～ 500円

　　　　 みどり町に すんでいない人：4さい～11さい 400円

　　　　　　　　　　　　　　　　　 12さい～ 600円

こうえんの 電車

電車を のりながら、いろいろな どうぶつを 見ましょう！ ひとり 1かい 250円

---

(9)

[9]　東京で　午前9時の　かいぎに　行きます。やすいほうが　よくて　トイ
　　　レが　いります。いくら　はらいますか。

1　5,500円
2　6,000円
3　7,500円
4　8,000円

大阪から　東京までの　バス

料金	時間	バス
8,000円	午後22：00～午前8：05	さくらバス
6,000円	午後21：00～午前7：15	ふじバス
7,500円	午後23：00～午前7：30	さくらバス
5,500円	午後22：30～午前9：45	ふじバス

※ふじバスは、トイレと　テレビが　ありません。

(10) あした ジェイソンさんは えいがかんの ちかくに すんでいるようこさん に 会って えいがを 見ます。ようこさんは 午後11時までに かえ りたいです。ジェイソンさんの しごとは 午後6時までです。しごとか ら えいがかんまで 1時間 かかります。やすいほうが いいです。

[10] どの えいがを 見ますか。

1 ともだちの いぬ
2 いい 先生
3 たのしかったりょこう
4 あきこが だいすき

あしたの えいが

ともだちの いぬ	17:30～19:30
いい 先生	18:00～20:00
たのしかったりょこう	19:30～21:30
あきこが だいすき	20:00～22:00※

※レイトショーは 500円 ひきます。

(11)

[11] リチャードさんは、6日の あさ 気分(きぶん)が わるくて、びょういんに
行(い)って くすりを もらいました。今日(きょう)は 13日(にち)ですが、あたまが
いたいです。 どのくすりを どう 飲(の)みますか。

1 ごはんを 食(た)べた後(あと)、リレーザを 1こ 飲(の)みます。

2 ごはんを 食(た)べた後(あと)、リレーザを 1こ 飲(の)んで、イタソウを
1こ 飲(の)みます。

3 あさごはんと よるごはんを 食(た)べた後(あと)、ヤマフルを 1こ 飲(の)んで、
ごはんを 食(た)べた後(あと)、リレーザを 1こ 飲(の)んで、イタソウを 1こ
飲(の)みます。

4 あさごはんと よるごはんを 食(た)べた後(あと)、ヤマフルを 1こ 飲(の)んで、
ごはんを 食(た)べた後(あと)、リレーザを 1こ 飲(の)んで、イタソウと オマビ
ルを 1こずつ 飲(の)みます。

7日分(なのかぶん)の くすりです。		
1.ヤマフル	1日(にち)2かい・5日間(いつかかん)	あさごはんと よるごはんを 食(た)べた 後(あと)、飲(の)んで ください。 1かいに1こ 飲(の)んで ください。
2.リレーザ	1日(にち)3かい・7日間(なのかかん)	ごはんを 食(た)べた後(あと)、飲(の)んで ください。1かいに1こ 飲(の)んで ください。
3.オマビル	1かい	すぐに 飲(の)んで ください。
4.イタソウ		いたいときに 1こを 飲(の)んで ください。

(12)

[12] 石川さんは、センターで えいがを 見たいです。今日は 3月6日
（月）です。月よう日から 金よう日まで 午前9時から 午後5時ま
で しごとを します。どう しますか。

1 4月1日に センターに 行って チケットを とって 4月2日に
センターで えいがを 見ます。

2 4月2日に としょかんに 行って 2かいに 行って えいがを
見ます。

3 4月2日に センターの 2かいに 行って えいがを 見ます。

4 3月11日に センターに 行って チケットを とって 4月2日に
センターで えいがを 見ます。

「山に のぼりたい」

いつ： 4月2日（日）午後1時から

どこ： さくら市センターの 2かいの ホール

料金： 0円！

※えいがを 見たい人は 4月1日までに センター（午前9時から
午後5時まで）に 行って えいがの チケットを とってください。
チケットは 250まいだけ ありますので はやいほうが いいです。

えいがの後で 1かいの としょかんで コーヒーと おかしが あります。

---

* チケット ー えいがの きっぷ

Part Five

Listening Comprehension

LESSON 1
Types of Listening Comprehension

The listening comprehension part of the N5 exam tests your ability to understand conversations as well as how to respond in conversation. There are four types of questions that you will see in this section—task-based comprehension, point comprehension, utterance expressions and quick response. Each tests a particular listening skill, so you will need to make use of different strategies for each to get the best score.

もんだい1 – Task-based comprehension

These questions test your ability to understand the task that is about to be completed based on the conversation. You'll hear a short introduction of the context and who is talking. There is almost always a man and a woman speaking. But, the dialogue will often identify the role of one or both. For instance, the conversation might be between a teacher and a student.

Then, you'll hear a question about what the man or woman is going to do next, and then the conversation. You'll hear a beep after the conversation and then the question one more time. You'll then have about 10 seconds to decide on the answer and mark it in the test booklet.

Tips

Before or while the dialogue is introducing the question, be sure to **skim through the possible answers and look for differences between them**. Are they different colored objects? Do they have different things printed on them? Think through the possible keywords they might use to describe the differences. For example, they may talk about different sizes: 大きい (**ōkii**, big) or 小さい (**chiisai**, small), or different locations—の前に (**no mae ni**, in front of) or の後ろに (**no ushiro ni**, behind).

Listen closely to the context the dialogue gives you at the beginning. Typically, there is a male and a female speaker, but listen closely to how the two speakers are related. Some common relationships include a teacher and student talking, two friends, two co-workers, or a boss and his staff.

Knowing the relationship of the two characters will give you clues as to what kind of words they will be using and what task they are trying to accomplish. For instance, if it is in a school setting, they might be talking about homework or what to do for class. If it is at the store, the speaker might be buying something or choosing a particular item.

Also **listen for the question** so that you can focus your listening on what the characters in the dialogue are going to do next. Common questions include the following:

男の人は はじめに 何を しますか。
Otoko no hito wa hajime ni nani o shimasu ka.
What is the man going to do first?

女の人は これから どうしますか。
Onna no hito wa kore kara dō shimasu ka.
What is the woman doing from now? (lit., from this)

女の人は こんしゅうまつは 何を 〜ますか。
Onna no hito wa konshū-matsu wa nani o ~masu ka.
What is the woman ~ing this weekend?

男の人は なんかいへ 行きますか。
Otoko no hito wa nan-kai e ikimasu ka.
What floor is the man going to?

男の人は 何を もってきますか。
Otoko no hito wa nani o motte kimasu ka.
What is the man bringing? (e.g. to the party)

女の人は どんなものを 買いますか。
Onna no hito wa donna mono o kaimasu ka.
What kind of item is the woman going to buy?

もんだい2 – Point Comprehension

These questions are quite similar to the Task-based Comprehension questions, but for these you will be looking to pick up one key point from the conversation. Just like the previous section, you will hear a short introduction that introduces who is speaking (almost always a man and a woman) and might get some hint as to the context. For instance, the dialogue might tell you where the conversation takes place (at a hospital, at a school, etc.), or identify one of the speaker's occupations (a teacher, doctor, student etc.) After that, you'll hear a question about the conversation before the actual conversation starts. You will hear a beep after the end of the conversation, and the question again, followed by 10 seconds of silence to mark your answer on the answer sheet.

Tips

These questions can sometimes be quite easy because you usually just have to listen to one key piece of information, and at the N5 level they typically don't try to trick you that much. Sometimes, all you need to do is listen to one sentence they say.

However, **they will try to trick you by giving you extra information that you do not need.** For instance, they might ask how long the woman studied today, but in the conversation, the male speaker might say how long he studied today. Or, the woman might talk about how long she usually (いつも, **itsumo**) studies, then be specific about how long she studied today.

And that is what these questions are designed to test, to see if you are able to listen and pick out the key point for the question asked. Or if you will be distracted by the extra information. Try to stay calm during this section and listen for the specific point. Try not to get hung up on some small detail that you don't understand. You may even want to cross off answers in your answer book that are definitely not correct. That way if you have to guess, you can do so quickly and have a better chance of getting a correct answer.

Common questions include the following:

2人は どこで いつ あいますか。
Futari wa doko de itsu aimasu ka.
Where and when are the two people going to meet?

だれと りょこうに 行きますか。
Dare to ryokō ni ikimasu ka.
With whom is (the woman) going on a trip?

どうやって 〜に 行きますか。
Dō yatte ~ni ikimasu ka.
How is (the man) going to ~? (by car, bus or by train?)

なにで てがみを 書きますか。
Nani de tegami o kakimasu ka.
With what is (the woman) going to write the letter? (with a pencil? A black pen?)

どのくすりを 飲みますか。
Dono kusuri o nomimasu ka.
What kind of medicine is (the man) going to take?

もんだい3 Utterance Expressions

For these questions, you are given a picture with two people talking to each other. One of them will have an arrow pointing to him/her. You are given some context about what the person wants to say, and then you must choose the best expression of the three that you hear. The expressions are not printed in the test booklet and will not be repeated. The context will not be repeated either.

Tips

Since **you will only hear the expressions once,** it is important to stay focused for this whole section. Don't get distracted by second guessing what you heard, just try your best to choose the most suitable answer, mark it on the sheet and move on.

While **you are listening to the three possible answers, you can make quick marks** depending on how 'correct' you think the answer is. For instance, if you think it is totally wrong—an X; if you think it might be right—a triangle; and if you think it is totally correct—a circle. That way, you can make a quick decision about what you are going to mark on the answer sheet before you listen to the next question.

Typically, this section will cover a few basic phrases like the ones you learned in grammar lesson 1 (pages 33-43). It might also cover the differences between transitive and intransitive verbs (page 170). It can also include basic questions (page 61).

もんだい 4 – Quick Response

For this series of questions, there is nothing printed in your test booklet. You will hear one line from the dialogue, and then three possible responses to it. You must choose the most appropriate response and mark it on your answer sheet. Nothing written in the test booklet will be graded, so be sure to record your answer on the mark sheet to each question before moving on.

Tips

Like the Utterance Expression questions above, you must stay focused during this entire section and answer the questions one by one. Don't spend too much time on one question or second guessing yourself. If you are not sure of the answer, make a quick guess and move on. The technique mentioned above—marking possibly correct answers—is a good strategy to follow here as well.

This section covers phrases and expressions as well. The difference is that for this section, there are no pictures and there is no context. You will only hear the first part of the conversation and you have to choose an appropriate response. These exchanges can sometimes not be very straightforward. For example, the following is **not** very typical:

A: 今は 何時ですか。　　　　　B: 今は 6時です。
Ima wa nanji desu ka.　　　　**Ima wa rokuji desu.**
What time is it now?　　　　　*It is now 6 o'clock.*

Instead, a correct response might be something like the following:

B: すみません、とけいが ありません。
Sumimasen, tokei ga arimasen.
Sorry, I don't have a watch.

Try to imagine the situation as best you can from the first line, and **listen to all the answers** before choosing one.

もうすぐ ゆうの ねこは たんじょうびです。今、
マットと ゆうが プレゼントを 買っています。
Soon, it will be Yu's cat's birthday. Now, Matt and Yu are buying a present.

さむく なっていますから、
うわぎを 買いませんか。
It's getting cold, so why don't we buy a jacket for my cat?

わあ、きれいだね。
いくらですか。
Wow, pretty, isn't it? How much is it?

わあ、そうですか。
Wow, really?

このシャツは どうですか。
How about this shirt?

へー。
Whoa!

1000円です。
やすいですよ。
1000 yen. That's cheap!

LESSON 2
Task-based Listening Comprehension

もんだい1

もんだい1では はじめに、しつもんを きいてください。それから はなしを
きいて、もんだいようしの 1から4の なかから、いちばん いい ものを
ひとつ えらんで ください。

Mondai 1
Mondai 1 de wa, hajime ni, shitsumon o kiite kudasai. Sore kara hanashi o kiite,
mondai yōshi no 1 kara 4 no naka kara, ichiban ii mono o hitotsu erande kudasai.

Question 1
As for question 1, listen to the question first. Then, listen to the conversation,
and from (the answers) 1 through 4 on the answer sheet, select the best one.

(1)

(2)

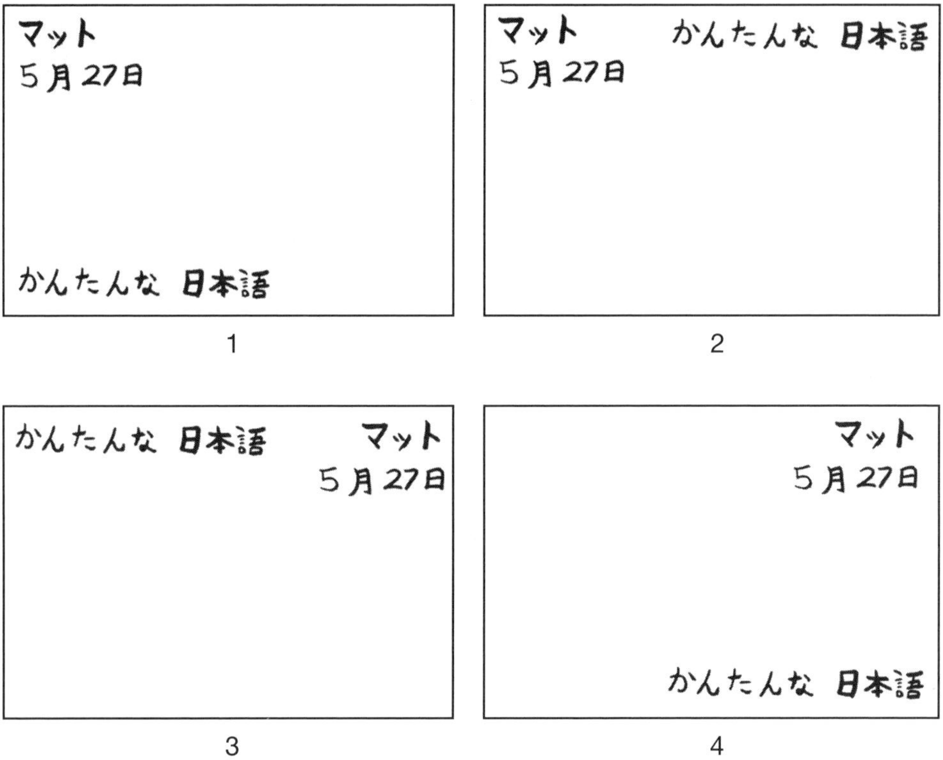

マット 5月27日 かんたんな **日本語**	**マット** かんたんな **日本語** 5月27日
1	2
かんたんな **日本語** **マット** 5月27日	**マット** 5月27日 かんたんな **日本語**
3	4

(3)

(4)

月	火	水	木	金	土	日

1

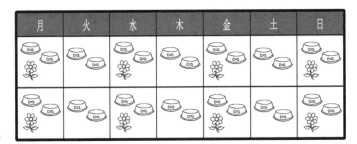

2

3

4

(5)

1 4かい

2 5かい

3 6かい

4 3かい

(6)

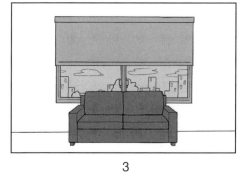

1

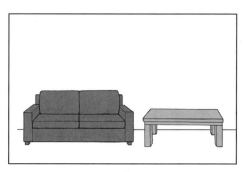

2

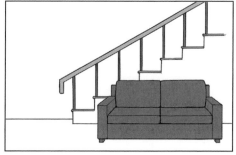

3

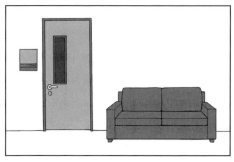

4

(7)

1 1:45

2 2:00

3 3:00

4 2:15

(8)

1 8がつに やまに のぼります。

2 6がつに うみに いきます。

3 8がつに うみに いきます。

4 6がつに やまに のぼります。

(9)

1 CD、おすし、プレゼント、のみもの

2 おすし、プレゼント、のみもの

3 CD、おすし

4 CD、プレゼント、のみもの

(10)

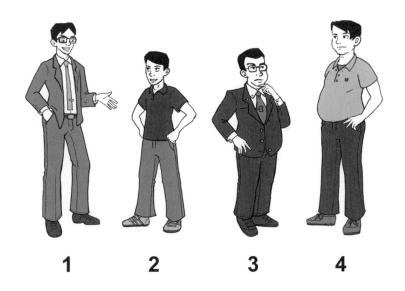

1　　**2**　　**3**　　**4**

LESSON 3
Understanding Key Points

もんだい2

もんだい2では、はじめに しつもんを きいて ください。それから はなしを きいて、もんだいようしの 1から4の なかから、いちばん いい ものを ひとつ えらんで ください。

Mondai 2
Mondai 2 de wa, hajime ni shitsumon o kiite kudasai. Sore kara hanashi o kiite, mondai yōshi no 1 kara 4 no naka kara, ichiban ii mono o hitotsu erande kudasai.

Question 2
As for question 2, first, listen to the question. Then, listen to the conversation, and from (the answers) 1 through 4 on the answer sheet, select the best one.

(1)

1　10まい

2　12まい

3　14まい

4　16まい

(2)

1　あたたかくした おちゃ

2　つめたい おちゃ

3　ジュース

4　女の人が つくった おちゃ

(3)

1

2

3

4

(4)
1 7:30
2 7:45
3 8:00
4 8:55

(5)

1 今日の　よる

2 あしたの　ごぜん

3 あしたの　よる

4 あさっての　ごご

(6)

1 15ほん

2 20ぽん

3 25ほん

4 30ぽん

(7)

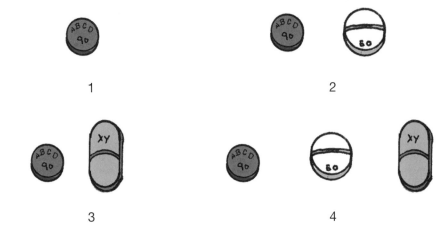

(8)

1

2

3

4

(9)
1 ゆきが ふる

2 あめが ふる

3 はれる

4 かぜが つよい

(10)
1 5ふん

2 10ぷん

3 20ぷん

4 25ふん

(11)

1 べんきょう する

2 がいこくに いく

3 うみに いく

4 じゅぎょうをうける

(12)

1　　　　**2**　　　　**3**　　　　**4**

(13)

1 にしまち2ー24ー4

2 はるまち2ー24ー4

3 はるまち2ー20ー44

4 にしまち2ー20ー44

(14)

1 おばさん

2 おかあさん

3 いもうと

4 あねえさん

(15)

1 バス

2 でんしゃ

3 ひこうき

4 くるま

パジャマを きます。
I'm putting on pajamas.

Correct – おじゃま します。

ありがとうございます。
Thank you very much.

Correct – すみません。

いらっしゃいませ。
Welcome!

Correct – いってらっしゃい。

おさけに 飲みます。
I'll go drinking first.

Correct – おさきに しつれいします。

このシャツは どうですか。
How is this shirt?

こわいですね。
Scary, huh?

Correct – かわいいですね。

こわい?!!
Scary?

ああ、これは たいへん。
Ahh, this is serious.

こわい – scary

LESSON 4
Understanding Verbal Expressions

もんだい3

もんだい3では、えを みながら しつもんを きいて ください。➡ (やじるし)
の ひとは なんと いいますか。1から3の なかから、いちばん いい もの
を ひとつ えらんで ください。

Mondai 3
Mondai 3 de wa, e o minagara shitsumon o kiite kudasai. (Yajirushi) no hito wa nan
to iimasu ka. 1 kara 3 no naka kara, ichiban ii mono o hitotsu erande kudasai.

Question 3
As for question 3, while looking at the picture, listen to the question. What is the
person with the arrow going to say? Choose the best answer from 1 through 3.

(1)

(2)

(3)

(4)

(5)

(6)

(7)

(8)

(9)

(10)

LESSON 5
Quick Response Questions

もんだい 4

もんだい4では、えなどが ありません。ぶんを きいて、1から3の なかから、
いちばん いい ものを ひとつ えらんで ください。

Mondai 4
Mondai 4 de wa, e nado ga arimasen. Bun o kiite, 1 kara 3 no naka kara, ichiban ii mono o hitotsu erande kudasai.

Question 4
As for question 4, there are no pictures etc... Listen to the sentences, choose the best answer from 1 through 3.

1)   ①   ②   ③

2)   ①   ②   ③

3)   ①   ②   ③

4)   ①   ②   ③

5)   ①   ②   ③

6)   ①   ②   ③

7)   ①   ②   ③

8)   ①   ②   ③

9)   ①   ②   ③

10) ① ② ③

11) ① ② ③

12) ① ② ③

13) ① ② ③

14) ① ② ③

15) ① ② ③

16) ① ② ③

Appendices

APPENDIX A
List of Grammar Points

Note: The last number in each entry refers to the Lesson in Part 2: Essential Grammar Points where the topic is covered, e.g., ああ **ā** is found in Lesson 3.

前に **mae ni** 7

Vstem + ません か Vstem + **masen ka** 5

Vました (past polite form) V**mashita** (past polite form) 3

Vstem + ましょうか Vstem + **mashō ka** 5

Vます (polite form) V**masu** (polite form) 2

N + も noun + **mo** 5

question word + も question word + **mo** 4

もう + past affirmative **mō** + past affirmative 6

もう + negative **mō** + negative 6

な-adj + な + N **na**-adj + **na** + noun 2

Vない (negative casual form) V**nai** (negative casual form) 6

Vない + で + ください V**nai** + **de** + **kudasai** 6

なんで・どうやって **nande・dōyatte** 2

なに・なん **nani・nan** 2

adj + なる adj + **naru** 7

sentence + ね sentence + **ne** 6

N + に noun + **ni** 4

Vstem + ながら Vstem + **nagara** 7

Vstem + に + 行く Vstem + **ni** + **iku** 5

N + の + N noun + **no** + noun 2

numbers 2

しか **shika** 8

そっち **socchi** 3

そちら **sochira** 3

そちらの + N **sochira no** + noun 3

そこ **soko** 3

そんな **sonna** 3

その + N **sono** + noun 3

それ **sore** 3

そう **sō** 3

suffixes 9

adj + する adj + **suru** 7

Vたい V**tai** 3

～たり～たり する **~tari ~tari suru** 8

Vて V**te** 4

Vて + ある V**te** + **aru** 6

Vて + いる V**te** + **iru** 6

Vて/Nを + ください V**te**/noun **o** + **kudasai** 4

Vて/Nを + くださいませんか V**te**/noun **o** + **kudasaimasen ka** 4

N + と + N noun + **to** + noun 5

とき **toki** 7

transitive verbs 9

は particle **wa** particle 2

sentence + わ sentence + **wa** 6

N + を noun + **o** 5

N + や + N noun + **ya** + noun 5

sentence + よ sentence + **yo** 6

N + より noun + **yori** 7

APPENDIX B
N5 Kanji List

[1 STROKE]

一   one   (e.g. 一日 *the 1st (day of the month)*; 一人 *one person*)

[2 STROKES]

七   seven   (e.g. 七日 *the 7th (day of the month)*; 七人 *seven people*)

人   person   (e.g. 人 *person*; 外国人 *foreigner*)

十   ten   (e.g. 十日 *the 10th (day of the month)*; 十人 *ten people*)

二   two   (e.g. 二月 *February*; 二人 *two people*)

九   nine   (e.g. 九日 *the 9th (day of the month)*; 九人 *nine people*)

入   go in; put in (e.g. 気に入る *to be pleased with*; 入る *to enter*)

八   eight   (e.g. 八日 *the 8th (day of the month)*; 八人 *eight people*)

[3 STROKES]

大   big; large   (e.g. 大きい *big*; 大家 *landlord*)

三   three   (e.g. 三日 *the 3rd (day of the month)*; 三人 *three people*)

上   up   (e.g. 上 *up*; 上手 *skillful*)

子   child   (e.g. 子供 *children*; 親子 *parent and child*)

下   down   (e.g. 下 *down*; 下手 *unskillful*)

小   small   (e.g. 小さい *small*; 小説 *novel*)

山   mountain   (e.g. 山 *mountain*; 富士山 *Mt. Fuji*)

女   woman   (e.g. 女性 *female*; 長女 *eldest daughter*)

川   river   (e.g. 川 *river*; 河川 *rivers*)

千   thousand   (e.g. 何千 *how many thousands*; 一千 *one thousand*)

口   mouth   (e.g. 口 *mouth*; 開口 *opening*)

土   soil; earth   (e.g. 土 *soil; earth*; 土曜日 *Saturday*)

万   ten thousand   (e.g. 万一 *by some chance*; 万歳 *Banzai! (celebratory cheer)*)

[4 STROKES]

日   day   (e.g. 毎日 *every day*; 休日 *holiday*)

中	middle	(e.g. 電話中 *during a telephone call;* 世の中 *the world*)
月	month	(e.g. 月見 *moon viewing;* 正月 *New Year's*)
分	minute; divide	(e.g. 気分 *feeling, mood;* 分 *minute*)
五	five	(e.g. 五日 *the 5th (day of the month);* 五人 *five people*)
六	six	(e.g. 六日 *the 6th (day of the month);* 六人 *six people*)
今	now; present	(e.g. 今夜 *tonight;* 今 *now*)
手	hand	(e.g. 手 *hand;* 一手 *move (in a game)*)
午	noon	(e.g. 午前 *morning; a.m.;* 午後 *afternoon; p.m.*)
水	water	(e.g. 水 *water;* 水曜日 *Wednesday*)
少	few; little	(e.g. 少数 *minority; few;* 少ない *a few; little*)
木	wood	(e.g. 木 *tree; shrub;* 木曜日 *Thursday*)
天	heaven	(e.g. 天気 *weather;* 天才 *genius*)
火	fire	(e.g. 火 *fire; blaze;* 火曜日 *Tuesday*)
友	friend	(e.g. 友達 *friend;* 友人 *friend (formal)*)
父	father	(e.g. 父 *father (humble);* お父さん *father (honorable)*)

[5 STROKES]

出	exit; leave	(e.g. 提出する *to hand in;* 出る *to leave*)
本	book	(e.g. 本 *book;* 本当 *truth*)
生	live	(e.g. 生活 *life;* 一生けんめい *with hard work*)
四	four	(e.g. 四日 *the 4th (day of the month);* 四人 *four people*)
立	stand	(e.g. 立つ *to stand;* 自立 *independence*)
目	eye	(e.g. 目 *eye;* 細目 *details*)
外	outside	(e.g. 外 *outside;* 外国人 *foreigner*)
北	north	(e.g. 北 *north;* 東北 *northeast*)
半	half	(e.g. 半分 *half;* 前半 *first half*)
白	white	(e.g. 白い *white;* 面白い *interesting*)
古	old	(e.g. 古い *old;* 中古 *used*)
母	mother	(e.g. 母 *mother (humble);* お母さん *mother (honorable)*)
右	right	(e.g. 右 *right;* 右手 *right hand*)
左	left	(e.g. 左 *left;* 左右 *right and left*)

[6 STROKES]

| 会 | meet | (e.g. 会う *to meet (somebody);* 会社 *company*) |
| 年 | year | (e.g. 来年 *next year;* 年 *year*) |

行	go	(e.g. 行く *to go;* 旅行 *trip*)
気	*spirit, air*	(e.g. 元気 *energetic;* 気分 *feeling; mood*)
多	*many, much*	(e.g. 多い *many;* 多少 *more or less*)
安	*cheap*	(e.g. 安い *cheap;* 不安 *unease*)
百	*hundred*	(e.g. 何百 *how many hundreds, hundreds of;* 八百屋 *greengrocer*)
先	*tip; ahead*	(e.g. 先 *previous; prior;* 先生 *teacher*)
名	*name*	(e.g. 名前 *name;* 有名 *famous*)
西	*west*	(e.g. 西 *west;* 西洋 *the West; Western countries*)
毎	*every*	(e.g. 毎週 *every week;* 毎晩 *every night*)
休	*rest*	(e.g. 休む *to rest;* 休暇 *holiday; day off*)
耳	*ear*	(e.g. 耳 *ear;* 耳鼻科 *ear, nose, and throat*)

[7 STROKES]

来	*come*	(e.g. 来る *to come;* 来年 *next year*)
社	*company; society*	(e.g. 社員 *company employee;* 社長 *company president*)
見	*see*	(e.g. 見る *to see;* 見える *to be seen*)
言	*say*	(e.g. 言う *to say;* 方言 *dialect*)
男	*man*	(e.g. 男性 *male;* 長男 *eldest son*)
車	*car*	(e.g. 車 *car;* 自転車 *bicycle*)
何	*what*	(e.g. 何 *what?;* 何か *something*)
足	*foot; leg*	(e.g. 足 *foot;* 遠足 *excursion*)
花	*flower*	(e.g. 花 *flower;* 花瓶 *flower vase*)

[8 STROKES]

国	*country*	(e.g. 外国 *foreign country;* 国 *country*)
長	*long*	(e.g. 長い *long;* 社長 *company president*)
東	*east*	(e.g. 東 *east;* 東京 *Tokyo*)
金	*gold*	(e.g. お金 *money;* 金曜日 *Friday*)
学	*study; learn*	(e.g. 学生 *student;* 大学 *university*)
空	*sky; empty*	(e.g. 空 *sky; air;* 空港 *airport*)
店	*store*	(e.g. お店 *store;* 店員 *store staff*)
雨	*rain*	(e.g. 雨 *rain;* 雨天 *rainy weather*)

[9 STROKES]

| 後 | *after; behind* | (e.g. 後で *after;* 後半 *last half*) |

前　*before; front*　　(e.g. 午前 *morning; a.m.;* 前に *before; in front of*)
食　*eat*　　　　　　(e.g. 食べる *to eat;* 食堂 *cafeteria*)
南　*south*　　　　　(e.g. 南 *south;* 南北 *North and South*)

[10 STROKES]

時　*hour*　　　　　(e.g. 時間 *time; hours;* 何時 *what time?*)
高　*high*　　　　　(e.g. 高い *high;* 最高 *the best*)
書　*write*　　　　　(e.g. 書く *to write;* 辞書 *dictionary*)
校　*school*　　　　(e.g. 高校 *high school;* 中学校 *junior high school*)

[11 STROKES]

魚　*fish*　　　　　(e.g. 魚 *fish;* 金魚 *goldfish*)

[12 STROKES]

週　*week*　　　　　(e.g. 今週 *this week;* 来週 *next week*)
道　*way*　　　　　(e.g. 歩道 *sidewalk;* 道 *road*)
間　*between*　　　(e.g. 間 *space; interval;* 一週間 *one week*)
買　*buy*　　　　　(e.g. 買う *to buy;* 買い物 *shopping*)
飲　*drink*　　　　(e.g. 飲む *to drink;* 飲み物 *drinks*)

[13 STROKES]

新　*new*　　　　　(e.g. 新しい *new;* 新聞 *newspaper*)
話　*talk; speak*　　(e.g. 話す *to talk;* 話 *talk; speech*)
電　*electricity*　　(e.g. 電気 *electricity;* 終電 *last train*)

[14 STROKES]

語　*language*　　　(e.g. 英語 *English;* 語る *to talk about*)
聞　*hear; listen*　　(e.g. 聞く *to hear;* 聞こえる *to be heard*)
読　*read*　　　　　(e.g. 読む *to read;* 読解 *reading comprehension*)
駅　*station*　　　　(e.g. 駅 *station;* 駅前 *in front of the station*)

N5 Vocabulary List

~ichi ～一 *SUF* best in

~kata ～かた *N-SUF* method of

abiru あびる *V1, VT* to bathe

abunai あぶない *ADJ-I* dangerous

achira, acchi あちら, あっち *N, UK* over there

ageru あげる *V1, VT* to give

aka あか *N* red

aka あか *ABBR* red light

akai あかい *ADJ-I* red

akarui あかるい *ADJ-I* bright

akeru あける *V1, VT* to open (a door, etc...)

aki あき *N-T* autumn

aku あく *V5K, VI* to open (e.g. doors)

amai あまい *EXP, ADJ-I, UK* sweet

amari, anmari あまり, あんまり *NA-ADJ, ADV, N, N-SUF, UK* (not) very

ame あめ *N* (hard) candy

ame 雨 *N* rain

anata あなた *N, UK, POL* you (referring to someone of equal or lower status)

ane あね *N, HUM* older sister

ani あに *N, HUM* older brother

ano あの *ADJ-PN, UK* that (someone or something distant from both speaker and listener, or situation unfamiliar to both speaker and listener)

ano, anō, anō あの, あのう, あのー *INT, UK* um...

ao あお *N* blue

ao あお *ABBR* green light

ao~ あお～ *PREF* immature

aoi あおい *ADJ-I* blue

apāto アパート *ABBR* apartment

arau あらう *V5U, VT* to wash

aru ある *V5R-I, VI, UK* to be (usually for inanimate or non-moving objects)

aruku あるく *V5K, VI* to walk

asa あさ *N-ADV, N-T* morning

asagohan あさごはん *N* breakfast

asatte あさって *N-ADV, N-T* day after tomorrow

ashi 足 *N* foot

ashita あした *N-T* tomorrow

asobu あそぶ *V5B, VI* to play

asoko あそこ *N, UK* over there

atama あたま *N* head

atarashii 新しい *ADJ-I* new

atatakai あたたかい *ADJ-I* warm (usu. air temperature)

ato 後 *N, ADJ-NO* behind; descendant; after

atsui あつい *ADJ-I* thick

atsui あつい *ADJ-I* hot (weather, etc...)

atsui あつい *ADJ-I* hot (thing)

au 会う *V5U, VI* to meet

ban ばん *N-ADV, N-T* evening

bangohan ばんごはん *N* dinner

bangō ばんごう *N* number

basu バス *N* bus

batā バター *N* butter

beddo ベッド *N* bed

benkyō べんきょう *N, VS* study

benri べんり *ADJ-NA* convenient

bōrupen ボールペン *N* ball-point pen

botan ボタン *N, UK* button

bōshi ぼうし *N* hat

bunshō ぶんしょう *N* sentence

butaniku ぶたにく *N, ADJ-NO* pork

byōin びょういん *N* hospital

byōki びょうき *N, ADJ-NO* illness

chairo 茶色 *N* light brown

chawan 茶わん *N* rice bowl

chichi 父 *N, HUM* father

chigau ちがう *V5U, VI* to differ (from)

chiisai 小さい *ADJ-I* little

chiisana 小さな *ADJ-PN* little

chikai ちかい *ADJ-I* near

chikaku ちかく *N-ADV, N* near

chikatetsu ちかてつ *N* underground train

chizu ちず *N* map

chōdo ちょうど *ADJ-NA, ADV, N, UK* exactly

chotto ちょっと *ADV, UK* somewhat

daidokoro だいどころ *N, ADJ-NO* kitchen

daigaku 大学 *N* university

daijōbu だいじょうぶ *ADJ-NA, ADV, N* all right

daisuki だいすき *ADJ-NA, N* very likeable

dandan だんだん *N, ADV-TO, ADV* gradually

dare だれ *N* who

dareka だれか *N, UK* somebody

dasu (1) 出す *V5S, VT* to take out

dasu (2) 出す *V5S, VT* to submit (e.g. thesis)

deguchi 出口 *N* exit

dekakeru 出かける *V1, VI* to go out (e.g. on an excursion or outing)

dekiru 出来る *V1, VI, UK* to be able to

demo でも *CONJ* but

denki でんき *N* electricity

denki sutōbu でんきストーブ *N* electric heater

densha でんしゃ *N* (electric) train

denwa でんわ *N, VS* telephone

depāto デパート *N, ABBR* department store

deru 出る *V1, VI* to appear

dewa では *CONJ, INT* with that

doa ドア *N* western style door

dochira, docchi どちら, どっち *N, UK* which way

doko どこ *N, UK* where

donata どなた *N, UK, HON* who

dono どの *ADJ-PN, UK* which

dore どれ *N, UK* which (of three or more)

dō, ikaga どう, いかが *ADV, UK* how

dōbutsu どうぶつ *N* animal

dōmo どうも *INT, ABBR* thanks

dōshite どうして *ADV, INT, UK* for what reason

doyōbi 土よう日 *N-ADV, N-T* Saturday

dōzo どうぞ *ADV* please

e え *N, N-SUF* picture

ē (1) ええ *INT* yes

ē (2) ええ *INT* huh?

eiga えいが *N* movie

eigakan えいがかん *N* movie theater (theatre)

eigo えいご *N* English (language)

eki 駅 *N* station

enpitsu えんぴつ *N* pencil

erebētā エレベーター *N* elevator

firumu フィルム *N* roll of film

fōku フォーク *N* fork

fuku 吹く（ふく）*v5K* to blow (wind, etc.)

fuku 服（ふく）*N, N-SUF* clothes (esp. western clothes)

furo ふろ *N* bath

furu ふる *v5R, VI* to precipitate

furui 古い *ADJ-I* old (not used for people)

futari 二人 *N* two people

futatsu 二つ *N* two (pieces)

futoi ふとい *ADJ-I* fat; daring

futsuka 二日 *N* two days, the second (day of the month)

fūtō ふうとう *N* envelope

fuyu ふゆ *N-ADV, N-T* winter

gaikoku 外国 *N* foreign country

gaikokujin 外国人 *N* foreigner

gakkō がっこう *N* school

gakusei 学生 *N* student (esp. a university student)

genkan げんかん *N* entry hall

genki げんき *ADJ-NA, N* health

getsuyōbi 月よう日 *N-ADV, N-T* Monday

ginkō ぎんこう *N* bank

gitā ギター *N* guitar

go 五 *NUM* five

gogo 午後 *N-ADV, N-T* afternoon

gohan ごはん *N* cooked rice

goshujin ごしゅじん *N, HON* your husband

gozen 午前 *N-ADV, N-T* morning

guramu グラム *N, UK* gram

gyūniku ぎゅうにく *N* beef

gyūnyū ぎゅうにゅう *N* (cow's) milk

ha は *N* tooth

hachi はち *NUM* eight

hagaki はがき *N, ABBR* postcard

haha 母 *N, HUM* mother

hai はい *INT, POL* yes

hairu 入る *v5R* to enter

haizara はいざら *N* ashtray

hajimaru はじまる *v5R, VI* to begin

hajimeni はじめに *EXP* in the beginning

hajimete はじめて *ADV, N* for the first time

hako はこ *N* box

haku はく *v5K, VT* to put on (lower-body clothing i.e. pants, skirt, etc...)

han 半 *N, N-ADV, N-SUF, N-PREF* half

hana 花 *N* flower

hana はな *N* nose

hanashi 話 *N* talk

hanasu 話す *v5S, VT* to speak

hanbun はんぶん *N* half

hankachi ハンカチ *N* handkerchief

hare はれ *N* clear weather

hareru はれる *v1, VI* to be sunny

haru はる *N-ADV, N-T* spring

haru はる *v5R* to stick

hashi 橋（はし）*N* bridge

hashi 箸（はし）*N* chopsticks

hashiru はしる *v5R, VI* to run

hatachi はたち *N* twenty years old

hataraku はたらく *v5K, VI* to work

hatsuka 二十日 *N* twenty days

hayai 早い（はやい）*ADJ-I* early (in the day, etc...)

hayai 速い（はやい）*ADJ-I* quick

hen へん *N* area

heta へた *ADJ-NA, N* unskillful

heya へや *N* room

hidari 左 *N* left

higashi 東 *N* east

hikōki ひこうき *N* airplane

hiku 引く（ひく） *V5K, VI, VT* to pull

hiku 弾く（ひく） *V5K* to play (an instrument with strings, including piano)

hikui ひくい *ADJ-I* low (height, tone, rank, degree, cost, etc...)

hima ひま *ADJ-NA, N* free time

hiroi ひろい *ADJ-I* spacious

hiru ひる *N-ADV, N-T* noon

hirugohan ひるごはん *N* lunch

hito 人 *N* person

hito~ 一 *PREF* one

hitori 一人 *N* one person

hitotsu 一つ *N* one (piece)

hitotsuki 一月 *N* one month

hoka ほか *ADJ-NO, N, N-ADV* other (esp. places and things)

hon 本 *N* book; main; (counter for) long cylindrical things

hondana ほんだな *N* bookshelf

hontō ほんとう *ADJ-NA, N* truth

hontōni, hontoni ほんとうに、ほんとに *ADV* really

hoshii ほしい *ADJ-I* wanted

hosoi ほそい *ADJ-I* thin

hoteru ホテル *N* hotel

hō ほう *ADV, PRT* one side (of a comparison)

hyaku 百 *NUM* hundred

ichi 一 *N, NUM* one

ichiban いちばん *N-ADV* best

ichinichi 一日 *N* one day

ie いえ *N* house

ii/yoi いい/よい *ADJ-I, UK* good

iie いいえ *INT, UK* no

ike いけ *N* pond

iku 行く *V1, VI* to go

ikutsu いくつ *ADV, UK* how many

ima 今 *N-ADV, N* now

imi いみ *N, VS* meaning

imōto いもうと *N, HUM* younger sister

inu いぬ *N* dog

ireru 入れる *V1, VT* to put in

iriguchi 入口 *N, ADJ-NO* entrance

iroiro いろいろ *N, ADJ-NA, ADJ-NO, ADV, ADV-TO* various

iru いる *V1, VI, UK* to be (of animate, and (potentially) moving objects)

iru いる *V5R, VI* to need

iru いろ *N* color

isha いしゃ *N, SENS* (medical) doctor

isogashii いそがしい *ADJ-I* busy

issho いっしょ *ADV, N* together

isu いす *N* chair

itai いたい *ADJ-I* painful

itsu いつ *ADV-NA, N, UK* when

itsuka 五日 *N* five days, the fifth (day of the month)

itsumo いつも *ADV, N, UK* always

itsutsu 五つ *N* five (pieces)

iu 言う *V5U, VI* to say

iya いや *ADJ-NA, N* unpleasant

ja, jā じゃ、じゃあ *CONJ, INT* well then…

jibiki じびき *N* dictionary

jibun じぶん *N* oneself

jidōsha じどうしゃ *N* automobile

jikan じかん *N-ADV, N* time

jisho じしょ *N* dictionary

jitensha じてんしゃ *N* bicycle

jōbu じょうぶ *ADJ-NA* strong

jōzu じょうず *ADJ-NA, N* skillful

jugyō じゅぎょう *N, VS* lesson

jū, tō 十 *NUM* ten

kaban かばん *N* (cloth, leather, etc... not paper, plastic) bag

kabin かびん *N* a flower vase

kaburu かぶる *V5R, VT* to wear (on head)

kado かど *N* (a) corner (of a desk, pavement, etc...)

kaeru かえる *V5R, VI* to go back

kaesu かえす *V5S, VT* to return (something)

kagi かぎ *N* key

kaidan かいだん *N* stairs

kaimono 買いもの *N* shopping

kaisha かいしゃ *N* company

kakaru かかる *V5R, VI, UK* to take (time or money); to hang

kakeru かける *V1, VI* to make (a call)

kaku 書く *V5K, VT* to write

kamera カメラ *N* camera

kami かみ *N* paper

kanji かんじ *N* kanji

kao かお *N* (person's) face

kappu カップ *N* cup

karada からだ *N, ADJ-NO* body

karai からい *ADJ-I* spicy; salty

karē カレー *N* curry

karendā カレンダー *N* calendar

kariru かりる *V1, VT* to borrow

karui かるい *ADJ-I* light (i.e. not heavy)

kasa かさ *N* umbrella

kasu かす *V5S, VT* to lend

kata かた *N* direction

katei かてい *N, ADJ-NO* household

kau 買う *V5U, VT* to buy

kawa 川, 河 *N* river

kawaii かわいい *ADJ-I* cute

kayōbi 火よう日 *N-ADV, N-T* Tuesday

kaze かぜ *N* wind

kaze かぜ *N* cold (illness)

kazoku かぞく *N* family

keikan けいかん *N, ADJ-NO* policeman

kekkon けっこん *N, ADJ-NO, VS* marriage

kekkō けっこう *ADJ-NA, N-ADV, N, UK* splendid

kesa けさ *N-T* this morning

kesu けす *V5S, VT* to erase; to turn off

ki 木 *N* tree

kieru きえる *V1, VI* to disappear

kiiro きいろ *ADJ-NA, N* yellow

kiiroi きいろい *ADJ-I* yellow

kiku 聞く *V5K, VT* to hear; to ask

kinō きのう *N-ADV, N-T* yesterday

kin'yōbi 金よう日 *N-ADV, N-T* Friday

kippu きっぷ *N* ticket

kirai きらい *ADJ-NA, N* hate

kirei きれい *ADJ-NA, UK* pretty

kiro, kiroguramu キロ, キログラム *N* kilogram

kiro, kiromētoru キロ, キロメートル *N* kilometer

kiru きる *SUF, V5R, VT* to cut (through)

kiru きる *V1* to put on (from the shoulders down)

kissaten きっさてん *N* coffee lounge

kita 北 *N* north

kitanai きたない *ADJ-I* dirty

kitte きって *N* (postage) stamp

kochira, kocchi こちら, こっち *N, UK* this way

kodomo こども *N* child

koe こえ *N* voice

koko ここ *N* here

kokonoka 九日 *N* nine days, the ninth (day of the month)

kokonotsu 九つ *N* nine (pieces)

komaru こまる *V5R, VI* to be worried

konban こんばん *N-ADV, N-T* this evening

kongetsu 今月 *N-ADV, N-T* this month

konna こんな *ADJ-PN* such (about something/someone close to the speaker (including the speaker), or about ideas expressed by the speaker)

kono この *ADJ-PN, UK* this

konshū 今週 *N-ADV, N-T* this week

kōhii コーヒー *N, ADJ-NO* coffee

kōto コート *N* coat

kopii コピー *N, VS* copy

koppu コップ *N* a glass

kore これ *N, UK* this (indicating an item near the speaker, the action of the speaker, or the current topic)

kotaeru こたえる *V1, VI* to answer

kotoba ことば *N* language

kotoshi 今年 *N-ADV, N-T* this year

kōban こうばん *N, VS* police box

kōcha こうちゃ *N* black tea

kōen こうえん *N* (public) park

kōsaten こうさてん *N* intersection

kuchi 口 *N* mouth

kudamono くだもの *N* fruit

kudasai 下さい *UK, HON* please (give me)

kumori くもり *N* cloudy weather

kumoru くもる *V5R, VI* to become cloudy

kuni 国 *N* country

kurai くらい *ADJ-I, UK* gloomy

kurasu クラス *N* class

kuro くろ *N* black

kuroi くろい *ADJ-I* black

kuru 来る *VK, VI, AUX-V* to come (spatially or temporally)

kuruma 車 *N* car

kusuri くすり *N* medicine

kutsu くつ *N* shoes

kutsushita くつした *N* socks

kyō 今日 *N-T* today

kyōdai きょうだい *N* siblings

kyonen きょねん *N-ADV, N-T* last year

kyōshitsu きょうしつ *N* classroom

kyū, ku 九 *NUM* nine

macchi マッチ *N* match (contest)

machi まち *N* town

mada まだ *ADJ-NA, ADV, UK* as yet

mado まど *N* window

mae 前 *N-ADV, N-T, SUF* before (some event)

magaru まがる *V5R, VI* to bend

maiasa まいあさ *N-ADV, N-T* every morning

maiban まいばん *N-ADV, N-T* every night

maigetsu, maitsuki 毎月 *N-ADV, N-T* every month

mainen, maitoshi 毎年 *N-ADV, N-T* every year

mainichi 毎日 *N-ADV, N-T* every day

maishū 毎週 *N-ADV, N-T* every week

man 万 *NUM* ten thousand

mannenhitsu まんねんひつ *N* fountain pen

marui まるい *ADJ-I* round

massugu まっすぐ *ADJ-NA, ADV, N* straight (ahead)

mata また *ADV, CONJ, PREF, UK* again

matsu まつ *V5T, VT* to wait

mazui まずい *ADJ-I, UK* unpleasant (taste, appearance, situation)

me 目 *N* eye

megane めがね *N* glasses

mētoru メートル *N* meter

michi 道 *N* street

midori みどり *N* green

migaku みがく *V5K, VT* to brush (teeth)

migi 右 *N* right

mijikai みじかい *ADJ-I* short

mikka 三日 *N* three days, the 3rd (day of the month)

mimi 耳 *N* ear

mina, minna みな, みんな *ADV, N* everyone

minami 南 *N* south

miru 見る *V1, VT* to see

mise 店 *N* shop

miseru 見せる *V1, VT* to show

mittsu 三つ *N* three (pieces)

mizu 水 *N* water (cold, fresh)

mochiron もちろん *ADV, UK* of course

mokuyōbi 木よう日 *N-ADV, N-T* Thursday

mon もん *N, N-SUF* gate

mondai もんだい *N* problem

mono もの *N* thing

motsu もつ *V5T* to hold

motto もっと *ADV* more

mō もう *ADV, INT, UK* already; soon

mōichido もういちど *EXP* again

muika 六日 *N* six days, the 6th (day of the month)

mukō むこう *N* over there

mura むら *N* village

muttsu 六つ *NUM* six (pieces)

muzukashii むずかしい *ADJ-I* difficult

nado など *N, N-SUF, PRT, UK* et cetera

nagai 長い *ADJ-I* long (distance)

naifu ナイフ *N* knife

naka 中 *N* middle

naku なく *V5K* to cry

naku なく *V5K* to bark

nakusu なくす *V5S, VT* to lose something

namae なまえ *N* name

nan, nani 何 *INT, PN, ADJ-NO* what

nanatsu 七つ *N* seven (pieces)

nanoka 七日 *N-ADV* seven days, the 7th (day of the month)

naraberu ならべる *V1, VT* to line up

narabu ならぶ *V5B, VI* to line up

narau ならう *V5U, VT* to learn

naru なる *V5R, VI, UK* to become

natsu なつ *N-ADV, N-T* summer

natsuyasumi なつやすみ *N* summer vacation

naze なぜ *ADV, UK* why

neko ねこ *N* cat

nekutai ネクタイ *N* tie

neru ねる *V1, VI* to lie down

ni 二 *NUM* two

nichiyōbi 日よう日 *N-ADV, N-T* Sunday

nigiyaka にぎやか *ADJ-NA* bustling

niku にく *N* meat

nimotsu にもつ *N* luggage

nishi 西 *N* west

niwa にわ *N* garden

noboru のぼる *V5R, VI* to climb

nomimono 飲みもの *N* (a) drink

nomu 飲む *V5M, VT* to drink

nōto ノート *N, VS* notebook

noru のる *V5R, VI* to get on

nugu ぬぐ *V5G, VT* to take off (clothes, shoes, etc...)

nurui ぬるい *ADJ-I, UK* lukewarm

nyūsu ニュース *N* news

obāsan おばあさん *N* grandmother; an old woman

obasan おばさん *N, HON* aunt

obentō おべんとう *N* (japanese) box lunch

oboeru おぼえる *V1, VT* to remember

ocha おちゃ *N, POL* tea (usually green)

ofuro おふろ *N* bath

ōi 多い *ADJ-I* many

oishii おいしい *ADJ-I, UK* delicious

ojiisan おじいさん *N, HON, UK* grandfather, an older man

ojisan おじさん *N, HON, UK* uncle

okāsan お母さん *N, HON* mother

okane お金 *N* money

okashi おかし *N* sweets

ōkii 大きい *ADJ-I* big

ōkina 大きな *ADJ-F* big

okiru おきる *V1, VI* to get up; to occur (usu. of unfavorable incidents)

oku おく *V5K* to put

okusan おくさん *N, HON* (your) wife

omawarisan おまわりさん *N* (friendly term for a) policeman

omoi おもい *ADJ-I* heavy

omoshiroi おもしろい *ADJ-I* interesting

onaji おなじ *ADJ-F, N* same

onaka おなか *N* stomach

onēsan おねえさん *N, HON* older sister

ongaku おんがく *N* music

oniisan おにいさん *N, HON* older brother

onna 女 *N* woman

onnanoko 女の子 *N* girl

oriru おりる *V1, VI* to descend (e.g. a mountain)

osake おさけ *N* alcohol

osara おさら *N* plate

oshieru おしえる *V1, VT* to teach

osoi おそい *ADJ-I* slow

osu おす *V5S, VT* to push

otearai おてあらい *N* bathroom

otoko 男 *N* man

otokonoko 男の子 *N* boy

otona 大人 *N* adult

ototoi おととい *N-ADV, N-T* day before yesterday

ototoshi おととし *N-ADV, N-T* year before last

otōsan お父さん *N, HON* father

otōto おとうと *N, HUM* younger brother

owaru おわる *V5R, VI* to finish

oyogu およぐ *V5G, VI* to swim

ōzei おおぜい *N, ADJ-NO* crowd (of people)

pātii パーティー *N* party

pan パン *N* bread

pēji ページ *N* page

pen ペン *N* pen

petto ペット *N* pet

poketto ポケット *N* pocket

posuto ポスト *N, VS* post

pūru プール *N* swimming pool

raigetsu 来月 *N-ADV, N-T* next month

rainen 来年 *N-ADV, N-T* next year

raishū 来週 *N-ADV, N-T* next week

rajikase, rajiokasetto ラジカセ / ラジオカセット *N* radio cassette player

rajio ラジオ *N* radio

rei れい *N, ADJ-NO* zero

reizōko れいぞうこ *N* refrigerator

rekōdo レコード *N* record

renshū れんしゅう *N, VS* practice

resutoran レストラン *N* restaurant

ringo りんご *N* apple

rippa りっぱ *ADJ-NA, N* splendid

roku 六 *NUM* six

rōka ろうか *N* corridor

ryokō りょこう *N, VS, ADJ-NO* travel

ryōri りょうり *N, VS* cuisine

ryōshin りょうしん *N* both parents

ryūgakusei りゅうがくせい *N* overseas student

sā さあ *CONJ, INT* well...

saifu さいふ *N* wallet

sakana さかな *N* fish

saki 先 *N, ADJ-NO, N-SUF, PREF* previous

saku さく *V5K, VI* to bloom

sakubun さくぶん *N, VS* writing

samui さむい *ADJ-I* cold

san 三 *NUM* three

sanposuru さんぽする *N, VS* to stroll

sarainen さらいねん *N-ADV, N-T* year after next

sasu さす *V5S, VI* to hold up (an umbrella, etc...)

satō さとう *N* sugar

se せ *N* height

sebiro せびろ *N* business suit

sētā セーター *N* sweater, jumper

seito せいと *N* pupil

sekken せっけん *N* soap

semai せまい *ADJ-I* narrow

sen 千 *NUM* thousand

sengetsu 先月 *N-ADV, N-T* last month

sensei 先生 *N* teacher

senshū 先週 *N-ADV, N-T* last week

sentaku せんたく *N, VS* washing

shashin しゃしん *N* photograph

shatsu シャツ *N* shirt

shawā シャワー *N* shower

shi, yon 四 *NUM* four

shichi, nana 七 *NUM* seven

shigoto しごと *N, VS, ADJ-NO* job

shikashi しかし *CONJ, UK* however

shimaru しまる *V5R, VI* to close

shimeru しめる *V1, VT* to close

shinbun 新聞 *N* newspaper

shinu しぬ *V5N, VN, VI, SENS* to die

shio しお *N* salt

shiro 白 *N* white

shiroi 白い *ADJ-I* white

shiru しる *V5R, VT* to know

shita 下 *N* below

shitsumon しつもん *N, VS* question

shizuka しずか *ADJ-NA* quiet

shokudō しょくどう *N* dining hall

shōyu しょうゆ *N* soy sauce

shukudai しゅくだい *N* homework

soba そば *N* near

sochira, socchi そちら, そっち *N, UK* that way (by you)

sōji そうじ *N, VS* cleaning

soko そこ there (place relatively near listener)

sono その that (something or someone distant from the speaker, close to the listener; actions of the listener, or ideas expressed or understood by the listener); um...

sora そら *N* sky

sore それ *N, UK* that (indicating an item or person near the listener, the action of the listener, or something on their mind)

sore dewa それでは *EXP, UK* in that situation

sore kara それから *EXP, UK* after that

soshite そして *CONJ, UK* and then

sōshite そうして *CONJ, UK* like that

soto 外 *N* outside

suguni すぐに *ADV, UK* instantly

suiyōbi 水よう日 *N-ADV, N-T* Wednesday

sukāto スカート *N* skirt

suki すき *ADJ-NA, N* liking

sukoshi 少し *ADV, N* few

sukunai 少ない *ADJ-I* a few

sumu すむ *V5M, VI* to live (of humans)

supōtsu スポーツ *N, ADJ-NO* sport

supūn スプーン *N* spoon

surippa スリッパ *N* slippers

suru する *VS-I, UK* to do

sutōbu ストーブ *N* heater

suu すう *V5U, VT* to smoke, to inhale

suwaru すわる *V5R, VI* to sit

suzushii すずしい *ADJ-I* refreshing

tabako たばこ *N, UK* tobacco

tabemono 食べもの *N* food

taberu 食べる *V1, VT* to eat

tabun たぶん *ADV, N* probably

taihen たいへん *ADV* very

taisetsu たいせつ *ADJ-NA, N* important

taishikan たいしかん *N* embassy

taitei たいてい *ADJ-NA, ADV, N, UK* mostly

takai 高い *ADJ-I* high

takusan たくさん *ADJ-NA, ADV, N, UK* many

takushii タクシー *N* taxi

tamago たまご *N* (hen) egg(s)

tanjōbi たんじょうび *N* birthday

tanomu たのむ *V5M* to ask

tanoshii たのしい *ADJ-I* enjoyable

tate たて *N* (the) vertical

tatemono たてもの *N* building

tatsu 立つ *V5T, VI* to stand

te て *N* hand

tēburu テーブル *N* table

tēpu テープ *N* tape

tēpurekōdā テープレコーダー *N* tape recorder

tegami てがみ *N* letter

tenki 天気 *N* weather

terebi テレビ *N, ABBR* television

tesuto テスト *N* test

to と *N* japanese style door

tobu とぶ *V5B, VI* to jump

toire トイレ *N, ABBR* toilet

tokei とけい *N* watch

tokidoki 時々 *ADV, N* sometimes

tokoro ところ *N, SUF* place

tomaru とまる *V5R, VI* to stop

tomodachi ともだち *N* friend

tonari となり next to (esp. living next door to)

tōi とおい *ADJ-I* far

tōka 十日 *N* ten days, the 10th (day of the month)

tori とり *N* bird

toru 撮る (とる) *V5R, VT* to take (a photo)

toru 取る (とる) *V5R, VT* to take

toshi 年 *N-ADV, N* year

toshokan としょかん *N* library

totemo とても *ADV, UK* very

tsugi つぎ *N, ADJ-NO* next

tsukareru つかれる *V1, VI* to get tired

tsukau つかう to use (a person, animal, etc...)

tsukeru つける *V1, VT, UK* to turn on

tsuku つく *V5K* to arrive at

tsukue つくえ *N* desk

tsukuru つくる *V5R, VT* to make

tsumaranai つまらない *ADJ-I, UK* boring

tsumetai つめたい *ADJ-I* cold (to the touch)

tsutomeru つとめる *V1, VT* to work for (someone, some company)

tsuyoi つよい *ADJ-I* powerful

ue 上 *N, ADJ-NO, N-ADV, N-SUF* above; before

umareru 生まれる *V1, VI* to be born

umi うみ *N* sea

uru うる *V5R, VT* to sell

urusai うるさい *ADJ-I, UK* noisy

ushiro 後ろ *N* behind

usui うすい *ADJ-I* thin

uta うた *N* song

utau うたう *V5U, VT* to sing

utsukushii うつくしい *ADJ-I* beautiful

uwagi うわぎ *N, ADJ-NO* jacket

waishatsu ワイシャツ *N, UK, ABBR* business shirt

wakai わかい *ADJ-I* young

wakaru わかる *V5R, VI* to be understood

warui わるい *ADJ-I* bad

wasureru わすれる *V1, VT* to forget

watashi, watakushi わたし、わたくし (hum) *PN, ADJ-NO* I, myself

watasu わたす *V5S, VT* to hand over

yama 山 *N* mountain

yaoya やおや *N* greengrocer

yaru やる *V5R, VT, UK, COL* to do

yasai やさい *N, ADJ-NO* vegetable

yasashii やさしい *ADJ-I* easy; kind

yasui やすい *ADJ-I* cheap

yasumi 休み *N* rest

yattsu 八つ *NUM* eight (pieces)

yobu よぶ *V5B, VT* to call out

yokka 四日 *N* four days, the 4th (day of the month)

yoko よこ horizontal (as opposed to vertical)

yoku よく *ADV, UK* well

yomu 読む *V5M, VT* to read

yori より *ADV, PRT* than (used for comparison)

yoru よる *N-ADV, N-T* evening

yottsu 四つ *NUM* four (pieces)

yōfuku ようふく *N* western-style clothes

yōka 八日 *N* eight days, the eighth (day of the month)

yowai よわい *ADJ-I* weak

yuki ゆき *N* snow

yukkuri ゆっくり *ADV, N, VS, ADV-TO* slowly

yūbe ゆうべ *N-ADV, N-T* last night

yūbinkyoku ゆうびんきょく *N* post office

yūgata ゆうがた *N-ADV, N-T* evening

yūhan ゆうはん *N* dinner

yūmei ゆうめい *ADJ-NA* famous

zasshi ざっし *N* magazine

zenbu ぜんぶ *N-ADV, N-T* all

zero ゼロ *N, ADJ-NO* zero

zubon ズボン *N* trousers

Answer Key

GRAMMAR

LESSON 1 JLPT-style Questions
1) 2   7) 3
2) 3   8) 3
3) 2   9) 1
4) 1   10) 3
5) 3   11) 2
6) 2   12) 3

LESSON 2 JLPT-style Questions
1) 4   6) 3
2) 4   7) 1
3) 4   8) 1
4) 2   9) 1
5) 2   10) 3

LESSON 3 JLPT-style Questions
1) 2   6) 1
2) 3   7) 3
3) 2   8) 1
4) 1   9) 2
5) 2   10) 1

LESSON 4 JLPT-style Questions
1) 4   6) 4
2) 1   7) 3
3) 2   8) 1
4) 4   9) 1
5) 1   10) 4

LESSON 5 JLPT-style Questions
1) 2   6) 4
2) 1   7) 1
3) 1   8) 1
4) 1   9) 1
5) 1   10) 1

LESSON 6 JLPT-style Questions
1) 1   6) 4
2) 2   7) 4
3) 4   8) 4
4) 2   9) 1
5) 2   10) 1

LESSON 7 JLPT-style Questions
1) 3   14) 4
2) 1   15) 4
3) 1   16) 1
4) 2   17) 1
5) 3   18) 2
6) 2   19) 2
7) 2   20) 3
8) 2   21) 4
9) 4   22) 4
10) 4   23) 3
11) 3   24) 4
12) 4   25) 2
13) 4

LESSON 8 JLPT-style Questions
1) 2   6) 4
2) 2   7) 3
3) 3   8) 4
4) 4   9) 1
5) 4   10) 2

LESSON 9 JLPT-style Questions
TRANSITIVE vs. INTRANSITIVE VERBS
1) 3
2) 4
3) 3
4) 3
5) 2

SUFFIXES
1) 2
2) 1
3) 2
4) 2
5) 2

SENTENTIAL GRAMMAR 2
1) 4 (2143)
2) 2 (1423)
3) 1 (2413)
4) 4 (3142)
5) 1 (4132)
6) 1 (3214)
7) 2 (1423)
8) 2 (4231)
9) 2 (4321)
10) 4 (3241)
11) 3 (2341)
12) 1 (3214)
13) 2 (1324)
14) 4 (1342)
15) 4 (1342)
16) 1 (3412)
17) 4 (1423)
18) 3 (4132)
19) 4 (1342)
20) 3 (4132)

TEXT GRAMMAR
Passage 1
1) 2
2) 2
3) 4
4) 2
5) 3

Passage 2
1) 4
2) 3
3) 2
4) 1
5) 4

Passage 3
1) 3
2) 1
3) 1
4) 3
5) 3

Passage 4
1) 3
2) 1
3) 4
4) 2
5) 4

VOCABULARY AND KANJI

Lesson 1
1) 3	11) 2
2) 2	12) 1
3) 3	13) 3
4) 2	14) 1
5) 1	15) 2
6) 2	16) 4
7) 2	17) 3
8) 2	18) 3
9) 3	19) 2
10) 1	20) 1

Lesson 2
1) 2	11) 3
2) 1	12) 2
3) 2	13) 4
4) 4	14) 2
5) 3	15) 1
6) 3	16) 3
7) 2	17) 4
8) 2	18) 3
9) 2	19) 2
10) 3	20) 2

Lesson 3
1) 3	6) 3
2) 2	7) 1
3) 3	8) 4
4) 3	9) 2
5) 2	10) 4

11) 4	16) 3
12) 2	17) 2
13) 3	18) 3
14) 1	19) 3
15) 2	20) 1

Lesson 4

1) 2	6) 1
2) 1	7) 4
3) 3	8) 4
4) 4	9) 2
5) 2	10) 3

READING COMPREHENSION

Lesson 2

1) 1	11) 1
2) 1	12) 1
3) 2	13) 1
4) 2	14) 4
5) 2	15) 3
6) 3	16) 3
7) 1	17) 4
8) 4	18) 4
9) 3	19) 1
10) 3	20) 4

Lesson 3 Give a Shot!

1) 1	11) 3
2) 1	12) 2
3) 2	13) 3
4) 4	14) 4
5) 4	15) 2
6) 4	16) 3
7) 3	17) 2
8) 2	18) 3
9) 3	19) 2
10) 2	20) 2

Lesson 4

1) 1	7) 2
2) 2	8) 2
3) 1	9) 3
4) 2	10) 4
5) 4	11) 2
6) 3	12) 4

LISTENING COMPREHENSION

Lesson 2

1) 3	6) 4
2) 4	7) 1
3) 1	8) 1
4) 2	9) 4
5) 4	10) 1

Lesson 3

1) 1	9) 1
2) 2	10) 2
3) 1	11) 1
4) 2	12) 4
5) 2	13) 2
6) 4	14) 3
7) 3	15) 1
8) 2	

Lesson 4

1) 3	6) 3
2) 1	7) 2
3) 2	8) 3
4) 3	9) 2
5) 3	10) 2

Lesson 5

1) 1	9) 3
2) 2	10) 2
3) 3	11) 3
4) 2	12) 1
5) 2	13) 3
6) 3	14) 1
7) 1	15) 3
8) 3	16) 3

"Books to Span the East and West"

Tuttle Publishing was founded in 1832 in the small New England town of Rutland, Vermont [USA]. Our core values remain as strong today as they were then—to publish best-in-class books which bring people together one page at a time. In 1948, we established a publishing office in Japan—and Tuttle is now a leader in publishing English-language books about the arts, languages and cultures of Asia. The world has become a much smaller place today and Asia's economic and cultural influence has grown. Yet the need for meaningful dialogue and information about this diverse region has never been greater. Over the past seven decades, Tuttle has published thousands of books on subjects ranging from martial arts and paper crafts to language learning and literature—and our talented authors, illustrators, designers and photographers have won many prestigious awards. We welcome you to explore the wealth of information available on Asia at **www.tuttlepublishing.com**.

Published by Tuttle Publishing, an imprint of Periplus Editions (HK) Ltd.

www.tuttlepublishing.com

Copyright © 2019 Periplus Editions (HK) Ltd.
Illustrations by Alan J Castree

All rights reserved. No part of this publication may be reproduced or utilized in any form or by any means, electronic or mechanical, including photocopying, recording, or by any information storage and retrieval system, without prior written permission from the publisher.

Library of Congress Control Number: 2019939994

ISBN 978-4-8053-1458-6

25 24 23 22   7 6 5 4 3   2201VP
Printed in Malaysia

TUTTLE PUBLISHING® is a registered trademark of Tuttle Publishing, a division of Periplus Editions (HK) Ltd.

Distributed by

North America, Latin America & Europe
Tuttle Publishing
364 Innovation Drive
North Clarendon
VT 05759-9436 U.S.A.
Tel: 1 (802) 773-8930
Fax: 1 (802) 773-6993
info@tuttlepublishing.com
www.tuttlepublishing.com

Japan
Tuttle Publishing
Yaekari Building 3rd Floor 5-4-12 Osaki
Shinagawa-ku Tokyo 141 0032
Tel: (81) 3 5437-0171
Fax: (81) 3 5437-0755
sales@tuttle.co.jp
www.tuttle.co.jp

Asia Pacific
Berkeley Books Pte. Ltd.
3 Kallang Sector #04-01
Singapore 349278
Tel: (65) 6741-2178
Fax: (65) 6741-2179
inquiries@periplus.com.sg
www.tuttlepublishing.com